ZULU WAR VCs

ZULU WAR VCs

VICTORIA CROSSES OF THE ANGLO-ZULU WAR 1879

James W. Bancroft

FRONTLINE
BOOKS

First published in Great Britain in 2018 by
Frontline Books

An imprint of
Pen & Sword Books Ltd
Yorkshire - Philadelphia

ISBN 9781526722645

A CIP catalogue record for this book is available from the British Library

Typeset in Palatino by SRJ Info Jnana System Pvt Ltd.

Printed and bound by TJ International Ltd, Padstow, Cornwall

Pen & Sword Books Ltd incorporates the Imprints of Aviation, Atlas,
Family History, Fiction, Maritime, Military, Discovery, Politics, History,
Archaeology, Select, Wharncliffe Local History, Wharncliffe True Crime,
Military Classics, Wharncliffe Transport, Leo Cooper, The Praetorian Press,
Remember When, Seaforth Publishing and Frontline Publishing.
For a complete list of Pen & Sword titles please contact

PEN & SWORD BOOKS LTD
47 Church Street, Barnsley, South Yorkshire, S70 2AS, England
E-mail: enquiries@pen-and-sword.co.uk
Website: www.pen-and-sword.co.uk

Or
PEN AND SWORD BOOKS
1950 Lawrence Rd, Havertown, PA 19083, USA
E-mail: Uspen-and-sword@casematepublishers.com
Website: www.penandswordbooks.com

Contents

Chapter 1	**The Victoria Cross Before 1879**	**1**
Chapter 2	**The Rise of the Zulu Nation**	**4**
Chapter 3	**The Disaster at iSandlwana**	**9**
	Lieutenant Nevill Josiah Aylmer Coghill VC	14
	Lieutenant Teignmouth Melvill VC	17
	Private Samuel Wassall VC	20
Chapter 4	**The Defence of Rorke's Drift**	**24**
	Lieutenant John Rouse Merriott Chard VC	55
	Lieutenant Gonville Bromhead VC	68
	Corporal William Wilson Allan VC	75
	Private Frederick Hitch VC	77
	Private Alfred Henry Hook VC	79
	Private Robert Jones VC	81
	Private William Jones VC	83
	Private John Williams (Fielding) VC	84
	Surgeon James Henry Reynolds VC	86
	Commissary James Langley Dalton VC	90
	Corporal Frederick Schiess VC	94
Chapter 5	**The iNtombe River Massacre**	**99**
	Sergeant Anthony Clarke Booth VC	102
Chapter 6	**Hlobane Mountain**	**111**
	Lieutenant-Colonel Redvers Henry Buller VC	117
	Major William Knox Leet VC	122
	Lieutenant Henry Lysons VC	128
	Private Edmund John Fowler VC	130
Chapter 7	**Khambula Hill**	**139**
	Lieutenant Edward Stevenson Browne VC	145

Chapter 8	**Operations at Ulundi**	**150**
	Captain William Leslie de la Poer Beresford VC	158
	Captain Henry Cecil Dudgeon D'Arcy VC	165
	Sergeant Edmund Joseph O'Toole VC	169
Appendix		**173**
Research Sources and Further Reading		**176**
Index		**181**

Chapter 1

The Victoria Cross Before 1879

The Distinguished Conduct Medal was instituted on 4 December 1854 for gallantry in the field performed by 'other ranks' of the British army, and the Conspicuous Gallantry Medal was established on 13 August 1855 as the naval equivalent of the DCM, but there was no universal medal that could be awarded for all ranks of the British armed forces. However, stories of the gallantry being performed by her soldiers in the Crimea, set against reports from the first war correspondents of their neglect and suffering which was causing discontent among the British public, prompted Queen Victoria to try to do something within her power to give them recognition. Consequently, the Victoria Cross was instituted by her royal warrant on 29 January 1856, and 111 men who fought in the Crimean campaign became the first recipients for 'conspicuous bravery and devotion to country in the presence of the enemy'. Rank, long service or wound was to have no special influence on who qualified for the award.

Queen Victoria took a great interest in the establishment of the award and in the design of the medal. Prince Albert suggested that it should be named after her, and the original motto was to have been 'For the Brave', but Victoria was of the opinion that this would lead to the inference that only those who had got the cross were considered to be brave, and decided that 'For Valour' would be more suitable. The design was not to be particularly ornate and not of high metallic value. All the medals have been cast from the bronze cascabels believed to be from two guns (said to be of Chinese origin), that the British had captured from the Russians at Sebastopol. The original ribbons for the medal were blue for the navy and crimson for the army. Queen Victoria thought that 'the person decorated with the Victoria Cross might properly be allowed to bear a distinctive mark after their name'. She pointed out that at that time 'VC' meant 'Vice-Chancellor', and she suggested 'DVC' (Decorated with the Victoria Cross) or 'BVC' (Bearer of the Victoria Cross). However, the simple 'VC' was finally agreed on. Upon its institution it carried an annuity of ten pounds. Many rank-and-file soldiers who gained the Victoria Cross are known to have felt great satisfaction at the fact that military regulations state that all officers must salute a man of any rank who passes by them wearing the Victoria Cross on his breast.

The first man to perform a deed that would be rewarded with the Victoria Cross was Mate Charles Davis Lucas on 21 June 1854, whilst serving aboard HMS *Hecla* during the bombardment of Bomarsund in the Baltic Sea. The first eighty-five recipient announcements were published in a supplement to the *London Gazette* for 24 February 1857, most of them extremely understated, and the first named was Lieutenant William Buckley of HMS *Miranda*, Royal Navy. The first investiture took place at Hyde Park in London on 26 June 1857, when sixty-two Crimean veterans received the medal from the Queen herself in a ceremony which is said to have taken only about ten minutes. She performed the deed in the rather awkward position of side-saddle on a horse, presumably because most of the men were tall and it would be easier for her to reach them, and she actually pinned the medal to the skin of Commander Raby, who was first in the queue and therefore became the first man ever to wear the Victoria Cross—literally! It seems she didn't get much better with practice, as she did it again to Lieutenant Graham who was twenty-fourth in line. The Queen recorded in her diary 'it was indeed a most proud, gratifying day'. However, even after seeing men in the line with limbs and eyes missing, and other disfigurements, it is unlikely that she or any British civilians really understood what horrors they had witnessed and experienced to gain the award.

Prior to the beginning of the Anglo-Zulu War in January 1879, the Victoria Cross had been awarded 345 times for actions in the Crimea and throughout the empire; the most being awarded in India—182 for the Indian Mutiny, and six more for other campaigns there.

Numerous sources have stated that the most Victoria Crosses awarded for a single action were gained for the defence of Rorke's Drift on 22-23 January 1879, during the Anglo-Zulu War. However, while the eleven Victoria Crosses for that battle has never been equalled since, and although it did produce the record of seven Victoria Crosses awarded to one regiment for a single action, my original research from 1992 to 1994 for compiling *The Chronological Roll of the Victoria Cross* first brought to light that there were three prior superlatives.

At that time, I carried out a comprehensive study of all the citations for the Victoria Cross which were announced in the *London Gazette* from 24 February 1857 to date, and my findings were published in my 1994 book *Deeds of Valour*, announcing that the superlative award of the Victoria Cross for a single action is the twenty awarded for the first attack on the Great Redan at Sebastopol on 18 June 1855, during the Crimean War. This is followed by the seventeen awarded for the assault on the Sikandar Bagh at Lucknow, during the Indian Mutiny, on 16 November 1857, and the twelve (probably thirteen) for the second attack on the Great Redan on 8 September 1855.

Some military enthusiasts I have consulted still want to believe that the eleven Victoria Crosses awarded to the defenders of Rorke's Drift should be recognised as the highest, based on the fact that it was an individual fight, while the assault on the Sikandar Bagh was part of a continuing battle (the twenty-four Victoria Crosses gained at Lucknow on 16-17 November 1857 was the most for a single twenty-four hour period), and the men who were awarded the Victoria Cross for both attacks on the Redan performed other acts of gallantry which were recorded. My theory is that if an action is mentioned in a Victoria Cross citation then it should be included in the total number for that particular man, and should not be devalued because other deeds are quoted in the same citation.

Chapter 2

The Rise of the Zulu Nation

For most of the nineteenth century, South Africa was disturbed by continuous friction between its mixed populations. After British troops had twice seized the Cape from the Dutch at the turn of the century, settlers began to arrive in 1820, and as they expanded the frontier there were many disputes over land boundaries between Cape Colonists and African Bantu tribes, which kept the British Army on constant alert. These disagreements sometimes escalated and led to confrontations which came to be known as Frontier Wars.

Soon after the British government abolished slavery in 1833, Boer farmers, who were of Dutch origin, began to push northwards into the interior to search the *veldt* for land where they could settle independently from British administration at the Cape. These 'treks' met with resistance from the natives, especially the Zulu, who, because of a series of bloody battles and subsequent reprisals, became their bitter enemies. The most well-known of these was the Battle of Blood River, which took place on 16 December 1837.

The Zulus lived in the area between the Drakensburg Mountains and the south-east coast. Boers continued to advance over the Drakensburg Mountains, and the British moved across the Great Kei River, which formed the north-east border of Cape Colony, and by the middle of the century the Zulus found their kingdom bordered on the west by the Orange Free State and the Transvaal Republic, both of which had been founded by the Boers, and in the south by the British colony of Natal. To the east was the Indian Ocean.

Early in the century the Zulus had been disciplined by a great military-minded chief named Shaka. Shaka had been born in 1787 near what is now named Melmoth in KwaZulu-Natal, the illegitimate son of Sezangakhona ka Jama (1762-1816), the chief of the Zulus, and a woman called Nandi of a neighbouring tribe. At that time the Zulus were only one of a number of small Nguni tribes, which also included the Swazi, the Xhosa and the Mthethwa.

Nandi was not one of Sezangakhona's sixteen wives, and because of the circumstances of his birth, Shaka and his mother led difficult lives as outcasts, which had a lasting effect on him. At an early age he began to show great courage and skill with weapons, which at that time consisted of a shield for defence, a throwing spear, and a long knobble-ended mace named a *knobkerrie*, which was used to bludgeon an opponent senseless before moving in for the kill. Tales abounded concerning Shaka's prowess. As a young herd boy he fought and killed a fierce leopard that had come to attack his cattle. There was also the saga of a mad giant who lived on a hill in Shaka's district. For years this wild warrior would come down from his lair to terrorise and take plunder from the local natives. However, one day he chose to approach the herd of cattle that was in Shaka's care. The madman was confronted by the six-feet-three-inch-tall and muscular young man who had learned to be a proficient fighter with his primitive weapons. Shaka triumphed after a duel which was still talked about across the *veldt* a century later.

Shaka became a fearless warrior with an outstanding reputation. His skill in battle soon caught the attention of Dingiswayo, a Mthethwa chieftain with great military talent. Dingiswayo initiated the promising man into one of his regiments. He mentored the young warrior, and in 1818 he was instrumental in making Shaka the king of the Zulus, before he himself was captured in an ambush and beheaded during the Zulu Civil War of 1817-19.

Shaka learned the advantages of an organised regimental system from Dingiswayo. As soon as young Zulus reached their teens they were put into age-regiments, led by chiefs, or *inDunas*, chosen by Shaka. Regiments of old warriors and regiments made up of young warriors were combined to form a corps, thus enabling the new recruits to learn from the experiences of the older men, and eventually to take their place. Each regiment had its own distinctive style of war regalia, and the warriors lived in military stockades which were segregated from the domestic settlements.

Shaka assured aggression in his warriors by depriving them of female companionship for long periods, particularly before a campaign, and the fact that warriors who had dared to be defeated were put to death on their return considerably enhanced their determination for victory. Killing became a custom of the Zulu nation and 'to conquer or to die' became their motto. The warriors were not allowed to marry without the permission of the king, and this was not given until the warrior had fought in battle and 'washed their spears' in human blood. The regiments who had proved themselves and had been allowed to marry carried light-coloured shields and wore a head-ring, or *isiCoco*, woven into the hair at the crown of their heads.

Shaka also made revolutionary improvements to their weaponry. He was an expert with the throwing spear, but he was not completely satisfied with its effectiveness. He had noticed in battles that no real harm was done to a foe until his warriors had closed in on them, and the spears could be picked up by an opponent and thrown back at them. So he re-armed his regiments with short, stabbing spears called *assegais*. These required very close combat, so swiftness of foot was important. Shaka believed that bare feet could move more surely across hard rocky ground, or become bogged-down in mud, so he ordered his warriors to discard their sandals. Some men disapproved of this idea because some of the terrain was also very thorny. Shaka solved this problem by ordering them to prepare beds of thorns on the ground, and to harden their soles by repeatedly marching over them.

Prior to Shaka's reign, tribal warfare had always been fought without any basic organisation. But Shaka introduced a tactical fighting formation based on an old hunting technique. His army, known as an *impi*, was divided into four groups. The bulk of the warriors formed a central group—the chest—which first engaged the enemy. Then two groups—the horns—moved swiftly around on each side to attack the flanks and rear, and encircle them. A reserve force—the loins—was kept at the rear, ready to be used when needed. Shaka's bold and well-trained warriors were well-drilled with their weapons and were highly disciplined in battle. They slept naked on military expeditions, whatever the weather threw at them.

Shaka revenged himself on all those who had treated him and his mother badly; one-by-one the Bantu tribes were crushed, and the Zulus took possession of all conquered lands. The few enemy warriors who were lucky enough to survive a battle were incorporated into the Zulu regiments, and within four years the land of the amaZulu—the 'children of the heavens'—covered over 20,000 square miles.

Shaka led the Zulus to greatness, but eventually his rule became one of terror. With no native tribes left prepared to wage war on his far superior forces, he had no means by which to relieve his aggressive urges. Consequently, he began to commit needless atrocities on his own people. He had four hundred women executed on suspicion of witchcraft, and any shield-bearer who allowed a single ray of sunshine to fall on him while he was shielding the king from its glare, was killed. And yet there was no shortage of men who were willing to take over the honour of shielding the royal head. The Zulu people were wise enough to realise that there was security in having a feared king and they were willing to put up with their precarious existence as long as they knew that Shaka commanded the reputation of a powerful leader.

However, after Nandi died in 1827, Shaka brooded, and he began to lose the respect he had built up for himself. He executed anyone who did not show continual grief at her death, and subjected his people to long periods of fasting. Sex was banned for a year, and the meaningless slaughter went on. He put to death anyone who sneezed while he was eating, and cut open a hundred pregnant women during a passing fad he had for embryology. Eventually the Zulus could stand him no longer, and some of his own family, including his successor, Dingane, conspired to stab him to death.

Dingane was the son of Sezangakhona and his sixth wife, Queen Mpikase, and it was during his reign that the Zulus began to resist the expansionist Boer farmers. But he and his successor, Mpande, who came to the throne in 1840 and was the son of Sezangakhona, and his ninth wife, Songiya, relaxed the strict military traditions. Consequently, it was not long before his family were squabbling about who should succeed him. A battle for succession followed between his two eldest sons, Cetshwayo, who was borne by Queen Ngqumbazi, and Mbuyazi. This came to a head when Cetshwayo's uSuthu faction pursued Mbuyazi's iziGqosa faction. The uSuthu trapped the iziGqosa at the river near the Ndondakuaka Kraal on 2 December 1856, where Mbuyazi and all his people, including five more of Mpande's sons, and all the women and children were slaughtered.

Mpande died in 1872, and Cetshwayo became King of the Zulus on 1 September 1873. He was the only grandchild of Sezangakhona, and was therefore the last bloodline king of the Zulus. He was a cunning and prudent leader who hated the way his father had allowed the Zulu to lose their great military reputation, and he loved to hear the wonderful stories of the great Shaka period. He patterned his mode of leadership on that of Shaka, being more intelligent and, at times, equally ruthless. Under his leadership the Zulu army became feared again. He added new regiments, and by 1878 these numbered no less than thirty-three.

Although the main structure of Zulu life was built on military lines, Cetshwayo did not keep a standing army as Shaka had done. Except for his personal bodyguard, most of his warriors enjoyed a comfortable life farming the fertile coastal land. With the fine, sub-tropical climate, inundated with regular rainfall, Zululand was perfect for agriculture and grazing sheep and cattle. They lived in circular homesteads called *kraals*, with dome-shaped thatched huts, each *kraal* being governed domestically by an *inDuna*. The king had become mainly a figurehead to whom the *inDunas* usually stayed loyal.

The women usually spent their day repairing basket-work for the huts, or preparing the food for the family. Some also boiled millet to make beer, or picked leaves to make pipe tobacco or snuff. When the men were not working the land they kept in shape through regular military exercises, which now included learning to use the firearms which Cetshwayo was able to acquire from white traders. But a Zulu warrior still prided himself on his ability to fight in close-combat, and was always restless to gain military honour. They saw themselves as invincible, and among the local native tribes they were. Cetshwayo had as many as 40,000 of these efficient warriors at his disposal, and this threat naturally caused great unease among his European neighbours.

Chapter 3

The Disaster at iSandlwana

Tension between British authority and various factions in South Africa had once again been building up, especially concerning the independent-minded Boer farmers and the warrior nation of the Zulu. Because of this, many British army units were already in South Africa taking part in the ninth Cape Frontier War. The area of unrest was the north-eastern Cape, where the Gaika and Gcaleka tribes were causing problems. The campaign followed the usual pattern of how the British dealt with such disturbances. The rebels used the bushy terrain and hill caves for refuge, and lines of troops formed up and entered the shrub to flush them out. By June 1878, Sindali, the chief of the Gaikas, had been killed, and the Gcaleka chief, Kreli, had been captured. The rebels lost heart and the uprising ended. These sweeping skirmishes in the Perie Bush gave most of the British troops their first experience of active service in South Africa.

However, the main threat to stability in the region came from the highly-disciplined army of fearless Zulu warriors. Lord Garnet Wolseley stated that 'these Zulus are a great danger to our Colony'. The British government knew that they had to be subdued before there could be any progress towards a united nation under one flag, which would be easier for administration and the hard-pressed British army.

In order to produce an excuse to deal with the Zulu threat, the British governor at the Cape, Sir Henry Bartle-Frere, devised a deliberately unworkable ultimatum and issued it to Cetshwayo, and British forces began to build up at three main strategic places along the border with Zululand even before Cetshwayo had responded. The 3rd (Central) Column, under the commander-in-chief, General Sir Frederick Thesiger (soon to become the 2nd Baron Chelmsford), marched towards a commandeered mission-station on the banks of the Buffalo River, known as Rorke's Drift. The backbone of this section of the invasion force was made up of soldiers of the 24th Regiment, the whole force totalling 5,000 troops and African auxiliaries.

The Buffalo River at Rorke's Drift was wide, but there was an island about halfway across. It was dangerous and rocky in some places, and the recent heavy rains had swollen it, making the current strong and treacherous. An Irishman called James Rorke had established the trading post ('KwaJim', or 'Jim's Place', in the local language), and he had cut away the banks to make it reasonably safe for transport. Engineers began to assemble two ponts for the purpose of ferrying the troops across. One was a raft on big barrels and the other was a pontoon supported on boats. These floating bridges were large enough to carry one Cape wagon and its team of oxen, or about eighty men at a time.

Cetshwayo was aware that to accept some of the terms of the ultimatum would mean the loss of Zulu independence and the eventual breakdown of Zulu society. No response to the ultimatum had been received from the Zulu king after twenty days, so a further ten days grace was allowed. This expired at midnight on 10 January 1879, and the invasion of Zululand began on the morning of 11 January. Lieutenant Coghill wrote in his diary: 'It was a raw and misty morning, the mist rising every now and then and disclosing the disposition of our forces as they pushed across, but there was no sign of the enemy'.

The column faced no opposition from the Zulus as they moved forward. The weather of late had been wet and the advance came to a halt when the condition of the track deteriorated further into enemy territory. They were forced to set up camp until the roads were repaired; a task which the Royal Engineers estimated could take as long as a week.

During this time, Lord Chelmsford planned an attack on the homestead of the Zulu chief of the amaQungebeni, named Sihayo kaXongo, situated among the rocks on the Ngedla Mountain overlooking the Batshe Valley a few miles ahead. Sihayo's son, Mehlokazulu, had been involved in the killing of two of his father's adulterous runaway wives, after abducting them from sanctuary in Natal, and the handing over of the king's son was one of the demands of the ultimatum. However, Sihayo was favoured by Cetshwayo, and the demand was unlikely to be met. Sihayo was not at home, but it was first blood to the British as they set fire to Sihayo's homestead and captured livestock. British casualties were minimal and the Zulus lost about sixty warriors.

Having been appointed orderly officer to Colonel Richard Glyn, of the 24th Regiment, Lieutenant Nevill Coghill and the column arrived at a distinctive sphinx-shaped rocky feature known as iSandlwana on 20 January 1879, and throughout the day a new advance camp began to take shape. Lieutenant Teignmouth Melvill, of the 24th Regiment, also took part in the invasion of Zululand with the 3rd Column and was present at the engagement at the stronghold of Chief Sihayo. Lieutenant Melvill strongly advised that some kind of defensive preparation should be made, but other officers thought that it was only a very temporary camp and his suggestions were not competently carried out.

As the camp was being set up that afternoon, Lieutenant Coghill accompanied Lord Chelmsford and a squadron of mounted men in a reconnaissance of the area. There was no sign of the enemy, but on the way back they came upon some chickens in a *kraal*. He was trying to catch one when he twisted his knee so badly that afterwards he could hardly walk, and he had to spend the following day laid up in his tent.

Zulus had been sighted to the north of the camp and early on the morning of Wednesday, 22 January 1879, Lord Chelmsford had taken a mobile column, amounting to about half of his force, further into enemy territory to try to locate them and coax them into a battle. There were now about 1,700 men left at iSandlwana, and Lieutenant Coghill was in the camp nursing his wound on light duties and, acting as galloper, he wore his blue patrol jacket. The camp was under the command of Lieutenant-Colonel Henry Pulleine, of the 24th Regiment, who was the son of a Yorkshire vicar.

For various reasons the large Zulu army of about 25,000 warriors had decided to shelter in a valley and advance into battle on the following day, but a detachment of colonial troops discovered them accidently, and having lost the element of surprise, they streamed out of the valley and deployed across a wide area in their traditional, and very effective, 'chest and horns' formation and raced towards the British camp at iSandlwana.

Lieutenant Horace Smith-Dorrien, a transport officer with the 95th (Derbyshire) Regiment, escaped to speak of how the Zulu attack developed:

> It was a marvellous sight, line upon line of men in slightly extended order, one behind the other, firing as they came, for a few of them had firearms, bearing all before them...They were giving vent to no loud war cries, but to a low musical murmuring noise, which gave the impression of a gigantic swarm of bees getting nearer and nearer.

Pulleine was not aware of the full extent of the massive Zulu attack and sent his men out in thin ranks with large gaps between them in an effort to protect as much of the front of the camp as he could. When the 'horns' of the Zulu attack appeared over the crest of the hills to the left and right, the British lines fell back about fifty paces to take advantage of rising ground closer to iSandlwana Hill, and even when the 'chest' began to pour over the ridgeline in full view of the defenders, the steady fire of the men of the 24th Regiment smashed into them and the attack showed signs of stalling.

However, the British line was too extended and the Zulus concentrated on racing into the gaps to attack the soldiers in flank. The British fell back again towards the tents below the mountain, which encouraged the warriors, and shouting their slogan '*Gwas Umhlongo! Gwas Inglubi!*' (which means 'Stab the white men! Stab the pigs!') they moved in for the kill. The last groups of men fought back-to-back on the *nek* of iSandlwana until they were overpowered and all were killed. Only about one hundred white men survived the carnage in what was the most devastating single defeat inflicted on the British army in the Victorian era. The Zulus had also suffered fearful losses, about 2,000 warriors killed and wounded, and on learning of the Zulu casualties Cetshwayo remarked 'an *assegai* has been thrust into the belly of the nation. There are not enough tears to mourn the dead'.

When the British lines were falling back, Lieutenant Coghill rode into camp and told Colonel Glyn's groom to strike the tents and load them into a wagon. When the situation became hopeless he told the groom to mount one of the colonel's horses and follow him out of the camp; which he did—and survived. As his horse stumbled across rocky ground, Lieutenant Coghill was anxious to remain mounted, aware that he would not be able to outrun the Zulus with an injured knee. A Zulu attacked him and sank an *assegai* into his horse's thigh, but the animal stayed on its legs and they wheeled around and escaped.

As adjutant of the 1st/24th Regiment, the care of the Queen's colour fell within Lieutenant Melvill's responsibility, and he collected the rolled-up standard and rode out of the camp in an attempt to save it from falling into enemy hands. He cut off across rugged country towards the Buffalo River, closely pursued by Zulus attracted by his red tunic. He had lost his sword, and was nearly unsaddled several times before he reached the river. The swollen water was running a torrent, but in the circumstances it was the lesser of two evils, so he and his horse plunged into the swirling water. He got into difficulty and was for a while stranded in mid-river holding on to a rock, before being swept away in the strong current, during which time he lost his grip on the precious flag and it was swept away and lost.

Having escaped from the 'field of blood', and on reaching the river, Lieutenant Coghill saw that the water was treacherous, but he plunged into the torrent and began to push his way across. He reached the Natal bank and was about to ride on, when he looked back and saw Lieutenant Melvill and Lieutenant Higginson, of the Natal Native Contingent, struggling in the water. He returned to the river to offer assistance, but his horse was hit by a Zulu bullet and its lifeless body fell on him, trapping his leg. He managed to free himself and helped Melvill to get to the Natal bank. They struggled over rocks for about one hundred paces with at least two Zulus close behind them. The warriors got to within thirty paces when the officers presented their revolvers and shot them down. They continued to clamber up a steep rock face with their wet and heavy clothing sapping their strength, until they could go no further. They stopped and prepared to defend themselves, but their heroic effort left them in a state of exhaustion and they were overpowered and killed.

Private Samuel Wassall, of the 80th Regiment, who was attached to the Mounted Infantry, was in the camp at iSandlwana. It soon became every man for himself and the possibility of survival depended on who could get onto a horse. Private Wassall threw his helmet away and, spurring his Basuto pony, he broke through the carnage clothed in his shirt sleeves and his bandolier belt strapped across his chest. He galloped the pony as fast as he could over the rocky terrain under enemy fire and with warriors in hot pursuit, and on reaching the river he was about to urge his mount into the roaring water when Private Thomas Westwood, who was also attached to the mounted infantry, cried out for help as he struggled desperately in the raging current. He was being swept away in danger of drowning.

With frenzied warriors wreaking carnage all around him, and at the imminent risk of his own life, he stopped his horse and dismounted on the Zululand side of the river and plunged into the water to try to offer assistance to his comrade. He waded out to Westwood and on reaching him he dragged him back to the Zululand bank, and helped him up into the saddle. With Zulus firing at them and getting perilously close, he spurred the horse into the river and urged it across. Mercifully reaching the Natal bank, they broke away and rode off towards Helpmekaar. On the following day he rode back to Rorke's Drift, where he learned of the gallant defence that had been performed there. Lord Chelmsford shook his hand and remarked 'you are a lucky man to have got away'.

Lieutenant Nevill Josiah Aylmer Coghill VC

Nevill Josiah Aylmer Coghill was born at Belvidere House in Drumcondra, Dublin, on 25 January 1852. He was the eldest of six children to Sir John Joscelyn Coghill, an Irish painter who became the 4th Baron Coghill, and his wife Katherine Frances, daughter of Lord John Plunket. Sir John was a justice of the peace, who owned 6,400 acres of land with properties at Glenbarahane, Castletownsend, County Cork; 3 Royal Marine Terrace at Strand Road in Bray, County Dublin; and 21 Bolton Studios, Redcliffe Road, south-west London. He had three brothers and two sisters. Egerton Bushe Coghill was also a well-known painter, and many of his pictures feature the landscapes of County Cork. The youngest sibling, Violet Alice Penrose, lived until 1951. The novelist, Edith Anna Somerville, was his cousin, and an uncle, Colonel Kendal Coghill CB, saw active service with the 2nd Bengal European Fusiliers in the Indian Rebellion of 1857-58, and commanded the 19th Hussars in Egypt in 1882.

Nevill was christened at St Matthias's Church in Killiney, Dublin, and his early years were spent in and around that city. As a young man he was nearly six feet tall, with blue eyes and fair hair. He became a member of the Leinster Lodge of Freemasons. The Coghill brothers were educated at Haileybury College in Hertford from the summer of 1865 to Christmas 1869, Nevill being in Trevelyan House. He was keen on outdoor activities, became a good horseman, and took his holidays mountain climbing in the Austrian Tyrol. The college prided itself on creating young men of officer material, and in July 1870 he sat the examination for an army appointment.

On 13 May 1871 he became an officer in the County of Dublin Militia, before gaining a commission as ensign in the 24th (2nd Warwickshire) Regiment on 26 February 1873. He was posted to the 1st Battalion depot at Warley, near Birmingham, on 20 April 1873. Nevill sailed to Gibraltar with his battalion on 22 May 1874, and when the unit transferred to the Cape in November of that year he returned to the new depot at Brecon. He attended a course at the Royal Military Academy in Sandhurst from 2 February to 2 April 1874, and passed an examination in the Course of Instruction in June 1875, being promoted to lieutenant on 13 August 1875.

He sailed from Southampton on the SS *European* to join his battalion in South Africa, arriving at the Cape on 16 February 1876. In August 1876, he was appointed aide-de-camp to General Sir Arthur Cunynghame, who was commanding the British forces in South Africa. From May to December 1877, he accompanied the general on a tour of inspection throughout the region. He served in the 9th Cape Frontier War, and played an important part during several skirmishes with native rebels in bush fighting around Ibeka Depot. General Cunynghame stated in his despatches from King William's Town on 20 February 1878 that 'Lieutenant Coghill, my aide-de-camp, has been most attentive to his duties; was well-spoken of at the Battle of Neumarka, and was present at many patrols in Galekaland'.

When General Cunynghame was replaced by Lord Chelmsford in March 1878, Lieutenant Coghill returned to Britain with him. He took back with him a number of native war trophies which his father later donated to the National Museum of Ireland. The family home had become 'Avonmore' at Ballybrack in Dublin, which Sir John had bought from the architect, William George Murray, after his death in 1871. After a short period of leave, he received news that hostilities with the Zulus seemed likely. 'I can smell sulphur!' he is reported to have said, and he said goodbye to his family and left home for the last time.

He sailed to South Africa on the SS *Tyne*, arriving at Cape Town on 12 September 1878, and he travelled to Pietermaritzburg to join the British forces being assembled there. He was originally considered for the job which was eventually given to Lieutenant Melvill, but he was appointed aide-de-camp to Sir Henry Bartle-Frere, the governor of the Cape. As the deadline for the Zulu ultimatum drew near and troops were being prepared for war, he was granted permission to rejoin his regiment. Arriving at Helpmekaar on 9 January, he was among the officers of both battalions of the 24th Regiment who dined together that evening, and was one of twenty-one officers present who would soon be killed in action.

Lieutenant Coghill met his death three days before his twenty-seventh birthday. A few weeks later, a mounted patrol found the Queen's colour and the bodies of the two officers, and on 14 April they were laid to rest on the side of the hill about ten paces from where they were killed. The place is marked by a stone cross and commemorative plaque. Lieutenant Coghill's diary was also recovered from the battlefield.

Nevill was entitled to the South Africa Medal with 1877-8-9 clasp. At that time the Victoria Cross was not awarded to men who did not live to wear it, so on 2 May 1879 the names of Lieutenants Coghill and Melvill appeared in a *London Gazette* memorandum, which, in the case of Lieutenant Coghill stated 'On account of his heroic conduct in endeavouring to save his brother officer's life, he would have been recommended to Her Majesty for the Victoria Cross had he survived'.

In 1902, a special plea on behalf of Sir John Coghill was made to King Edward VII in respect of a posthumous Victoria Cross award to his son. After Sir John died in 1905, his wife made a stronger plea, and a month after the Victoria Cross warrant was revised in 1907, a Victoria Cross was sent to Sir Egerton Coghill on 6 February 1907.

The memorials to his name are numerous: a memorial plaque and a commemorative headstone dedicated to him and Lieutenant Melvill was placed below Itchiane Hill at Fugitive's Drift in 1974; he is named on the memorial at Brecon Cathedral; his name is inscribed on the colour pole of the 24th Regiment, which is laid up in Brecon Cathedral; he is named on the Victoria Cross honours board in the regimental museum; there is a memorial in the Royal Military Academy Chapel in Camberley; he is named on the war memorial; there is a portrait of him and a stained-glass memorial at Haileybury College; he is named on a memorial plaque at St Winnow's Church; his name is commemorated on the Coghill Memorial at Drumcondra Church; there is a memorial plaque at St Fin Barre's Anglican Cathedral in Cork; and a memorial plaque and window at St Barrahanes Church in Castletownsend, County Cork.

Several commemorative poems and verses were composed in honour of the two men and their heroic deed, and Sir John received a letter of sympathy from Horse Guards. His family presented his Victoria Cross to the regimental museum at Brecon in 1976, and when the Queen's colour of the regiment is on parade, Lieutenant Coghill's sword is carried by the colour ensign. *Whom the God's Love: a Memoir of Neville Coghill* was published in 1966. Fifty-two of his letters and two diaries still survive. The earliest 1877-78 diary is held at the regimental museum of the Royal Welsh, and the 1879 diary was donated to the National Army Museum in London by Sir Patrick Coghill.

In a letter I received from a family descendant it is stated:

> For your interest, my past relatives in the British and Indian Army include: Colonel J. G. B. Walker, 14th/11th Sikhs (my father); Lt-Colonel J. R. B. Walker, Gurkhas [*sic*] (my uncle); Lord Birdwood; Uncle Gunny; Nevill Coghill (yes, the same as died at iSandlwana);

> and others. Coghill and Gunny did not know that their families would be related by marriage. Coghill was closely related (uncle?) to an eminent Oxford professor of English.

The Victoria Cross awards to Lieutenants Coghill and Melvill were not universally appreciated, and some were even of the opinion that they did not deserve the medal. General Garnet Wolseley, who seems to have had an aversion to the awarding of gallantry medals of any kind, stated:

> I am sorry that both of these officers were not killed with their men at iSandlwana instead of where they were. I don't like the idea of officers escaping on horseback when their men on foot are killed. Heroes have been made of men like Melvill and Coghill, who, taking advantage of them having horses, bolted from the scene of the action to save their lives. It is monstrous making heroes of those who saved or attempted to save their lives by bolting or of those who, shut up in buildings at Rorke's Drift, could not bolt, and fought like rats for their lives which they could not otherwise save.

Lieutenant Teignmouth Melvill VC

Teignmouth Melvill was born at 4 Clarendon Place, Marylebone, London, on 8 September 1842 and was baptised at St Mary's Church, Paddington Green, London, on 9 December 1842. He had five sisters, and he was the younger of two sons to Philip Melvill FRGS (born at Topsham, Helston in Cornwall on 26 October 1795 and died at Bodmin in Cornwall on 4 October 1882) and his wife Eliza (born at Helston on 21 June 1805 and died in Bournemouth on 14 December 1890). His father was originally a Bengal Army officer who became secretary in the Military Department of the Honourable East India Company, and his mother was the daughter of Colonel William Sandys of Lenarth, Helston. His brother, Philip Sandys Melvill, went on to become agent to the viceroy and governor-general of India, at Baroda.

Teignmouth was sent away for his education, first to Cheltenham College in Gloucestershire, then to Harrow School from 1856 to 1858. His father retired from the Indian service when the East India Company was nationalised after the Indian Rebellion in 1858. The family home became Ethy House in Lostwithiel, on the banks of the River Fowey in Cornwall, and they regularly attended the local St Winnow's Parish Church. The 1861 census records that Teignmouth was living away from home as a pupil of Bonchurch School at Ventnor, on the Isle of Wight. His next studies took him up to Trinity College, Cambridge, where he was active with the university 'drag' hunt, and was a member of the Athenaeum and Amateur Dramatics Society. He graduated with a Bachelor of Arts in February 1865.

Teignmouth fatefully chose the army as his calling and he was commissioned by purchase as ensign in the 24th (2nd Warwickshire) Regiment on 20 October 1865, joining the 1st Battalion in Ireland. He served on the island of Malta, where he became a Freemason, being promoted by purchase to lieutenant on 2 December 1868. He was appointed adjutant on 7 March 1873 while serving at Gibraltar. In the same year, the regiment acquired a new depot at Brecon in Wales. Early in 1875 the 1st Battalion received orders to go to Cape Colony, and Lieutenant Melvill sailed for South Africa, where he took part in bush fighting at Griqualand West, and was noted for his hard work and intelligence throughout the Cape Frontier War of 1877-78.

He met Sara Elizabeth, daughter of Mr George Thomas Reed, of Port Elizabeth, Cape Colony, and they married in the town in February 1876. They had two sons: Teignmouth 'Tim' Philip was born in Cape Town on 13 February1877; and Charles William was born at St Winnow in Cornwall on 5 September 1878. Lieutenant Melvill passed the examination for entry into the Staff College at Camberley, but Lord Chelmsford required his services in South Africa so he stayed on; a decision which was to cost him his life.

Teignmouth was aged thirty-six when he was killed in action at iSandlwana, and Queen Victoria placed his widow and two boys on the civil list. He was entitled to the South Africa Medal with 1877-8-9 clasp, and on 2 May 1879, only a memorandum appeared in the *London Gazette*, which in his case stated that had he survived he would have been recommended for the Victoria Cross 'on account of the gallant efforts made by him to save the Queen's colour of his Regiment after the disaster at iSandlwana'.

In 1906, Sarah Melvill was one of several people to petition King Edward VII to revise the Victoria Cross warrant to include posthumous awards. As a result, the *London Gazette* for 15 January 1907 carried notification of Victoria Cross awards to both Melvill and Coghill, and Mrs Melvill received the medal five months later. It is now with the regimental museum at Brecon.

There are several memorials to Teignmouth Melvill at Cheltenham College: he is named on the Big Classical VC Roll of Honour in the Assembly Hall; there is a display and name in the 'For Valour' memorial book in the library; he has an entry in the 'Honours Book' in the Archives

Department; and a framed citation and picture in classroom number five in the Centenary Block. There is a memorial dedicated to him in the Harrow School Chapel; there is a stained-glass memorial window at St Winnow Parish Church in Cornwall, and on a memorial at St Fin Barre's Anglican Cathedral in Cork; his name appears on the Victoria Cross Honours Board; his name is inscribed on the colour-pole of the regiment laid up in Brecon Cathedral, and a memorial was erected on the bank of the Buffalo River by the South African War Graves Board in 1974.

Sarah and the two boys went to live with Philip and Eliza at Ethy House, and the boys eventually went on to distinguished military careers. Tim was commissioned into the South Wales Borderers from Sandhurst in 1896, before transferring to the 17th Lancers, with whom he gained the Distinguished Service Order in France during the Great War. He attained the rank of colonel, commanding the regiment. He played for the celebrated 17th/21st Lancers polo team, won an Olympic gold medal at Antwerp in 1920, and represented his country against the United States in 1924. He was appointed Assistant Military Attaché in Madrid, and was the polo correspondent with the influential sport magazine *The Field*. He died at King's Lynn on 12 October 1951.

Charles was commissioned into the South Lancashire Regiment in 1897 and served in the Boer War. He served in India until 1906, after which he went to New Zealand to take up farming in Otago, and worked in administration with the New Zealand Military Forces. On the outbreak of the Great War he served with the South Lancashire Regiment on the Western Front. He was commandant of the New Zealand military forces when he died suddenly at Wellington on 15 September 1925.

Of the twenty-three Victoria Crosses awarded to the 24th (2nd Warwickshire) Regiment of Foot (later the South Wales Borderers, and now the Royal Welsh), ten were gained for the Anglo-Zulu War of 1879, and the regiment has served with distinction in many campaigns in Europe and the empire.

Raised in Kent in 1689 as Sir Edward Dering's Regiment of Foot, the unit did its first of many tours of Ireland, serving in that troubled country until 1692. John Churchill, Duke of Marlborough, one of England's greatest commanders, took over as colonel in 1702, and the regiment took part in the War of the Spanish Succession (1702-1713), gaining many famous battle honours. It became known as the 24th Regiment of Foot in 1751, and a 2nd Battalion was formed in

1757, which later became the 2nd Welch Regiment. 1776 saw the 24th Regiment in North America, and after Quebec had been relieved, they were in frequent action as part of the advance guard during the British Army's march south for the American War of Independence. Through a lack of provisions and reinforcements, the campaign was a disaster, and the 24th Regiment was part of the outnumbered British force which had to surrender at Saratoga in 1777.

In 1782 the unit was instructed to style itself the 24th (2nd Warwickshire) Regiment, and in 1801 it was sent to Egypt. It took part in the capture of Alexandria, for which it was awarded the battle honour 'Egypt', and adopted the 'sphinx' as an insignia on the regimental colour and the collar badge. It then saw its first tour of service at the Cape of Good Hope 1805-1810.

In 1804, a 2nd Battalion was raised at Warwick, and took part in the Duke of Wellington's campaigns. It served with distinction in the Peninsular War, gaining nine battle honours. It was disbanded in 1814. The Regiment then served in India 1846-61, during which time it took part in the Sikh Wars, and during the Battle of Chillianwallah in 1849 it succeeded in breaking through enemy lines and capturing guns, but suffered heavy losses. In 1858, a 2nd Battalion was raised in Sheffield, being presented with colours in the following year.

It was this unit which gained the regiment's first Victoria Crosses, when five soldiers manned a boat and risked their lives in perilous water attempting to rescue comrades from cannibalistic natives on the shore of Little Andaman Island in 1867. One of these soldiers was Private Griffiths, who was killed in action at iSandlwana. A sixth Victoria Cross was gained by the battalion during the Ashanti Expedition in 1874. In 1873, the regiment moved their depot from Warley in Birmingham to Brecon in Wales. In 1872 the 1st Battalion returned to South Africa to deal with inter-tribal fighting in the Transkei. When the 2nd Battalion arrived there in 1878 to assist in the Cape Frontier War, the two battalions operated in the same country for the first time. This campaign consisted mainly of sweeping skirmishes to flush rebel natives out of the bush, and was over by mid-1878.

Private Samuel Wassall VC

Samuel Wassall was born on 28 July 1856 at number 11 Court, Alcester Street, St Mary's Parish in the industrial Deritend district of Birmingham, not far from where the St Andrew's football ground was built in 1906.

He was the second-youngest son in the family of seven children to a wire worker named Thomas Wassall (1819-1881) and his wife Elizabeth (formerly Silk, 1824-1869). The 1871 census records the family as living at 21 Ayres Yard in St Edmunds Parish, Dudley, Birmingham, and Sam was listed as a bricklayer. He was apprenticed to a dyer in 1874.

He enlisted into the 80th Regiment (Staffordshire Volunteers) at Dudley on 28 November 1874, as no. 427 Private Wassall. On 2 November 1875, the governor of the tin-rich province of Perak, in Malaysia, was murdered, and nine days later Private Wassall was among three companies of the regiment who sailed to Singapore on the SS *Kashgar* as reinforcements sent to deal with the situation. Also among the troops was fellow Brummie, Private Thomas Westwood. The culprits were soon captured and the fighting ceased. For his service he was awarded the Indian General Service Medal with Perak clasp.

After returning to the Hong Kong station, Private Wassall sailed with the regimental headquarters bound for Mauritius, but when measles broke out among the children on board the ship they were diverted to the Cape, arriving at East London, but they were refused permission to land because of the sickness until 6 March. Private Wassall's company reached Pretoria on 13 March, where they were attached to the brigade being prepared by Colonel Hugh Rowlands VC, for an expedition against Sekhukhune, chief of the Pedi tribe. The Pedi and the Boers had disputes over land boundaries along the Transvaal border, and several confrontations had occurred. When Britain annexed the bankrupt Boer state in 1877, the problem was inherited.

On 13 August 1878, Private Wassall was one of thirty-four men of the 80th Regiment who became attached to the Imperial Mounted Infantry as Carrington's Horse, under Lieutenant John Russell (of the 12th Lancers), bringing the squadron's strength to 120. The brigade also consisted of the 1st Battalion 13th Light Infantry and 400 mounted volunteers. They moved to Fort Weber and were ready to assault Sekhukhune's mountain stronghold by 4 October. However, a serious drought ground the operation to a halt through lack of water and pasture for the transport animals. When sickness began to hit them it was decided to postpone the campaign until a more favourable time, and the British withdrew.

Most of the force moved to Utrecht in the Transvaal, where Colonel Evelyn Wood VC was establishing a base for the 4th (left flank) Column in preparation for the invasion of Zululand. The mounted infantry were sent to Rorke's Drift to join the central column, and after the troops crossed the border on 11 January they formed an escort for Lord Chelmsford when he travelled north to rendezvous with Colonel Wood, who was advancing towards Ulundi from the north-west, and on the following day Private Wassall's unit formed an advance guard during the attack on Sihayo's stronghold. Three days later he was on the move again when he was with a detachment of mounted troops sent to reconnoitre eastwards beyond iSandlwana, about thirty-five kilometres into enemy territory, where they encountered a body of Zulus and shots were fired, but there were no casualties.

Captain Barton recorded a statement after visiting the hospital at Helpmekaar on 11 February 1879, where Private Westwood overheard him relating the events he had witnessed and the action of the unknown soldier who he thought had perished. Westwood cried out that it was Private Wassall who had saved his life and that the hero was still alive. Captain Barton's testimony set in motion a recommendation that Private Wassall should be awarded the Victoria Cross in recognition of his gallant conduct. Three further officer statements were acquired before Private Wassall was tracked down, and on 11 April he made a formal statement that he signed in the presence of the Pietermaritzburg District Magistrate.

He returned to the destroyed camp with the 17th Lancers on 21 May, being asked to comment on the battle and describe the events of his miraculous escape. The award of the Victoria Cross to Private Wassall appeared in the *London Gazette* of 17 June 1879, and he received the medal from Lord Wolseley at Utrecht on 11 September. He also received the South Africa Medal with 1877-8-9 clasp. He was the first soldier of the 80th Regiment to be awarded the medal, and he was the youngest recipient serving with the British army at that time. He remained with the mounted infantry when the unit moved to Utrecht to prepare for the re-invasion, and after being present during the pitched battle at Hlobane Mountain, he took part in the subsequent operations with the Flying Column, being present at the Battle of Ulundi for the final crushing defeat of the Zulu army on 4 July 1879.

He was discharged from the army in the summer of 1880. He stood for a photograph to be taken at a studio in Dublin before he arrived back in England. The October 1879 issue of the popular children's periodical, *Aunt Judy's Magazine*, included a story entitled 'Jackanapes', which is believed to have been based on Private Wassall's Victoria Cross action. It was written by the editor herself, Juliana Horatia Ewing, who was an army officer's wife.

Samuel went to live at the home of his brother, William, at 28 Exmouth Street in Barrow-in-Furness, Lancashire (now in Cumbria). He was living at 5 Bath Street when he met a girl named Rebecca, who lived in the same street, and was the daughter of John Round. They married at St Matthew's Church in Barrow on 10 April 1882. The 1891 and 1901 censuses record the family living at 30 Exmouth Street, St James the Great Parish, Hindpool, Barrow, and he is described as a steelworks labourer. They had four sons and five daughters between 1883 and 1903. Samuel became employed as an electrical worker in the ship construction department at the Barrow shipyard, and the 1911 census records him living at 32 Lyon Street, Barrow-in-Furness.

He welcomed King George V and Queen Mary at Furness Abbey Station when they visited the town on 17 May 1917, and he met them again on 26 June 1920 when he was one of 324 holders of the Victoria Cross who attended a garden party at Buckingham Palace as guests of the sovereign. His wife went with him and he described the occasion as 'one of the greatest experiences of my life'. He was always proud to represent ex-servicemen at ceremonies and he was present at the unveiling of the cenotaph in Barrow Public Park. He placed the memorial wreath on several occasions.

Samuel Wassall was one of three surviving Zulu War VC-holders when he died at the North Lonsdale Hospital in Barrow on 31 January 1927, aged seventy. After a service at St James's Church, he was buried in Barrow Cemetery with military honours provided by the King's Own Regiment. Later that year, his Victoria Cross was presented to the South Staffordshire Regiment at Whittington Barracks in Lichfield. He is named on a memorial in the Garrison Church of St George at Whittington Barracks. His action is depicted on *The Victoria Cross Heroes* cigarette card number twelve.

A new memorial stone was placed at the grave in 1986, during a dedication service which was attended by many of his family descendants. Among them was 'Genial' Johnny Wassall, who had gained the Military Medal serving as a sergeant with the Royal Marines in the Falklands War. One of his assignments was to report on enemy movements for two months while disguised as a Merino sheep. During the First Gulf War in Iraq he served with the Special Air Service and was commended for his bravery by General Schwarzkopf.

Chapter 4

The Defence of Rorke's Drift

On the day of the invasion, the mission station at Rorke's Drift became all hustle as the soldiers began to pitch their tents between the back of the buildings which made up the post and a craggy hill known as the Oscarberg or Shiyane, about four hundred paces away; a sprawling military camp was quickly forming.

At that time the men of the Commissariat and Transport Department were considered to be civilians and they were officered by men of the Army Service Corps. Assistant Commissariat Officer Walter Dunne was in charge of the stores. He was joined by Acting Assistant Commissary James Langley Dalton, a tall, red-haired Londoner, who was in his late forties and therefore the oldest man at the post. He was a veteran of a line regiment which had taken part in the Red River Expedition in Canada in 1870 and had experience of service in the previous two Cape Frontier Wars. For the latter, he was mentioned in despatches for his efficiency as the sole officer at Ibeka Depot, during which time he provided three columns of troops with supplies on a regular basis. He had ridden up to the border with a young clerk named Louis Byrne in torrential rain on New Year's Day.

Their immediate duty was to supervise the establishment of a supply depot in the former chapel building. It measured eighty feet by twenty feet, and he and his men began the arduous task of stocking it with stores. There were bags of corn weighing 200 pounds each, heavy wooden boxes filled with biscuits, smaller wooden boxes containing two-pound tins of corned beef, and ammunition boxes each containing sixty packets of ten cartridges.

The medical team on ambulance wagons rolled up to the front of Witt's former house. The ambulances were ordinary Cape wagons that had been fitted with a sprung frame to act as a kind of rudimentary suspension which was intended to make life more comfortable for casualties in transit. James Henry Reynolds, a Dublin-born surgeon with the Army Medical Department, was well aware of the difficulties of military operations in South Africa. He had served with the 1st Battalion 24th Regiment in Griqualand in 1875, and he was with them again during the Cape Frontier War when they were besieged by Gcaleka rebels at Impetu for several months.

Doctor Reynolds eyed Witt's thirty-year old ramshackle house that they would have to somehow utilise as a field hospital. The two buildings were about forty paces apart, and each had a veranda facing away from the Oscarberg. This building was slightly smaller than the other, at sixty feet by eighteen feet, and Jim Rorke had somehow crammed eleven poky compartments into it, that were separated by thin partitions made from bricks and mud, with slight wooden doors. Doctor Reynolds decided to use one of the rooms to store medical supplies and stretchers and two front rooms were prepared as casualty stations. The patients would have to be put into seven dismal 'wards' that stretched in an 'L' shape at the western end and along the back of the building, the doors of which faced south towards the mountain. Only one of the rooms had access to the interior, which meant that the doctor would have to walk around the outside of the building to attend to most of his patients. The beds were straw-stuffed mattresses on hard boards placed on bricks to elevate them off the dusty floor, and these were already filling up with men nursing injuries suffered while unloading heavy bags and boxes off wagons as the camp was being established, and ailments such as bowel disorders caused by drinking bad water, or general debility as a result of the climate. The medics were also responsible for a water barrel on a cart and several appliances for filtering the dirty water.

Among the patients was Christian Ferdinand Schiess, of the Natal Native Contingent, known as Friederich, who was a hefty young Swiss veteran of the Franco-Prussian War, and he had gained a good reputation for his service in the most recent Cape Frontier War. He was limping about the place nursing a severely blistered foot caused by wearing ill-fitting boots.

Men of B Company, 2nd Battalion 24th Regiment formed the main bulk of the unit that was left behind to garrison the depot. They were under the command of a stocky, thirty-three-year old lieutenant named Gonville Bromhead, who had twelve years of home service behind him. He was from Lincolnshire, and was of a distinguished military family. However, his own career was being hampered by a hearing problem. Indeed, some disgruntled men in his company were apt to state that their officer's hardness of hearing was the reason why they were given such secondary tasks as guarding supply dumps. They could only watch the men as they slowly marched into hostile territory and disappeared from view, imagining that they would be marching on to glorious triumphs and wishing they were marching to war with them. However, they hoped to re-join the rest of their regiment when reinforcements arrived at Rorke's Drift to take their place.

Lieutenant John Chard was a thirty-one-year old Devonian serving with the 5th Company Corps of Royal Engineers. On arriving at Durban on 5 January he was greeted by a torrential downpour in which the Engineers had to unload hundreds of tons of stores and equipment. To add to his dilemma his vaccination injection had become inflamed and his right shoulder was very sore, but he received the order from the commander and with no time to recover he took a small party of engineers to join the 3rd Column at Rorke's Drift. The party included Driver Charles Robson, who was the officer's batman and groom, a corporal and three sappers. A small mule train was organised on which the men and their equipment were loaded. Chard rode on horseback with Charles on his spare mount. Because the rains had drenched the tracks the movement of wagons was slow and it was not until 19 January that the party of tired men rattled by the mission station and down to the river, where the sappers set to the task of fixing and securing the ropes that were used to pull the ferries across the river.

A drizzly rain fell during the night, and the morning of 22 January 1879 was cold, damp and misty. Lieutenant Horace Smith-Dorrien rode into the camp to attend to some transport business, and while he was there he told Lieutenant Bromhead that Zulus had been sighted and Lord Chelmsford had taken half the force further into enemy territory to locate and engage them. Everyone was expecting action soon.

Lieutenant Chard had also been to the camp at iSandlwana, where he learned that his duties were specifically on the Natal side of the river, keeping the ponts in working order and maintaining the tracks back to Helpmekaar. Through field glasses he had seen groups of Zulus moving about on the distant hills in a westerly direction towards the vicinity of Rorke's Drift, so he became concerned that they might try to cut off the supply line by attacking the depot. He set off back and arrived at the post in time for lunch. There he found a note in his tent from Major

Henry Spalding, who was the depot commander, stating that a small guard was to be placed at the ponts to protect them until a company which had been ordered forward from Helpmekaar arrived. Chard considered the guard to be too small for the task and went up to the post to express his feelings. There he told Major Spalding what he had seen at iSandlwana, and in light of this the major agreed and decided to go to Helpmekaar himself to see what was delaying the reinforcements. As he set off he told Chard that he was in charge of the depot in his absence, but 'nothing will happen' and he would be back before dark. With that, Lt Chard went back to his duties at the river.

Some men were out of the camp doing various duties, and several sergeants heard the pounding of artillery coming from the direction of iSandlwana. They could make out what they believed were clouds of smoke rising in the distance, but it was difficult to see clearly with the naked eye. The hills around the post seem to have muffled the sound of the ordnance from the men in the camp, for all seemed normal. Lieutenant Bromhead and Mr Dunn were relaxing, smoking their pipes under a tarpaulin they had propped up with tent poles to shield them from the hot sun. The officer had allowed most of his unit to idle near their tents. Some were entertaining themselves in playing cards and other kinds of gaming schools, while others were trying to write letters home to their families.

Private Henry Hook, usually known as Harry, was the hospital cook that day and he was busy at the cookhouse ovens behind the store brewing tea for the sick and injured. Private Frederick Hitch was also working at the ovens preparing food for dinner. The army owed much of its field kitchen arrangements and gadgets to a Frenchman named Alexis Soyer, a former chef at the fashionable Reform Club in London. He had designed a form of portable stove for use in camp during the Crimean War. It was essentially a steam boiler fired by wood, or coal when it was available, with a removable oven on top, and a chimney attached to take away any smoke. The 'Soyer stove' was considered such a useful appliance that they were still being used during the Gulf War, the only new improvisation being that they were fired by bottled gas.

He also improved the method of making tea—a real advantage to British soldiers in the field. It had previously been brewed in the same copper boiler which had just been emptied of soup. To put this right he had invented his 'scutari teapot', a large kettle in which there was a removable filter to hold the loose tea and enable it to be used to better effect.

When the sergeants returned and reported what they had heard Surgeon Reynolds, Otto Witt and Reverend Smith decided to go up the Oscarberg hoping to get a better view of what was happening. When they arrived at the summit they were disappointed to discover that the slopes of iSandlwana blocked their view, but they could hear the artillery pounding. About half an hour after the eclipse they saw a large body of natives moving around iSandlwana coming on in their general direction. They took them to be a unit of the Natal Native Contingent, which disappeared from view as they descended into low country, presumably in pursuit of fugitive Zulus. At about 1.00 p.m. many men used their hands to make visors to look up at the sky as it went dark during an eclipse of the sun.

The men at the post were not too concerned as they believed there was a large body of troops between them and the Zulu army, and reinforcements were presumably on their way from Helpmekaar. However, at about 3.00 p.m., two riders caught the attention of some of the men as they galloped hell-for-leather towards them from the direction of iSandlwana. The first man rode on, but the second stopped, and as he dismounted he called out 'you will all be murdered and cut to pieces!' This is believed to be Trooper Charles Fletcher, of the Natal Carbineers, and as the panic-stricken man approached the command tent they listened with horror as he gasped out the news that the camp at iSandlwana had been taken by the Zulus and most of the men left in it had been wiped out. The identity of this man and some others who passed by the mission station that day has caused much debate among some modern researchers, but I doubt the men of the 24th Regiment cared too much who they were considering the fact that they rode away and left them to their fate.

From the top of the hill, Surgeon Reynolds had seen four colonials riding frantically towards the depot on the Natal side of the river from the direction of iSandlwana. He thought they might need his assistance, so he rode back down the hill and arrived just as they pounded into the camp. They were visibly anxious, and to the doctor's surprise one of them was on Surgeon-Major Shephard's horse. The first man simply shouted 'they're coming', and rode on to Helpmekaar, but the other dismounted and asked to be shown to the officer's tent. When Bromhead appeared he hastily handed him a pencilled note that had reached them because of the combined efforts of three officers who had escaped the carnage and bloodshed at iSandlwana, and he shouted uncontrollably 'good God, the camp is taken and they are coming here!'

The note confirmed the previous report, and a look of urgency came onto the officer's face when he read that, with the column in disarray, a large Zulu *impi* was at that moment making its way towards Rorke's Drift. This he was to hold at all costs. The officers found it hard to believe that such a disaster could have happened. Nobody could grasp the full significance at first and they didn't quite know what to do. However, Bromhead regained his composure and his first act was to send a man down to the river to warn Chard.

By this time, the men in the depot were looking at each other with apprehension as they suspected that there was some kind of alarm. They were ordered to fall in and Bromhead wasted no time in telling them the unbelievable news, and said that whatever had happened they would stand firm to the last man. The fugitives tried to make them realise that the Zulus were in overwhelming numbers and their only chance of survival was to retreat; which they themselves promptly did, leaving the soldiers to realise the implications of the serious disaster which had occurred.

The officers also came to realise they were in a somewhat dire situation and there were some quick decisions to be made. There was a feeling among the ranks that the safest thing to do was to try to reach the troops back at Helpmekaar, but if they did retreat could they get there before a fast-moving *impi* caught up with them? Also, if Lord Chelmsford's advance force was falling back they might be in desperate need of supplies and ammunition, and the Rorke's Drift depot was their only lifeline. They had no idea of the size of the force that was coming and they had done nothing to put the post in a state of defence. If the Zulus arrived soon they were open to attack on all sides and were sure to be massacred. Could they throw up a makeshift barricade in time? Then, Mr Dalton joined them and took the initiative by strongly suggesting that they should stay and make a defence. He strengthened his opinion by bringing to notice the good supply of building material they had in the store.

Mr Dunne said to Mr Dalton, 'do whatever you think best', and they began to work out a line of defence as the men started to pull down the tents, and with the help of Sergeant Windridge and the men of the 1st Battalion, the commissariat began to empty the store of anything that could be used to build a barricade, as all ranks put their backs into it and worked with great determination. Colour-Sergeant Bourne posted look-outs, selected six men to be posted inside the hospital in preparation to guard the bedridden sick as soon as it had been barricaded, then he was instructed to organise skirmishers. According to Corporal Lyons it was he and Corporal Allan who took out sixteen skirmishers each, Allan taking his party to the left of the Oscarberg. The men were also instructed to loophole the walls of the buildings.

At about 3.15 p.m., Lieutenant Chard was in his tent dealing with some correspondence when his attention was brought to two riders galloping towards the Drift from the east. When they reached the makeshift jetty on the far bank they dismounted and began to edge their way tentatively into the water. One of them was Lieutenant Adendorff, of the Natal Native Contingent. It would seem that they had left iSandlwana quite early on, but their escape would still have been hazardous as Zulu warriors were marauding everywhere. Neither of them could swim, so they hugged the bed of the river nervously as they grasped their way forward and called out to be ferried the rest of the way. Lieutenant Chard was concerned on witnessing their anxious behaviour as he ordered the pont to be sent across to collect them, and when they reached the Natal bank Adendorff quickly took him out of earshot of the men and told him the shocking news that the camp at iSandlwana was in the hands of the enemy. His companion confirmed the report before he quickly rode off, stating that he wanted to take the news to Helpmekaar. At that time, the men at the river were not aware of the *impi* that was on its way to attack Rorke's Drift.

Lieutenant Chard could hardly believe what he was hearing, but he tried to keep calm as he had his horse saddled. He was suggesting to Adendorff that perhaps he had left iSandlwana too soon to be so sure of the outcome when Bromhead's message arrived asking him to go up to the post as soon as possible. He gave orders to prepare the wagon and oxen and posted his men in good positions to overlook the ferry before making haste to the depot. On arriving, and being told of the approaching enemy, he had a quick consultation with the officers and approved all the decisions that had already been taken. He added his knowledge of field fortification to suggest improvements, and when he was satisfied that everything was under control he returned to the river.

The hospital building formed the western end of the perimeter, and a barricade of bags and boxes connected the back of the hospital with the front of the storehouse. Two wagons were included in this wall to save time and the gaps under them were filled with bags and boxes. More bags were stacked on top of them for further height and to form embrasures between them through which the men could fire. The high stone wall at the back of the store completed the south section of the fort, with the exposed windows blocked and the wall loopholed.

There was a stone *kraal* to the west of the perimeter, with walls that were only chest-high and too thin to stack materials on for extra height, but it was too close to the store veranda and had to be included in the perimeter, the opening between it and the store being blocked with bags. A natural ledge of rock about two feet high ran along the course of the front of the post, and bags and boxes were stacked three or more high along the top of the ledge to form a breastwork of convenient height to fire over, and a six foot obstacle to an assailant. However, in front of the hospital veranda the ledge veered outwards and the rampart continued in a straight line along the top of the slope, before curving round to meet the far corner of the building, and there was an area here where only a long plank filled the gap. This was the most vulnerable part of the barricade. The length of the north wall was about one hundred paces, and the length of the whole perimeter was about 400 paces.

When Lieutenant Chard arrived back at the ponts the fatigue party was ready to move. The hawsers and cables had been sunk out of sight of the enemy, and Sergeant Millne, Mr Daniells and the detail of men offered to moor the ponts in the middle of the river and try to defend them from the decks. This was a brave request and the officer was greatly heartened by their pluck, but he decided that they would be better deployed defending the depot and they all made their way up to the post.

Several more fugitives arrived from iSandlwana, but most, or all, of them rode on. They may have made a useful addition to the numbers, but their morale had been shattered and the officers decided that Rorke's Drift was no place for faint hearts, and they would probably be better off without them. Each time a fresh gruesome tale was told the natives became more and more nervous, and their numbers too were dwindling. Then an encouraging reinforcement arrived. Lieutenant Henderson led a troop of about one hundred mounted colonials into the depot. Chard told him to send a detachment down to the river to watch over the Drift, and another to reconnoitre behind the Oscarberg, and if necessary to check the enemy's advance and give them more time to finish the fort. When they fell back they were to help in the defence of the depot. Mr Dalton asked him, and a man named Hall, to try to rally the edgy natives and try to stop them from sneaking off until the work was done.

Chaplains Smith and Witt had watched several fugitives riding towards Rorke's Drift, and while it began to bother them that the column may be falling back, they were reassured because none of them were red-coated imperial troops. A large number of natives suddenly came into view moving up from the river and they saw them squat down. This was presumably to take snuff, but modern research has suggested that they were indulging in concoctions far more potent. About thirty minutes later they rose up again in a mass and continued their advance towards the Oscarberg. The two clerics were deceived by their leisurely approach, but their suspicions were aroused when they saw that they were not wearing the red rag of the Natal Native Contingent around their heads. The oncoming force was within rifle range when they realised that the two men on grey horses who were leading them were not Europeans. They looked at each other with horror in their widened eyes when they realised that the oncoming horde was a large Zulu *impi*. They turned and fled quickly down the hill. On arriving at the now bustling camp, Witt became angry at the sight of what had been done to his property, but he stated that he was concerned for his family so he and Lieutenant Purvis, along with a native who was believed to be a cousin of the Zulu king, rode away. Chaplain Smith decided that the presence of a man of God was never more needed so he elected to remain at Rorke's Drift.

Satisfied that as much as possible had been done to put the post in a reasonable state of defence, the officers told the men to stop work and saw to it that every man was allocated a specific position at the barricade to defend. The six men who had been posted inside the hospital were ordered to barricade the windows and doors with whatever they could and try to defend the patients who could not be moved. It was also important to give them a breather before the attack began. The water cart was already within the enclosure, ammunition had been issued, and the opened boxes of reloads had been placed in convenient places for the men to get at.

Private Hitch had just brought the last of four kettles of tea into the compound when Lieutenant Bromhead requested him to get onto the roof of the store as lookout, which gave him a panoramic view of the area around the post. There were indeed several features which the warriors could use to their advantage. The heights of the Oscarberg loomed menacingly over the depot, and there were some deep *dongas* (dry water holes) on the approach from the south-west and from the east towards the river. Only about twenty paces to the south of the back of the store stood the shed that had been used as the cookhouse, and beside it were two round stone ovens. There were two shallow drainage ditches, one running in a southward direction away from the store and the other running almost parallel with the wagons in the south barricade. Beyond them the tents of the 24th Regiment littered the ground. To the north, thick bushes grew right up to the ledge of rocks and there had been no time to cut them down. Some thirty paces away from the hospital veranda, running parallel with the ledge, there was a wall about five feet high. Just beyond the wall there were two poplar trees to which some horses had been tied, while a rutted track ran by, and beyond that there was a fenced garden. There was rising ground to the west, where some haystacks and the toilet stood. The ground sloped down towards the river to the east, where there was an additional, larger, rough-stone *kraal*, and beyond that stood the engineer wagon.

At about 4.20 p.m. the sound of rifle fire could be heard from behind the hill, which triggered a mass colonial desertion. The detachment under Lieutenant Henderson could be seen retreating towards Helpmekaar, and the hundred or so natives that were left took to their heels, with their officer following on his horse. Chard's native wagon driver scampered towards the hill and hid in a cave, where he presumably remained throughout the fighting. Corporal Anderson had been ordered to leave the hospital to fight at the wall but he lost his nerve and fled after them. To see them deserting like that was too much for some of the men of the 24th, and they shouted curses and some even fired after them. Anderson was hit in the back of the head and his lifeless body went sprawling among the trees in the orchard at the front of the post.

The sound of pounding hoofs then caught their attention as Henderson and Hall came galloping up to the post. Henderson reported that his men had refused to obey orders, and Hall shouted at the top of his voice that the Zulus, 'as black as Hell and as thick as grass', were almost upon them. They both rode off afterwards, and it was generally agreed it was fortunate that these troops had shown their weakness before the attack and not during it.

With this reduction in manpower, Lieutenant Chard decided that the line of defence was too extended and he ordered that more boxes should be used to construct an inner barricade reaching about seventy paces from the north-west corner of the store to a point at about the middle of the front wall. This would provide a valuable entrenchment if the defenders were forced to fall back from the original perimeter.

Lieutenant Chard knew that his men had superior weapons to those carried by the enemy. He could also gain confidence from the fact that the reputation of bravery attributed to the Zulus was matched by the tradition of coolness and gallantry of the British infantryman. Such bravery was shown at the Alma, Balaclava, Inkerman, and in the trenches around Sebastopol during the Crimean War, at Lucknow and Gwalior, and across Central India during the Indian Mutiny, at the Taku Forts in China, and during the Ashanti Expedition.

The feeling of isolation must have been terrifying, particularly in the face of an as-yet unseen foe. The warriors who were about to attack them and try to cut them to pieces would give no mercy, and expect none for themselves in their desire to 'wash their spears' in the blood of their enemy. Some men made pacts to kill each other if all seemed lost to save themselves from the horror of Zulu ritual savagery. There was no safe refuge, and whether they survived or not seemed to depend on the strength of the defences and how heavily outnumbered they might be. Hearts began to pound, and all each individual could do now was to put his faith in the rifle in his hands and the fighting ability of the tense comrades beside him.

A cry of 'stand to!' echoed around the post, and as Corporal Allan and the rest of the skirmishers ran in and took their places at the barricade, all eyes turned to the western flank of the Oscarberg where about fifty Zulus had come into view. They extended into open order as they edged forward cautiously, prancing about trying to draw fire from the barricades it would seem, so that a solitary *inDuna* (chief) who had appeared on the crest of the Oscarberg could count their guns. There was a clicking noise all around as the men in red tunics, dark trousers and low-brimmed tropical corked helmets fixed the 24-inch bayonets to their rifles. They were ordered to present arms, and nervous fingers eased pressure on the triggers, but the warriors were some distance away and a second voice rang out ordering them to hold their fire.

Private Hitch called down to Lieutenant Bromhead that he could see the main body of the Zulus behind the skirmishers, and he caused a flurry of mixed remarks when he estimated their numbers to be as many as 4,000, their columns stretching right across the pass from the Oscarberg to another hill. He reported that several hundred were forming a long, curved line preparing for an attack. He could also see many warriors creeping along the low terraces of the hill, where they were taking cover at the mouths of caves and settling down behind rocks. These warriors carried rifles, and as he took a prone position below the apex of the roof they exchanged a few shots, and he also took a pot shot at the dark figure of an *inDuna* he saw on the hill, who stood out against the bright blue sky, but his target was out of range.

The *inDuna* on the hill waved a signal and a stout mounted *inDuna* brought forward a mass of Zulus into full view of the men in the garrison. Their war regalia was designed to give them a fierce appearance. They wore loin cloths with horse-hair fringes and animal tails streamed from their elbows and knees. Many wore cow tail necklaces and beadwork ornaments. They carried black shields with a white splash, and their deadly stabbing *assegais* (spears). These were warriors of the inDlu-yengwe regiment, believed to be 1,000-strong and in their early thirties. The overall leader of the *impi* that was massing at the Oscarberg was Dabulamanzi, Cetshwayo's ambitious brother. His warriors had acted as reserves at iSandlwana and resented having not taken any major part in the battle. They were defying orders from Cetshwayo, who warned them not to enter Natal or attack fortified places, but they had been driven on by their desire to prove their prowess. After one loud chant of their war-cry '*Usuthu! Usuthu!*' they began to advance at a steady trot in sections of about fifty at a time. They swerved right and made a mad rush at the south barricade.

Lieutenant Bromhead gave the order for three volleys, and at about 600 paces the defenders' rifles thundered the first shots and clouds of black smoke rose from the barricade. Chamber levers clicked back and used cartridge cases tinkled onto the rocky ground. The first shots were wild, but at about 500 paces the firing steadied and a bullet from Private James Dunbar's rifle brought the *inDuna* crashing from his horse. The firing quickly gained momentum, and as the lead slugs smashed into the attackers, who were so thick that it was impossible to miss them, the force of impact lifted some of them off their feet before they fell, tumbling and rolling, and sprawling over each other as they did so. Some just dropped to the ground 'as if they had been cut off at the knees'. The sight of this gave the soldiers confidence, but their volleys were failing to stop the onrush. The warriors at the rear simply leaped over the ones who were falling before them and stooped forward as they ran in an effort to make more difficult targets. Their legs made a strange whooshing noise as they pushed through the long grass, and regardless of their dreadful losses and the danger to their lives, they gallantly raced forward.

The onrush was getting perilously close, and the men behind the wagons and bags were bracing themselves to receive the enemy with their bayonets, when at about fifty paces the Zulus were caught between such heavy volleys from the south barricade, with a tremendous crossfire from the back of the store and hospital, that the attack was checked. Warriors who carried rifles took cover behind the cookhouse and ovens, while others scrambled into ditches or took advantage of anything that would shield them from the rain of bullets. Some ran up to the back of the storehouse and threw themselves against the wall, but there was no cover and they were shot down. The greater number veered to their left without stopping and rejoined the main bulk of the warriors, which Dabulamanzi was leading in a wide swoop around the hospital. Some came in to attack the defences in front of the hospital veranda, while the rest rushed into the thick bushes and trees to the north-west, and, under this cover, they pushed even further around the post until they had almost completely surrounded it.

The warriors on the Oscarberg began to fire down at the post, as did those who had taken cover in front of the south ramparts. They made as much noise as possible for the purpose of drawing the fire from the soldiers, while the Zulus hidden in the bushes on the other side of the position made an assault at the north wall. It was a good tactic, but it did not come off successfully as a look-out on the top floor of the storehouse gave warnings of any such danger. The British gritted their teeth as they met the rush, and there was the rattle of bayonet on shield and the clatter of rifle barrel on spear as the Zulus threw themselves at the breastwork, and with fanatical bravery they tried to get over. There was a desperate struggle as some of the warriors succeeded in climbing onto the bags and boxes and slashed and stabbed at the defenders in their frenzy, while the redcoats parried, prodded and thrust at them with their bayonets, or blasted them off the walls at point blank range. Some warriors fell screaming with dreadful injuries. Sometimes the butt of a rifle or even a swift left hook was enough to keep out a man.

The determined attack was pushing the men back from the area in front of the hospital, to a dog-leg breastwork that jutted in from the outer perimeter. There was a certain space of about nine yards where there had been no time to complete the barricade and only a plank of wood had been placed across it, and the Zulus were not long in discovering the weakness. At this vulnerable position, Lieutenant Bromhead led Hitch, Nichols (Nicholson), Fagan, Cole, Dalton, Schiess and Williams in a counter-strike with the point of the bayonet which threw the attackers back, and it was here that the hardest work was done at the beginning of the struggle.

Private Hitch shot a Zulu as he and several more warriors scaled the step to get at the men. As he tried to re-load, a warrior broke through, dropped his weapons, and grabbed the muzzle of Hitch's rifle, trying to wrench it from him. Fortunately, Hitch had a firm grip on the butt and somehow managed to reload as they struggled to and fro. He pulled the trigger and shot the Zulu, who held onto his grip for a while before he fell dead.

In spite of his problem, Corporal Schiess had chosen to fight alongside the regular soldiers, and he was helping at the barricade. On several occasions he climbed over the bags and got among the Zulus on the rocky step, smashing them off with the butt of his rifle and thrusting his bayonet at them as they pounced forward and tried to stab him. When some Zulus actually managed to clutch hold of his bayonet, he got it out of their hands, and, springing over the parapet, bayoneted some six or seven straight away. The men fighting near him were impressed by his gallant conduct, and they were alarmed when a bullet caught him on the instep of his already injured foot. However, it boosted their morale when he ignored the wound and carried on fighting. Schiess could not restrain himself in wanting to get at the Zulus each time they began to cause problems. He behaved with the greatest coolness and gallantry throughout the attack.

These successful actions gave the men renewed spirit. The tide changed, and the surviving Zulus were forced to scramble back out of the compound and take refuge in the bushes. However, the whole place was now alive with Zulus. The main body of them had moved right around the perimeter under cover of the thick bushes. Many were crouching behind Witt's wall, and they occupied the ditches, the garden and the hollow formed by the wear and tear of the use of the track. The defenders could not see them, but they could hear the rustling of branches and leaves, and some fired into the foliage in the hope of scoring an unseen hit. The Zulus crept right up to the ledge of rocks extending as far to the left as the bushes gave them enough cover to do so, from where they rose up, sprang out and surprised the soldiers as they attacked the breastwork.

These were mostly of the uDloko regiment, which totalled about 2,000 men aged forty-one, and the uThulwana, the regiment that Cetshwayo had once belonged to, which totalled about 1,000 men aged about forty-five. The inDluyengwe and the uThulwana were known collectively as the uNdi Corps. A fourth regiment, known as the iNdlondlo, had also set off towards Rorke's Drift, but for some reason they had turned back; perhaps they thought better of defying their king? Some warriors carried white shields and others brown shields with white spots, and most wore the head ring of battle-experienced married regiments. They wore monkey-skin earflaps, the plumes of exotic birds such as the crane and ostrich, otter-skin headbands, and ornaments of beadwork. Snuff boxes dangled from their earlobes and ivory snuff spoons were fastened to their heads.

Some Zulus started to run in at the doors of the hospital and smash their spears at the wooden panels. Surgeon Reynolds and the A. H. C. men realised that they would have to abandon the medical supplies unless they acted quickly and tried to move as much as they possibly could. He and Privates Luddington and McMahon dashed to the dispensary, while Corporal Miller and Mr Dalton covered them with their rifles. As they were grabbing as much as they could a Zulu crept up, sprang forward and pulled Miller towards him by the muzzle of his rifle and he was about to thrust his *assegai* into his stomach when Mr Dalton shot the warrior and saved the corporal's life. All the medical men then burst through the Zulus and ran to the entrenchment.

Once again the fighting became fierce, and Lieutenant Bromhead and his men drove the Zulus out of the compound near the hospital. Weapons clashed as the Zulus held one side of the barricade while the British kept their ground on the other. Each time the warriors were driven back into the bush they shouted their war cry of '*Usuthu!*' clashed their spears against their shields, then just as before they rose up and attacked the breastwork. The defenders replied with defiant shouts and met them with rapid fire. As the defenders fired, and then stabbed with their bayonets, the Zulus grabbed at them and some were wrenched from the rifles. But they were constantly driven back into the bush. There were acts of bravery on both sides, as they were locked in the brutality of battle.

Surgeon Reynolds, or one of his medics, was by the casualties as quick as he could, putting cold water on the injury and applying a cold compress to stop the bleeding. The doctor was looking after a terrier dog called Pip, which belonged to an officer who had moved up with the column. The excited animal scampered along at his feet barking at the Zulus. The Reverend Smith spent his time moving along the ramparts with his native servant, handing out cartridges from his hat, as well as reproving curses and foul comments, and stopping to give spiritual comfort to the wounded and dying. Birds were flirting through the smoke overhead, disturbed and confused by the cries and turmoil of the fighting. Above them, vultures hovered and waited in scavenging anticipation.

As Corporal Scammel was putting his rifle to good use from behind the front rank of soldiers, he cried out in pain as a bullet ripped into his shoulder and he dropped to the ground. He crawled up to Lieutenant Chard and handed him his cartridges. He asked for a drink of water and Mr Byrne brought him one. But while Byrne was helping his comrade, he himself was shot through the head and fell dead. Scammel was taken to the doctor, who by this time was using the storehouse veranda as the casualty station, calmly busying himself with organising and attending to his casualties, not allowing the violence all around him to stop him from doing his duty.

Lieutenant Chard was now well aware that the post was in great danger on all sides, so he gave the order that two heaps of sandbags which had been left outside the store should be constructed into a high redoubt to give them a second line of fire. This would also be the place where they would make their last stand if they had to. Mr Dunne and a few men at once started to pull the sacks from the top of the pile and stack them in two heaps, leaving a hollow in the middle where the wounded could be put away from enemy fire.

It was beginning to get dark, and they suddenly realised that they might be overrun by the Zulus under cover of darkness. However, at about this time the Zulus managed to set fire to the roof of the hospital and when it burst into flames the light illuminated the area. It seemed that fortune was on the side of the defenders, because now they would be able to see the Zulus as they attacked.

It was time for Lieutenant Chard to assess the situation and consider the chances of survival. Lieutenant Bromhead had secured the area around the stone *kraal*, but now the men inside the hospital were dangerously hard pressed. If he decided to abandon the outer perimeter, the men would be in even greater peril. But a large body of Zulus was pushing forward again and he could see that the men would not be able to hold the west barricades for very much longer. Eventually he found that he had no choice but to call all the men in the firing line to fall back to the biscuit box entrenchment. As they retired, a mass of warriors occupied the hospital veranda, and many more ran in on the outer perimeter and used it as cover from British bullets and from where they could continue to launch attacks.

Some of the men of the 24th stated that Corporal Schiess fought like a tiger. After the retreat to the biscuit boxes, without orders he crept out a few feet along the wall the British had just abandoned, to dislodge one in particular of the enemy who seemed to have got the hang of how to aim his rifle and was particularly annoying as he was shooting better than usual. He slowly raised himself up to get a shot at some of the enemy. The closest Zulu to him on the other side of the wall fired at him and blew his hat off. He immediately jumped up, bayoneted the Zulu, shot a second, and bayoneted a third who came to their assistance. With this good work done he returned to the cover of the inner entrenchment.

The hospital building was now completely isolated from the rest of the compound and the men inside were in great peril. All this time they were engaged in a desperate fight with warriors swarming all around the building and smashing at the doors to try to break them down. The thatch was packed tightly so the roof only smouldered at first, but it sent dense, black, choking smoke into the rooms.

Private Waters was stationed in an inner room defending a window at the veranda. Gunners Howard and Evans were defending their north-west corner room, which also had access to the veranda, and a window from which they were firing at Zulus who were massing at the front of the building. Behind this was the middle end room where the Zulus were fiercely assaulting the flimsy outer door. The doorway was completely out of the line of cover fire and there was no communication with the interior. Privates John Williams and Joseph Williams were defending this dangerously-exposed room, which contained four patients. Private Horrigan was able to offer assistance, but Private Beckett was too ill and the other two were bedridden.

Joseph had smashed bricks out of the wall to form a loophole the size of a small window to gain a wider line of fire. He was concentrating his aim at warriors who were creeping up as close as they could get, then running in and throwing their weight against the door, smashing at the panels in an effort to break it down. The patients were becoming anxious and the defenders more desperate as they realised that they were running out of ammunition and the door was gradually beginning to give way. In addition to this, the choking smoke was beginning to get thicker and causing them to cough and splutter. They knew that they would all be slaughtered by the Zulus or suffocated by smoke fumes and eventually burned to death if they did not get out very soon.

As soon as he had fired his last cartridge, John Williams began to poke and hack his bayonet into the mud which held the blocks together at the back petition in an effort to make a hole big enough to fit a man through, while Joseph started to thrust his bayonet at the warriors who were forcing their way through the splintering door. By the time John had succeeded, frenzied hands were grabbing at Joseph trying to disarm him. He must have known by this time that he had little chance of survival as he fought hard to hold the warriors back to give his comrades time to escape. However, as John and Horrigan struggled to get Beckett through the hole, the Zulus finally forced their way in. The gallant defender was seized by the warriors and manhandled out of the door, where they stabbed and smashed at his body, while others attacked the defenceless Privates Hayden and Adams in their beds. All three suffered the slaughter of Zulu ritual killing. They were stabbed repeatedly and their stomachs ripped open, which the Zulus believed released the spirits from within and prevented their own stomachs from swelling. Sergeant George Smith stated 'Drummer Hayden…was stabbed in hospital in sixteen places, his belly cut open right up in two places, and part of his cheek was cut off'.

The three breathless men who got out of the room now eyed the area they had escaped to. They could not go left towards the veranda, because Zulus were trying to get in that way. Through the thick smoke they could just make out the welcome form of Private Waters, who was standing in a doorway to their right, and beckoned them to follow him. Privates Williams and Beckett did so, but it was too late for Private Horrigan. Zulus came through the hole and from the veranda and set about him. They dragged him out through the front of the building, threw him violently to the ground and began to stab and rip at his body. Several warriors raced forward and tried to get at Private Waters, but he managed to close the door just in time.

Inside the room with Private Waters were Private Hook and eight patients. Private Waters had been shot in the arm as he fought to keep out the Zulus and he had retired to the inner room, where he found Hook single-handedly protecting the sick from the Zulus, who were trying to force their way in through a back door. At least here there was some cover cross-fire from the ramparts, and Hook had strapped up Waters' injured arm to try to stop it from bleeding.

Hook and Private Cole had defended a Xhosa native who had been wounded at Sihayo's *kraal* in a small room at the north-west corner. There was a door facing south and an interior door which connected with the room they were now in. However, it was above this room where the Zulus had first set light to the thatch, and Private Cole had run outside when the tension and fumes got too much for him to endure. Private Hook had then fought back the warriors for as long as he could, with the native groaning at him and asking him for a weapon to defend himself. The struggle became hopeless. Realising he could not hold on any longer, Hook had no option but to retire and escape through the interior door. The native cried out to him to help him to take off his bandages so that he could come, but Hook knew there was not enough time and there was nothing he could do. When the Zulus burst in they questioned the man before they stabbed him to death.

The two defenders were now in a room containing twelve men, and they continued to fight desperately to keep the maddened Zulus back from the interior doors. Private Williams realised quickly that their only path of escape was to get through the partition again. His bayonet had snapped from the muzzle of his rifle, so he took up one of the pickaxes that had been used to make loopholes and began to hack at the far wall, which would get them into two rooms that were closer to the compound. He had to continually avoid the blades of spears that kept thrusting at him as the warriors assaulted the doors, and one of them hit him on the front of his helmet which caused a scalp wound. The Zulus continued to grab at the rifles to try to snatch them away, but the determined defenders gripped them tightly. Several times they managed to load the weapons as they wrestled for possession and shot the foremost attackers at point-blank range.

Private Williams broke through at last, and with sharp, slicing blows he began to widen the hole. When the gap was large enough, the patients were helped through it one by one. Hook managed to hold the Zulus at bay until there was only Private Connolly left in the room. He was sat near the opening nursing his painful knee. A Zulu pressed his weight against the door and tried to force his way in, but Hook put the muzzle of his rifle on the warrior and fired. The blast threw the Zulu and all the men behind him sprawling back from the doorway, so Hook took advantage of the situation by grabbing hold of Connolly with both arms and dragging him out. The patient cried out in pain, but he was relieved to escape the raging horde that burst into the room behind them.

Private Hook stayed at the partition and thrust his bayonet at the Zulus who tried to follow, while John Williams wasted no time and began to repeat his task of picking at the wall to make another escape hole. The last two rooms had a communication door between them, and a high window leading out into the abandoned area of the compound.

Privates Robert and William Jones had defended seven patients in these rooms. There was a big age gap between the two soldiers, and

Robert had only been born a few months before William enlisted. There was a door and a window in the back wall, but it could be covered by fire from the barricades. The Zulus who managed to dodge the bullets were met at the doorway by the two Joneses, who were bayoneting them as soon as they got there. Robert had received three *assegai* wounds to his body, two in his right side and one in the left, when several warriors attacked them all at once and they could not bayonet them quickly enough. At the same time they were trying to help the sick men up to the high window, from where they were able to drop down into the compound. As Trooper Lugg was in the process of escaping he saw one bold Zulu creep into the kitchen to light his pipe. Lugg gained his escape and several more patients followed him, but Sergeant Maxfield was delirious and the defenders were struggling to dress him.

Corporal Allan and Private Hitch had kept up a communication with the hospital defenders via the escape window and the nearest back door. It seems that at one point during the evacuation they got together on a flight of steps which led up to the upper floor of the storehouse to give them an elevated view of the compound, and from where they could see warriors creeping up to the outside of the north wall preparing to climb over the barricade and attack the patients. This left them dangerously exposed to rifle fire from the armed warriors on the hill to their rear, but they were in a better position than most to shoot at the warriors who were putting the patients in peril.

When Doctor Reynolds had no casualties to attend to he was keeping them, and as many defenders as he could, supplied with bullets. This area was dangerously exposed to enemy cross-fire, and on one occasion, as the doctor was running to the hospital with his arms full of cartridges, a Zulu slug hit his helmet and gave him a jolt.

All of a sudden the entire roof of the hospital burst out in flames and became a blazing inferno, making it far too hazardous for anyone who stayed inside the building. The Joneses had managed to dress Sergeant Maxfield, but in his delirium he was being difficult and they could not get him to move. They had no choice but to leave him. 'We did not know of anyone being left inside the hospital, only the Zulus', so they made a determined effort to force the warriors away from the doorway to give themselves time to make their escape. William Jones climbed up to the window and eased his way out. With a complete disregard for his own safety, and aware that Zulus may well have entered the room, Robert passed his rifle out of the window and decided to make one last attempt at a rescue. He groped his way across the smoke-filled room, only to witness frenzied Zulus stabbing the helpless sergeant as he lay on his bed. There was nothing he could do, so he quickly climbed up to the window and heaved himself out before the Zulus could get at him. He had no sooner dropped down from the window on the other side when part of the roof collapsed behind him—'a complete mass of flames and fire'.

Private Williams, his hands cut and blistered, had started to shepherd the patients into the last room. By this time the fire was blazing out of control and it had burned to the rafters of the roof, causing fierce flames that curled menacingly above their heads. It was becoming unbearably hot and everyone was coughing and spluttering from the effect of the smoke, fumes and dust. Eight more patients were evacuated through the hole. However, Private Beckett was demoralised, and Private Waters became weak from loss of blood, and they both became aware that either the flaming hot roof material or the Zulus would be upon them before they got out. Hook yelled at them to get a move on, but as the Zulus broke in they took advantage of the screen of black smoke and both climbed into a cupboard that was standing in the corner. They pulled items of clothing over themselves and hoped they were not discovered—or burnt to death!

The warriors piled into the room, but they did not bother about the cupboard and made their way to the hole in the wall, where they were once again stopped in their tracks by Private Hook's lunging bayonet and Private Williams smashing at them with the butt of his rifle.

Hook and Williams got their patients out of the window, and quickly followed them. Zulus attempted to attack this second batch of hospital refugees as they dropped down from the window and began to hobble slowly or crawl frantically across the compound to get to the relative safety of the biscuit box entrenchment. Private Savage limped desperately across the fort and scrambled over the boxes, but Private Robert Cole got into difficulty and a number of Zulus were approaching him. Private McMahon ran to his assistance, and Private Hitch added some firepower by shooting down three warriors as McMahon helped the soldier to the boxes. Gunner Cantwell ran from the store to assist Bombardier Lewis, and as he did so Private Hitch levelled his rifle at his hip and shot down a warrior who was about to attack them.

Corporal Allan was helping the last of the invalids to get to the entrenchment when a Zulu bullet struck him and travelled right through his arm. The already wounded Corporal Lyons said, 'give it to them, Allen, I am done; I am dying', to which Corporal Allan replied, 'all right, Jack!' Then Lyons noticed a hole in his arm and said, 'Allan, you are shot', and William replied, 'yes. Goodbye'. He walked away with blood running from his arm. Surgeon Reynolds attended to him and dressed his wound and he went back to his duties, but being too injured to fight, he spent the night distributing ammunition to his comrades at the barricade.

Most of the fourteen patients who reached the entrenchment were taken to Doctor Reynolds to be attended to at the casualty station in the veranda of the storehouse, but some were able to assist in the fighting and took their places alongside their comrades who were valiantly defending the inner fort. Private Savage was able to lay on his side and fire through a gap in the boxes, and Trooper Lugg took up a position beneath the eaves of the storehouse roof.

When the hospital was set on fire it was a disaster for the men inside. However, when it went dark the light from the blazing roof proved to be their salvation, as it illuminated the warriors as they continued to run in and assault the barricades. Such was the cunning of the enemy that some warriors used the shadows created by the light from the fires, and sprang up onto the ramparts, only to be shot down as soon as they got there.

Mr Dalton was using his rifle well. A warrior fell almost every time he fired it, and he continually moved along the barricade encouraging the men. He brought attention to a warrior running in to assault a section of the barricade, and had raised himself up to full height to get a better aim and fire at another, when he was shot through the right side of his chest. He turned pale with shock, but he managed to stay on his feet and hand his rifle to Lieutenant Chard. He asked Chard to take his remaining cartridges from his pockets, and the doctor was soon at his side bandaging his wound to stop the bleeding. The stretcher-bearers then helped him to the redoubt, where he was made as comfortable as possible. Mr Dunne was totally exposed to enemy fire as he stood high up on the bags directing the construction. The men toiled relentlessly until the sides were about eight feet high, and they had totally exhausted themselves. Between twenty and thirty men climbed inside, and the most serious casualties were also placed there.

It was now gone seven o'clock and the fierce Zulu onslaughts were becoming general almost all around the perimeter. The defenders used the same tactic to face most of these attacks, which was to hold firm with the bayonet, and then thrust it forward repeatedly at the warriors as they came over the barricade. Therefore, the Zulus found themselves faced with a line of bayonets, a kind of palisade of cold steel, which they either fell onto, or it stabbed at them and either killed them or forced them back out of the fort, as Private Caleb Wood recalled:

> When our ammunition began to run short the order was given to use cold steel. We stood back from the wall and received the enemy's charges with the bayonet at the 'shorten arms'—a point which is almost impossible for any man to turn aside, for there is so much weight behind it. This was very well to stop the first ranks, but points from the guard in quick succession was the method we adopted.

Driver Robson was among the men who were trying to defend the *kraal* at the eastern end of the barricade. He was concentrating his fire at the Zulus who were ransacking the wagon with all the engineering equipment in it. Because the *kraal* was some distance from the light given off by the flames it was not as well lit as the rest of the fort, and many warriors were able to creep up close to the stone wall undetected. One warrior crawled along the rampart and grabbed hold of Private Michael Minehan's leg. The frantic soldier prodded the straw with his bayonet to locate the Zulu and killed him. Eventually, the defenders of this area were pushed back from the barricade to the inner wall of the *kraal* below the mealie bag redoubt, and the Zulus occupied the abandoned wall. The men defending the redoubt were well elevated above them, and each time a warrior presented himself above the *kraal* he was easily picked-off by rifle fire.

Lieutenant Bromhead and the men he had brought back from the outer perimeter were fiercely defending the area where the biscuit boxes met the bags that formed the north perimeter, and several men were wounded or killed at this point. A Zulu bullet hit Lance-Sergeant Williams in the left side of his chest and he fell, seriously wounded, and the stretcher-bearers took him to the redoubt. Private Fagan, 'aged about twenty-one', was also hit in the chest. He fell against the biscuit boxes, but he got back up again looking dazed and confused. He managed to keep hold of his rifle and fired two more shots before he collapsed and died. Privates Chick and Scanlon were shot down by Zulu cross-fire, and Lieutenant Chard would also have been killed had not Private Jenkins shouted a warning and pulled his officer's head down just as a Zulu round whizzed over him. Private Desmond was nicked in the fleshy part of his thumb by a Zulu slug, and another enemy bullet found its way through a gap in the boxes and hit Corporal Lyons in the right side of his neck. He fell sprawling into the biscuit boxes and landed outside the enclosure, but some men quickly dragged him back and Doctor Reynolds attended to him at the storehouse casualty station.

Lieutenant Bromhead was keeping his eye on the ammunition, and he was continually ordering his men to take careful aim and not to waste a single bullet. As he himself took careful aim at a warrior who appeared near the hospital, another warrior scrambled over the breastwork and came up behind him with his spear raised ready to strike. Private Hitch saw the danger, but his rifle was not loaded and he had lost his bayonet. He could do nothing but try to bluff the Zulu by putting the muzzle of his rifle on him and pretend he was going to fire. The ruse worked, and the horrified Zulu clambered back out of the enclosure without delivering the fatal blow. Private John Smith received an *assegai* thrust to his abdomen, which seems to have been the only officially recorded casualty caused by an enemy spear.

More Zulus sprang up out of the bushes and attacked the wall, so Private Hitch joined the men fighting to keep the enemy back from the north perimeter. A Zulu attempted to climb the breastwork, so Hitch blocked him and tried to force him back. As he did so, he noticed a Zulu to his left out of the corner of his eye who was aiming his rifle straight at him. As he was already dealing with a warrior there was nothing he could do to defend himself and the Zulu shot him in the right shoulder. He reeled back from the force of impact and fell to the ground as the Zulu moved in for the kill. Lieutenant Bromhead had positioned himself behind Hitch to provide a second line of fire and he saw the danger; he levelled his revolver and shot dead the Zulu. Private Hitch was bleeding badly, but he got to his feet, stripped to his shirt, and put his injured arm into his waist belt for support. Private George Deacon tore the lining out of Mr Dunne's greatcoat (presumably with his permission) and tied it around Hitch's shoulder to secure it. Hitch borrowed Lieutenant Bromhead's revolver for a short while, mainly for protection in his weakening state, but he began to feel sickly from pain and loss of blood, so he decided to make himself useful by giving out ammunition.

The Zulus who were crouching outside the perimeter were causing problems with their short-range fire, and Corporal Schiess was concerned about the amount of damage they were doing, so he slipped stealthily over the boxes and crept along the inner side of the wall towards a group of the enemy. He suddenly raised himself up before them and aimed his rifle, but one of them fired first and blew off his hat. The corporal quickly jumped onto the bags, his body illuminated by the glare from the blazing fire, and bayoneted a warrior. He shot the next Zulu who appeared, and as a third warrior was coming to their assistance he met him with the point of his bayonet. The gallant man then returned to his post.

Dabulamanzi was directing the movements of his warriors from behind Witt's garden wall, and although even the defenders had admiration for their determination and bravery, he had launched numerous fierce attacks and he was becoming anxious at the lack of success they were having. He had disobeyed Cetshwayo's orders and could only justify what he had done by taking back news of an unqualified victory. But, the soldiers were still secure in their corner of the defences. Even if he did succeed, his losses were heavy, and mounting. Being deprived of his fellow *inDuna* by Private Dunbar, he was finding it increasingly difficult to stir up morale in such a large *impi*, and there were signs that they were losing heart. They were used to fighting out in the open and not against men behind protective walls with rapid-fire rifles. They had not eaten properly for several days, and they had moved at a brisk run for about sixteen miles before reaching Rorke's Drift.

The three defenders outside the perimeter shivered in the cold night air. Private Waters nursed his wound as Zulus prowled around nearby. He was trodden on several times, but the darkness hid his identity and they presumed he was just a dead body. Private Becket was curled up unconscious in a drainage ditch, with his abdomen saturated in blood. Gunner Howard had also nearly been discovered several times. He contemplated making a dash for the enclosure, but there were too many warriors around so he had no choice but to stay motionless, shivering with cold and fear.

For the defenders inside the fort thirst had become as much an enemy as the Zulus, especially among the wounded. The water cart was within the compound close to the hospital wall, where it was impossible to reach without great personal risk. Some men decided that any kind of liquid would be acceptable to quench their thirst and they tried to get at the casks of rum, but Sergeant Millne was having none of it. He reminded them of his orders, and as he jumped onto the barrel he warned that he would shoot any man who tried to get at it. However, the cries of the wounded were hard to bear, so a few men jumped over the boxes and ran to fetch some water. One soldier stated, 'this battle had various effects on our men. Some who had always been ready to crack a joke could not now seem to speak a word. One man, unbearably vexed at our position, cried like a child, fought like a lion and swore like a demon'.

However, many men were beginning to think that their situation was hopeless, but they still intended to fight to the end. They could see no hope of being rescued and no chance of escape. It would only be a matter of time before the Zulus broke through their defences and the battle was lost. They had been firing continually for five hours, changing shoulders when they became bruised and sore from the recoil of their rifles, until both shoulders hurt so much that they had to hold their weapons out in front of them to fire. The rifle barrels became so hot that their fingers and palms became scorched, forcing them to have to use a rag to enable them to hold the weapon. Others picked up the rifles of their dead or wounded comrades and used them alternately. They had to use a ramrod to clear the barrels when they fouled-up and jammed, and their hands became cut and splintered as they fumbled for cartridges in the ammunition boxes. The bayonets were effective of course, but they were not strong, and most of those that had not been snapped off by the enemy had bent during the struggle. Their uniforms were ripped and begrimed, and their faces were dirty and splashed with blood; some of it their own and some of it not. Some men could no longer speak from exhaustion and the dank smoke that parched their throats.

Lieutenants Chard and Bromhead joined the men in the redoubt to get a better view of the situation. The hospital fire blazed on, and although it had destroyed most of the medical supplies, it continued to be their salvation and allowed the men to detect the warriors as they ran in to attack the barricades. Chaplain Smith was praying that the warriors would go away, and the men who could no longer fight encouraged those who could.

Private Hitch continued to do good work in handing out ammunition, but he was thirsty and he began to feel faint. He collapsed, and dragged himself to sit up with his back against the biscuit boxes. Private Deacon was close by and, on seeing that Hitch was losing consciousness, had asked him if he would prefer to be shot when it came to the end. Hitch declined, and after passing out he was taken to the shelter of the storehouse.

Towards midnight the attacks became less frequent, but the Zulus kept the soldiers on constant alert. Dabulamanzi was still trying to stir up aggression in his tired warriors, and the ground shook as they stamped their feet and clashed their shields in the darkness. On one side of the post the commands of Zulu leaders would call out, and cries of '*Usuthu! Usuthu!*' would follow. The men in that part of the barricade would strain their already weak and sore eyes to scan the darkness, or prick up their ears to detect any movement as they prepared to receive an attack. Then the same thing would happen at another section of the perimeter and the men there would be alerted; they could never be sure from where the next attack would come. Dark, shadowy figures would then run in at the barricade, and as they became illuminated by the light from the flames, the defenders shot most of them down as they approached. The few who reached the wall clambered up the bodies of their dead and pounced on the soldiers, but the shock of sharp, cold steel always met them and they died in the effort.

The fire began to burn itself out, but fortune favoured the brave yet again, because as it did so a pale light began to show across the skies. As the new morning dawned, it also dawned on the defenders that they might live to see another day. The battlefield became still and quiet, but now and again a rafter or other timbers fell from the roof, and as they hit the ground a few embers would spark up from within the burnt out shell of the hospital; as this happened new targets were illuminated and a few shots were exchanged. Then all became silent again, but for the heart-rending cries of the wounded and dying. Warriors who were too gravely wounded and beyond help of survival were put out of their pain by their fellow natives with a swift and sharp spear thrust under the armpit. Brave and gallant men from totally diverse cultures had been brought together in terrible conflict and had learned to hold a deep respect for each other.

Towards morning the British became suspicious of a longer-than-usual silence. But, when the dull light rose from behind the hills and glimmered across the sky, the defenders looked out beyond the hundreds of black corpses scattered all around, some groaning in agony among the carnage; they saw groups of dejected and spent warriors retiring over the rise from where they had come twelve hours earlier. They dragged many of their wounded and dying away on their shields.

The early light revealed a devastating scene of carnage, and the defenders could hardly believe their eyes at what men are capable of doing to their fellow men under the dreadful banner of war. The burned-out hospital was still smouldering, and the charred remains of the men who had died there smelt awful. Hundreds of Zulu corpses were scattered all around the perimeter, some piled in masses against the ramparts. All had terrible injuries. Some warriors had been pinned to the ground by the bayonet which had killed them. Trampled grain, pot-holed tins and used cartridge cases from the 20,000 rounds of ammunition that had been used were strewn all around, and the fortifications were stained with blood.

Private Waters had taken refuge in the cook house, and he was so relieved to see red coats moving about the post that he came out of hiding and walked towards the barricades. Suspecting he was a Zulu in a British jacket, several rifles were trained on him at once, but he managed to identify himself before a shot was fired. Gunner Howard had also survived his ordeal, and Lieutenant Chard's wagon driver came stumbling back into the depot unharmed.

Nobody believed that they had seen the last of the Zulus, and although many men could hardly move their aching limbs, the officers kept them busy repairing the barricades and preparing for any renewed surprise attack. He also hoped that keeping them busy would prevent them from dwelling on their still precarious situation. They tied ropes around the now unstable walls of the hospital building and pulled them down, and the thatch was stripped from the roof of the storehouse and piled into the *kraal*. The bushes and trees that had provided so much cover for the Zulus were cut down as much as possible, with the dead horses being left tied to the trees. Two men were told to tie a piece of white material to a length of wood and get up onto the rafters of the store roof to act as lookouts to give warning by waving the flags if they saw any Zulu advance towards the post. Patrols were sent out, cautiously watching for any surprise attack. They collected all the Zulu rifles and ammunition they could find, and they brought in hundreds of Zulu *assegais* that had been left around the defences.

Many warriors were still alive, and shots rang out as they were discovered and tried to get away. A Zulu who was lying in the *kraal* pretending to be dead suddenly got to his feet and fired his rifle at the soldiers as they moved around the ramparts, and then he fled towards the river. His shot did no harm, and he had taken everyone so much by surprise that by the time a few shots were fired after him it was too late and the plucky warrior got away. As Trooper Lugg limped about among the dead he came upon a rifle on the ground, and he was about to pick it up when a Zulu lying close by took hold of the weapon and jammed it against his body.

The trigger clicked, but the rifle misfired and before the Zulu could react, Lugg dropped on him and stabbed him to death with his hunting knife. Private Hook was following the course of a dry stream as he was patrolling down by the river carrying a bundle of spears when he came upon a Zulu lying motionless on the ground. The man was unarmed, but the soldier noticed blood running from a wound in his leg and he suspected a trap. As he passed by, Hook watched for any other Zulus who might be about to ambush him, but the seemingly lone warrior sprang up and grabbed hold of his rifle. As the man tried to wrestle Hook to the ground he dropped the spears and hit the Zulu in the chest. He stepped back as he loaded the rifle and shot the warrior through the head. After all these incidents the men were not allowed to leave the fort unless they were in numbers.

There were twenty-seven casualties. Eleven soldiers of the 24th Regiment had been killed, and another was added that day when Private Beckett was found mortally wounded. Doctor Reynolds did all he could to try to save his life, but he had lost too much blood and had deteriorated beyond help. The bullet that hit Lance-Sergeant Williams had passed right through him, but he was seriously ill. Doctor Reynolds applied a temporary dressing and he intended to cut the bullet out, but Williams succumbed to his injuries two days later. The official total of killed in action was seventeen, including Corporal Anderson and the Xhosa native. The bodies of the dead men the warriors had got hold of had been treated horribly. The corpse of Joseph Williams was found mutilated, but he had sold his life dearly for there were many Zulu dead scattered about the area he had defended. The bodies of Privates Hayden and Adams had been badly burned, but it was still possible to tell that they too had been mutilated. Their corpses, along with those of Sergeant Maxfield, Private Horrigan and the native were placed under the straw in the *kraal*. One man's head had been split open, and another man, who still had his rifle presented over the parapet, had been hit between the eyes by a Zulu slug which had taken the back of his head away, leaving his face with just a hole in it. Trooper Hunter had received six stab wounds, and one of the Zulus had been shot and killed as he was cutting up the corpse of a man, and his stiffened body was still leaning over his victim when he was found.

Doctor Reynolds continued to attend to the wounded. He extracted thirty-nine pieces of bone from Hitch's shattered shoulder joint, and dressed the neck wound suffered by Corporal Lyons. The slug had passed down his body and struck his spine, where it lodged. There was little the doctor could do under the circumstances but try to nurse him back to strength. Several other men had multiple lacerations and other kinds of less serious wounds.

Lieutenants Chard and Bromhead got together to assess the situation as it now stood. There were fewer than two full boxes of ammunition remaining in reserve, which meant that each defender had about twenty cartridges left. Some men had slumped down behind the barricades to rest their aching limbs, while others shivered in the cold morning air in the effects of shock after a hard-fought battle. They had no idea if and when another Zulu attack might come, but even though they had fought far beyond what they expected of their capabilities, and morale was still high, they knew that if help did not come the constant Zulu assaults would eventually wear them down and they might lose the will to fight on. When the work of repairing and securing the defences was done, they returned to their posts around the perimeter and waited in an almost unbearable state of uncertainty.

At about seven o'clock the signalmen drew attention to the south-west, where a large body of the enemy had come into view over the rise, and were waiting menacingly. The officers called out for most of the force to take their places at that side of the perimeter ready to meet the attack, but then the white flags were waved for a second time, and the lookouts brought attention to a line of men winding their way down through the Bashee River valley, coming towards the river about an hour's march away. It was impossible to tell at first if they were British or Zulu, but if they were the latter they knew that their terrible fate was sealed. They had no real idea what had become of the rest of the column, and even if they had survived they may have assumed that Rorke's Drift had fallen to the enemy and had marched directly on to Helpmekaar. A young native came running up to the barricade, and as Mr Daniells could speak a little Bantu, Chard asked him to interrogate the boy. He was found to be friendly, so Chard sent him on to Helpmekaar with a note explaining the dire situation and requesting reinforcements as a matter of urgency.

Eventually, the defenders could see the approaching column more clearly through field glasses, and hopes were raised when they could make out red tunics among them. But, it was suggested that they could be Zulus dressed in the tunics of their dead comrades from iSandlwana. It was a tense time, as the Zulus on the hill were gradually moving forward, and they too seemed equally unsure about the identity of the advancing force. The weary men in the fort watched anxiously, not knowing what to expect. Suddenly, there came hysterical shouts from the store roof and the signallers began frantically waving their flags, shouting that a body of men in red tunics and white faces was approaching the river. They were British. The defenders were overcome with relief and some cried with emotion. Wild cheers rang out and helmets were thrown into the air. Seeing this, Dabulamanzi turned his dejected and tired warriors away, and they disappeared around the hill.

At 8.15 a.m. Major John Cecil Russell, of the 12th (Prince of Wales' Royal) Lancers, brought an advance detachment of mounted troops up to the post. He was anxious to know if any of the troops from iSandlwana had managed to escape to Rorke's Drift, but Chard informed him that very few men had reached the garrison, and those that did were colonials who had ridden on to Helpmekaar. They were stricken with grief at this news. Lord Chelmsford and his staff arrived shortly afterwards. He was dejected and emotional, and he thanked the defenders for what they had done. The column then began to arrive. They had lost everything, including their pride, their morale was at rock bottom, and they were weary and hungry. While Rorke's Drift had been under attack, they had spent a restless night among the carnage at iSandlwana. Zulu campfires could be seen on the hills all around them, and as they looked towards Rorke's Drift the light from the burning hospital had lit up the sky. As they had approached the river they passed Dabulamanzi's *impi* as it was moving away from the Drift. A few stragglers at the back of the column had exchanged shots, but nobody was in the mood for another fight. The commissariat provided them with bread, biscuits and tins of corned beef, and there was reasonably fresh water; Colour-Sergeant Bourne at last gave the order to issue a welcome tot of rum to each man. Some men walked about the post anxiously looking for their friends, and Privates Camp and Gee were told of the fate of their brothers. Pip's master was not among the survivors, and many areas of South Wales would be devastated by the loss of so many of their men.

The defenders had been on alert for eighteen hours, but they were far too tense to find any kind of relaxation. As they began to allow themselves to reflect on the events, they were gradually coming to realise that they might have been involved in an action that would be considered special. Every man was thankful that he had survived the terrible ordeal.

Henry Harford described the scene: 'I wandered about the fort, looking at the wreckage which gave the appearance and feeling of devastation after a hurricane, with the dead bodies thrown in, the only thing that remained whole being a circular miniature fortress constructed of bags of mealies in the centre'.

Lieutenant Chard was without his tunic as he washed his powder-blackened face in a muddy puddle, along with Private Bushe, of the 24th Regiment, who was covered in blood from his injury. Bushe offered to share his dirty towel with the officer and Chard accepted thankfully. Chard then went to check his ransacked Royal Engineers wagon. It was wrecked, but the Zulus had left an unbroken bottle of beer, which he and Lieutenant Bromhead used to celebrate their good fortune in surviving the battle thus far. Private Hook was sent back to his duties of making tea for the sick. However, a sergeant came up to him and said he had to drop everything and report to the officers at once. So he found himself standing before Lord Chelmsford in his shirt sleeves and with his braces dangling by his side, explaining his part in the action within the hospital. Captain William Penn-Symons, of the 24th Regiment, wrote down everything that was reported.

For their valour during the defence of Rorke's Drift eleven men were awarded the Victoria Cross, a total which has never been equalled since, and seven went to soldiers of the 24th Regiment; the most Victoria Crosses awarded to one regiment for a single action. There were also five awards of the Distinguished Conduct Medal: Gunner John Cantwell, Royal Regiment of Artillery; Private William Roy, 1st Battalion, 24th Regiment; Colour-Sergeant Frank Bourne, 2nd Battalion, 24th Regiment; Corporal Francis Attwood, Army Service Corps; and Corporal Michael McMahon, Army Hospital Corps—but this last award was later withdrawn.

Lieutenant John Rouse Merriott Chard VC

John Rouse Merriott Chard was born at Boxhill, in the Pennycross district of Plymouth, on 21 December 1847. He was the second son of three in the family of six children to William Wheaton Chard, described as a landed proprietor, of Pathe near Othery in Somerset, and his wife Jane, daughter of Doctor John Hart Brimacombe, of Stoke Climsland in Cornwall. They were wealthy enough to afford home tutorship for the family and keep several servants. His older brother, William Wheaton junior, followed family tradition and became a colonel in the 7th Royal Fusiliers and commanded the regiment from April 1887 to September 1890, while his younger brother, Charles Edward, became a vicar. His great-nephew, Lieutenant-Colonel Michael Chard, stated during the centenary of the defence of Rorke's Drift in 1879 that 'all my family are Royal Regiment of Fusiliers and he was the black sheep, because he became a sapper—but he ended up doing rather well'.

The 1851 census records the family as living at Mount Tamar, Kingstaunton, St Budeaux, Plymouth, and gives his place of birth as Weston Peverell in Devon. The 1861 census gives much the same information, except his place of birth as Pennycross, Devon. There were three sisters named Jane, Florence and Margaret, and the family worshipped at St Budeaux Church.

John was educated at the Plymouth New Grammar School, and attended the Royal Military Academy at Woolwich, where he was remembered for always being late for breakfast. He passed-out in 1868 and was commissioned as lieutenant in the Corps of Royal Engineers on 15 July 1868. After two years at Chatham he sailed to Bermuda in October 1870, being employed in the building of fortifications at the Hamilton Dockyard. His father died in 1873, and he returned to England in January 1874. In the following month he was posted to Malta, where he was again employed in the construction of defences. He returned to England in April 1876, and after a short stay at Chatham, he was appointed to the Western District at Exeter.

As the situation in South Africa worsened he was ordered to report to Aldershot to join the 5th Company, Corps of Royal Engineers for active service at the Cape. The unit set sail from Gravesend on 2 December 1878, arriving at Durban on 5 January 1879. His vaccination injection had become inflamed and his right shoulder was very sore, but British troops were already assembling on the Natal-Zululand border, so with no time to recover he was ordered to take a small party of engineers to join the 3rd Column at Rorke's Drift. For almost the entire journey the tracks were bad, and by the time he arrived at his destination on 19 January the column had already invaded enemy territory. One of the ponts which was used to ferry the troops across the Buffalo River had broken down, so Chard and his men set up camp on the Natal bank to work on repairing it.

The citation for the award of the Victoria Cross to Lieutenant John Chard, published in the *London Gazette* of 2 May 1879, states:

> The lieutenant-general commanding the troops reports that, had it not been for the fine example and excellent behaviour of these two officers under the most trying circumstances, the defence of Rorke's Drift post would not have been conducted with that intelligence

and tenacity which so essentially characterised it. The lieutenant-general adds that its success must, in a great degree, be attributable to the two young officers who exercised the chief command on the occasion in question.

A colonial trooper stated 'the men spoke highly of Chard,' and his cool leadership proved invaluable that day. He was appointed captain and brevet-major dated from 23 January 1879, thus becoming the first man in history to move from a lieutenancy to a majority in the army in a single day. He and his fellow defenders received the thanks of the government.

This is how the British public received news of the defence of Rorke's Drift, when Lieutenant Chard's report appeared in newspapers in March 1879:

THE ZULU WAR
Madeira, Monday

The following has been received here from Cape Town:-

Lord Chelmsford has issued the following general order:-

The lieutenant-general commanding Her Majesty's forces in South Africa has much satisfaction in publishing the subjoining official report of the gallant defence of Rorke's Drift Post made on January 22 and 23. The lieutenant-general feels sure that the gallant conduct of the garrison will receive most ample recognition, and trusts the example set by a few brave men, and the success attended their noble efforts, will be taken to heart by all under his command. The odds against them were nearly thirty to one; but taking advantage of the material which lay to hand, and hastily constructing with it such cover as was possible, this heroic little garrison was able to resist during the space of twelve hours the determined attacks made upon them, and, further, inflicting heavy loss on the enemy, the killed alone being more than three times their number.

Rorke's Drift, January 25:

My Lord—I have the honour to report that on the 22nd instant I was left in command at Rorke's Drift by Major Spalding, who went to Helpmekaar in order to hurry forward a company of the

24th Regiment. I was specially ordered to protect the ponts. At 3.15 p.m. that day I was watching at the ponts when two men came towards us from Zululand at the gallop. They shouted out and were taken across the river; and I was then informed by one of them—Lieutenant Adendorff, of Commandant Lonsdale's regiment, who afterwards remained to assist in the defence—of the disaster befallen at the iSandlwana camp, and that the Zulus were advancing upon Rorke's Drift. The other, a carbineer, rode on to take the news forward to Helpmekaar.

Almost immediately afterwards I received a message from Lieutenant Bromhead—commander of the company of the 24th Regiment at the camp near the commissariat stores—asking me to come up at once. I gave instructions to strike tents, and to put all stores into the wagon, while I instantly made my way to the commissariat store, and there found that a note had been received from the Third Column, stating that the enemy was advancing in force against our post, which we were to strengthen and hold at all costs. Lieutenant Bromhead was already most actively engaged loop-holing and barricading the store-building and hospital, and also in connecting the defences of the two buildings' walls constructed of mealie-bags and wagons. I held a hurried consultation with him and Mr Dalton, of the commissariat—who was actively superintending the work of defence, and whom I cannot sufficiently thank for his most valuable services—and I entirely approved all his arrangements. I then went round our position down to the ponts, and brought up along with their guard one sergeant and six men, the gear, wagon &c. I desire here to mention for approval the offer of these pont guards, Daniels and Sergeant Milne, of the 3rd Buffs, who, with their comrades, volunteered to moor the ponts out in the middle of the stream, and there to defend them from the decks, with a few men to assist.

We arrived back at our post at 3.30 p.m. and, shortly after, an officer with some of Durnford's Horse came in and asked orders from me. I requested him to send a detachment to observe the ponts and drift, and to throw out vedettes in the direction of the enemy, in order to check their advance as much as possible, his men falling back on the post when forced to retire, and thereafter to assist in the defence. I next requested Lieutenant Bromhead to station his men, and, having seen every man thoroughly knew his post, the rest of the work went quickly on.

At 4.20 p.m. the sound of firing was heard behind the hill to our south. The officer of Durnford's Horse returned, reporting that the enemy was now close upon us. His men, he told me, would not obey orders, but were going off towards Helpmekaar, and I myself saw them in retreat, numbering apparently about one hundred, going in that direction. About the same time Captain Stephenson's detachment of the Natal Native Contingent left us—as did that officer himself. I saw that our line of defence was too extended for the small number of men now left, and at once commenced an inner entrenchment of biscuit boxes, out of which we had soon completed a wall two boxes high.

About 4.30 p.m. 500 or 600 of the enemy came suddenly in sight around the hill to our south. They advanced at a run against our south wall, but were met by a well-sustained fire; yet, not withstanding heavy loss, they continued to advance to within fifty yards of the wall, when their leading men encountered such a hot fire from our front, with a cross one from the store, that they were checked. Taking advantage, however, of the cover afforded by the cook-house, and the ovens, they kept up thence heavy musketry volleys; the greater number, however, without stopping at all, moved on towards the left round the hospital, and thence made a rush toward our north-west wall and our breastwork of mealie bags. After a short, but desperate, struggle those assailants were driven back with very heavy loss into the bush around our works.

The main body of the enemy close behind had meantime lined the ledge of rocks, and filled some caves overlooking us at a distance of a hundred yards to the south, from whence they kept up a constant fire. Another body, advancing somewhat more to the left than those who first attacked us, occupied a garden in the hollows of the road and also the bush beyond it in great numbers, taking especial advantage of the bush, which we had no time to cut down. The enemy were thus able to advance close to our works, and in this part soon held one whole side of the wall, while we on the other kept back a series of desperate assaults which were made on a line extending from the hospital all along the wall as far as the bush. But each attack was most splendidly met and repulsed by our men with the bayonet, Corporal Ferdinand Schiess, of the Natal Native Contingent, greatly distinguished himself by conspicuous gallantry. The fire from the rock behind our post, though badly directed, took us completely in reverse, and was so heavy that we suffered very severely, and at six o'clock was finally forced to retire behind the entrenchment of biscuit boxes.

All this time the enemy had been attempting to force the hospital, and shortly afterwards did set fire to the roof. The garrison of the hospital defended the place room by room, our men bringing out all the sick who could be moved before they retired. Privates John Williams, Henry Hook, Robert Jones and William Jones, of the 24th

Regiment, were the last four men to leave, holding the doorway against the Zulus with bayonets, their ammunition being quite expended. From want of interior communication and the smoke of the burning house, it was found impossible to carry off all the sick, and, with most heartfelt sorrow and regret, we could not save a few poor fellows from a terrible fate. Seeing the hospital burning, and the desperate attempts being made by the enemy to fire the roof of our stores, we now converted two mealie-bag heaps into a sort of redoubt, which gave a second line of fire all along, Assistant Commissary Walter Dunne working hard at this though much exposed; thus rendering most valuable assistance.

Darkness then came on. We were completely surrounded, and, after several furious attempts had been gallantly repulsed, we were eventually forced to retire to the middle and then to the inner wall of our *kraal* on the east of the position we first had. We were sustaining throughout all this a desultory fire, kept up all night, and several assaults were attempted, but always repulsed with vigour, the attacks continuing until after midnight, our men firing with the greatest coolness, not wasting a single shot. The light afforded by the burning hospital proved a great advantage.

At four o'clock on the morning of 23 January firing ceased; and at daybreak the enemy were passing out of sight over the hill to our south-west. We then patrolled the ground, collecting arms from dead bodies of the Zulus, and strengthening the position as much as possible. We were still removing thatch from the roof of the store, when about seven o'clock, a large body of the enemy once more appeared upon the hills to the south-west. I now sent a friendly kaffir, who had come in shortly before, with a note to the officer commanding at Helpmekaar, asking help. About eight o'clock, however, the British Third Column appeared, and at sight of this the enemy, who had been gradually advancing towards us, commenced falling back as our troops approached.

I consider the enemy which attacked us to have numbered about three thousand; we killed about three hundred and fifty. Of the steadiness and gallant behaviour of my whole garrison I cannot speak too highly. I wish especially to bring to your notice the conduct of Lieutenant Gonville Bromhead, of the 2/24th Regiment, and the splendid behaviour of his Company, B, 2/24th. Of Surgeon James Reynolds in regard of his constant attention to our wounded under fire, assisting them where they fell. Of Acting Commissary Officer James Dalton, to whose energy much of our defences were due, and who was severely wounded while gallantly assisting in the fight. Assistant-Commissary Walter Dunne, Acting Storekeeper.

Colour-Sergeant Frank Bourne, 2/24th; Lance-Sergeant Thomas Williams, 2/24th, wounded dangerously; Sergeant Joseph Windridge; Corporal Ferdinand Schiess, Natal Native Contingent, wounded; Private Joseph Williams, 2/24th; Private William Jones 2/24th; Private Michael McMahon, Army Hospital Corps; Private Robert Jones, 2/24th; Private Henry Hook, 2/24th; and Private William Roy, 2/24th.

The following is the list of killed: Sergeant Robert Maxfield, Privates John Scanlon, Garret Hayden, Robert Adams, Thomas Cole, John Fagan, James Chick and Joseph Williams, all of the 2/24th Regiment; Privates Edward Nicholas, William Horrigan and James Jenkins, 1/24th; Mr Louis Byrne, Commissariat Department; Trooper Sydney Hunter, Natal Mounted Police; Corporal Michael Anderson, Natal Native Cavalry; a private of the NNC. Total: fifteen, and twelve wounded, of who two have since died; Sergeant Thomas Williams, 2/24th; and Private William Beckett, 1/24th.

[*Signed*] JOHN R. M. CHARD, lieutenant, RE.

To Colonel Glyn, CB, commanding, 3rd Column

Major Chard remained at Rorke's Drift to supervise the burial of hundreds of dead Zulus in mass graves, and to work on a more permanent stone perimeter. Suffering the hardships of atrocious conditions, he was struck down with fever, and on 17 February he was taken by ambulance wagon to Ladysmith, where he was looked after by a Doctor Park and his wife. After showing signs of improvement he suffered a relapse, and just after the announcement of his Victoria Cross award it was reported in local newspapers that he had died. However, he was nursed back to health, and was able to report back for duty in time for the re-invasion of Zululand.

He joined Colonel Wood's column at Khambula to inspect the fortifications, and he was involved in all the engineering activities during the Flying Column's advance on the Zulu capital at Ulundi. His unit followed up Colonel Buller's scouting activities, building bridges and repairing roads. While the Second Division was halted at Fort Newdigate to await supplies, Chard was out on picket duty when he was caught up in a false alarm which caused the British to open fire. Several men were wounded and some horses were killed, and he and his men spent an uncomfortable time sheltering in a muddy trench with British bullets whizzing about above them. He survived the ordeal and he was in the British square at Ulundi on 4 July 1879 to witness the final crushing defeat of the Zulu army. He was decorated by General

Sir Garnet Wolseley during a parade of the troops at St Paul's Camp in Zululand on 16 July 1879. For his service at the Cape he also received the South Africa Medal with 1879 clasp.

However, John Chard may have been too modest for his own good, and seems to have been a man with no particular ambitions. This attitude caused animosity towards the already-reluctant hero, and he began to find himself on the rough end of some jealousy-fuelled criticism. Some senior officers, including General Wolseley, who was not a supporter of the awarding of gallantry medals, and General Buller, a fellow West Countryman, made less than complimentary remarks about his ability in the field, and some unnecessary personal insults. On recording the presenting of the award of the Victoria Cross to Major Chard, Wolseley wrote:

> A more uninteresting or more stupid-looking fellow I never saw. Wood tells me he is a most useless officer, fit for nothing. I hear in their camp also that, the man who worked hardest in defence of Rorke's Drift Post was a commissariat officer, who has not been rewarded at all. The only one who behaved badly was the doctor and reports say he was a coward. Bromhead, of the 24th Regiment, who was the second-in-command of the post, is a very stupid fellow also.

The commissariat officer was of course Mr Dalton, who, thanks in part to Major Chard, was later awarded for his gallantry.

For some unknown reason, Colonel Wood had taken a dislike to Major Chard and made no secret of the fact that he disapproved of his gallantry award. As Wolseley stated, Wood considered Chard to be 'a most useless officer,' and did his best to damage Chard's reputation whenever he could—which unfortunately to some extent he succeeded in doing. Captain Walter Jones, of the Royal Engineers, who was a friend, said of Chard:

> He is a most amiable fellow, but as a company officer he is so hopelessly slow and slack...With such a start as he got, he stuck to the company doing nothing. In his place I should have gone up to Lord Chelmsford and asked for an appointment. He must have got it, and if not he could have gone home soon after Rorke's Drift, at the height of his popularity and done splendidly at home. I advised him, but he placidly smokes his pipe and does nothing.

Major Chard arrived at Spithead aboard the *Eagle* on 2 October 1879, where the Duke of Cambridge welcomed him and delivered a message from Queen Victoria inviting him to an audience with her at Balmoral Castle. He was invited to a second audience with the queen on 21 February 1880, when he presented the sovereign with a more detailed account of the action at Rorke's Drift than his official version. He was received at Plymouth as a local hero, being presented with a gold chronometer and a superb sword of honour that had been specially manufactured and richly carved. He was presented with an illuminated address by freemasons in Exeter, and he was guest of honour at dinner receptions in Taunton and at the Wanderers Club in Chatham. He was held in the highest regard in the West Country for the rest of his life. Queen Victoria was appreciative of his unassuming manner and the modest way in which he told of the events at Rorke's Drift, and it was said at the time when he submitted his official report, which was modest and to the point, that 'he has spoken of everybody but himself'.

During his first visit to Balmoral he gave a verbal account of the battle to Queen Victoria, after which she presented him with a gold ring. He did the same to the queen's private secretary, who was not influenced by regimental jealousy, and noted:

> Chard has been here this morning. He explained the difference of Rorke's Drift to the queen, Prince Leopold, the Grand Duke of Hesse, and Princess Beatrice, in the queen's private room, and did it all very clearly and modestly. After dinner he did likewise to us in the billiard room on the table, where store and hospital were books and boxes, and mealie bags and biscuit tins were billiard balls. I gather from all I hear that Dalton was quite as much (if not more) of the presiding genius here, as himself. He conceived the idea of joining the two buildings with mealie bags, etc. before Chard's arrival on the scene; though perhaps Chard would have done so, had he not found it in operation. The inner line, which was their great safeguard, was Chard's own idea, I fancy, and when they were deserted by so many of the defenders (natives, etc.) it was soon found that the first line of defence was too extended. Bromhead (commanding B Company, 2/24th Regiment) had of course great influence over his men, and kept them in their places or moved them about, controlled their fire with great judgement. Only one and a half boxes of ammunition were left when morning came, beside what they had in their pouches. Chard made no complaint, but it seemed odd to me that he was not consulted as to the distribution of the Victoria Cross. He is not a genius and not quick, but a quiet, plodding, dogged sort of fellow who would hold his own in most of the situations in which, as an Engineer officer, his lot may be cast…

His niece, Dorothy, who remembered him from when she was a child, recalled him as a man who never seemed to come to terms with what he had done and never considered his deed to have been as heroic as people thought. Her story of his arrival back in Somerset sums up the type of man he was. Major Chard was met at Taunton by civic dignitaries, and after some speeches he was driven to North Curry, where he was met by admiring crowds. Told by his sister to take off his hat and wave back to them, he reluctantly did so, muttering sheepishly 'all I did was my duty'. Whatever people thought of him, civilian or military, Queen Victoria grew very fond of him.

John Chard never married, but he is said to have had a relationship with a woman called Emily Rowe, who bore a daughter to him at Exeter, believed to have been on 16 February 1882, who was named Violet Mary. Emily Rowe married Lawson Durant, and had a second daughter, named Irene, born on 6 January 1884. Emily Durant died in 1939. Violet's birth would have been kept secret because of the stigma of illegitimacy at the time, and because of Chard's fame and association with the queen. He left an annuity to Emily and Violet for the duration of her lifetime, and the family have preserved two letters written by Chard and addressed to Emily telling her about his trip to Japan. At his funeral it was recorded that an anonymous wreath bearing the inscription 'That day he did his duty' took pride of place beside a tribute from Queen Victoria on the coffin. It is interesting to wonder who might have sent this wreath. This information is gleaned from letters I received from a family descendant, which state:

> I was particularly interested to read about Lt Chard, as he is my great-grandfather. Although you are quite correct in your book when you say he was not married, he had had a relationship with an Emily Rowe who gave birth to a daughter, Violet, on 16 February 1882. Emily Rowe subsequently married a Lawson Durant. Violet Durant (Rowe) was my father's mother.
>
> As well as some letters from John Chard to Emily, Chard left £50 annuity for Emily and her daughter Violet for her lifetime. This money was duly received by my grandmother.
>
> I feel that at Rorke's Drift, Chard was just an ordinary man who kept his head and used common sense and training to good effect.

A second letter states:

> I do have some information which you may find useful. Violet Mary Rowe/Durant (Chard's daughter) was born on 16 February

> 1882 at Exeter, or so we believe, but my parents think that the year of birth might be suspect. It is possible that Emily, her mother, lied about her birth as she was illegitimate. Violet had a younger sister, Irene Durant, who was born on 6 January 1884, making her just two years younger than Violet. I would also add that although Emily married Lawson Durant, we are not certain that Irene was in fact his child.
>
> The only information I have about Emily Rowe is that she was born on 4 January (but no year), and died in January or February 1939.
>
> My parents have in their possession a couple of letters from John Chard written to Emily, telling her about his trip to Japan.

In January 1880 he began service at Devonport, and the 1881 census records him as living with his mother and sister, Margaret, at 19 Portland Villas, in the district of Charles the Martyr in Plymouth.

He went to Cyprus in December 1881, where he was appointed regimental major on 17 July 1886, and during which time his mother died in 1885. He returned home in March 1887. He was posted to Fulwood Barracks, in Preston, in May 1887. The 1891 census records that he lived in a house close to the barracks at 80 Victoria Road in Fulwood (which still exists), and had a twenty-five-year-old Cypriot servant, named George Theodoulie, working for him.

He remained in Preston until being posted to Singapore on 14 December 1892, where he was commanding Royal Engineer for three years, and was promoted to lieutenant-colonel on 18 January 1893. On his return to Britain in January 1896, he took up his final post as commanding royal engineer in the Perth District. In May that year he presented Queen Victoria with Japanese mementos he had brought back from the East especially for her. He was promoted to colonel on 8 January 1897.

While in Scotland he was diagnosed to have cancer of the mouth. In November 1896, he was too ill to visit Balmoral at the request of Queen Victoria, and he underwent an operation in Edinburgh. In March 1897 surgeons had to remove his tongue. He was still able to converse quite well, but his condition became critical, and in August 1897 doctors diagnosed that the cancer was terminal. He was placed on sick leave from 8 August 1897. He spent the last days of his life with his brother in the rectory at Hatch Beauchamp, where many friends, including Queen Victoria, expressed their concern about his condition. On 11 July 1897, he had received the Diamond Jubilee Medal and a book containing a signed portrait of his sovereign.

After suffering terrible distress towards the end, he died peacefully in his sleep at Hatch Beauchamp Rectory on 1 November 1897, aged fifty. He was buried in the churchyard at Hatch Beauchamp, where a rose-coloured marble cross marks the spot. Queen Victoria sent a wreath bearing an inscription written in her own hand: 'A mark of admiration and regard for a brave soldier from his sovereign'. There was a wreath from Colonel Bourne, and the officers of the South Wales Borderers, and there were tributes from all over the world. For many years the queen's wreath lay beneath a memorial window which was placed in Hatch Beauchamp church.

There is a bust of him and he is named on the 'For Valour' board at the Royal Engineers Museum in Chatham, where there is an officer's sword and a water bottle, and a Zulu shield, *assegai* and *knobkerrie*, taken by Chard at Ulundi. There is a plaque at the YMCA Sports Centre at Pennycross in Plymouth; the Territorial Army Centre in Swansea has a 'John Chard VC House'; and Chard Street in Nottingham and Chard Road in Plymouth were named after him. A memorial plaque has been placed in Jesus Chapel at Rochester Cathedral; there is a bronze bust of him in Taunton Shire Hall; and a brass plaque on the south wall of St Michael's Church in Ottery states:

> In loving memory of the three sons of William Wheaton CHARD, of Pathe House, Somerset, and Mount Tamar, Devon: Colonel William Wheaton Chard; he served for thirty years abroad in the Royal Fusiliers and commanded the 1st Batt. in Egypt and in India. Born 24 Dec. 1841, died 12 Sept. 1890, buried at St Budeaux, Devon. Colonel John Rouse Merriott Chard, VC, RE. The hero of Rorke's Drift; born 21 Dec. 1847, died 1 Nov. 1897, buried at Hatch Beauchamp. The Rev. Charles Edward Chard, BA. Rector of Hatch Beauchamp, Somerset, for twenty-five years; born 4 Dec. 1856, died 12 Sept. 1910, buried at Hatch Beauchamp.

The John Chard-Dekarasie Medal in silver was awarded to all ranks of the South African Union Defence Forces from 1952 to 2003 for twenty years' long and efficient service, with the John Chard-Medalje in bronze being awarded for twelve years of service.

The location of Chard's Victoria Cross had remained a mystery for many years. Then, in 1972, what was described as his South Africa Medal and a 'cast copy' of his VC, was offered for auction in London.

Sir Stanley Baker, who had portrayed Chard in the film *Zulu*, purchased the set for £2,700. It was offered for auction again in 1996, and one of the most extraordinary stories in the history of the Victoria Cross began to unfold. Prompted by the mystery surrounding the whereabouts of the original Victoria Cross, the auctioneers decided to send it to the Royal Armouries at Leeds to be examined. The tests revealed it to be identical to all authentic VCs cast from the cascobels of cannon captured by British forces in the East, and therefore proved to be the genuine original medal. His Victoria Cross is now displayed on rotation at the Lord Ashcroft Gallery, as part of the 'Extraordinary Heroes' exhibition at the Imperial War Museum in London.

Most of the earliest applications of engineering were for military purposes, in the building of fortifications, bridges and roads. Before 1855, as war raged in the Crimea, the technical elements of the British army, such as artillery and engineering, were provided by the Board of Ordnance. Both artillery and engineer officers formed part of the early 'artillery trains' and the ancestor of the Corps of Royal Engineers emerged from The Board of Ordnance in 1717. Before 1782 the officers of the Royal Engineers did not have a military title, but in that year they were first granted commissions. It was not until 1787 that the military officers of the engineer department were constituted the Corps of Royal Engineers, the men being regimented into the Corps of Royal Military Artificers.

When Napoleon invaded Egypt, a detachment was sent to Constantinople to train the Turkish army; other companies performing good service in Egypt, Malta, Italy, Sicily and the West Indies. In 1813 the title the Corps of Royal Sappers and Miners replaced that of the Military Artificers, and did effective work under Wellington in the Peninsular and Waterloo campaigns.

The Crimean War was the scene of manifold activities by the engineers in the construction of trenches to get closer to the Sebastopol fortifications, during which time they gained the unit's first eight Victoria Crosses, and afterwards the officers and men were united to form one corps under the title Royal Engineers. After the Indian Mutiny of 1857-58, the Bengal, Madras and Bombay Corps of Engineers were transferred to the Royal Engineers. As the Corps developed in a progressive world it became responsible for such things as the construction and repair of ports and airfields and the operation of railways. When an army is retreating, the engineers are responsible for the demolition of roads and bridges behind them; when advancing, they are occupied in repairing those blown up by the enemy. To date the Corps has received thirty-seven Victoria Crosses.

Lieutenant Gonville Bromhead VC

Gonville Bromhead came from a distinguished military family. He was born on 29 August 1845 at Versailles, Yvelines, France, the youngest of four sons in a family of nine children to Edmund de Gonville Bromhead (1791-1870) of Thurlby Hall, with land and property in County Galway, Ireland; a retired major and 3rd Baronet; and Judith Christine Cahill (1804-1873), the daughter of the pioneering archaeologist James Wood, of Woodville, County Sligo, Ireland. At the time of the 1861 census he was the only boy left at home, and records that the family lived at Thurlby Hall, situated at 18 Main Street in Thurlby, Bassingham, near Lincoln, and not far from the medieval church of St Germain, where they worshipped and which contains many impressive memorials to the family. Some of the following facts published here concerning the Bromhead family are disputed by modern historians, but the information is based on the documentation I have consulted. It has to be said that a history of the Bromhead 'family of warriors' is long overdue.

His great-grandfather, Boardman, served as ensign under General James Wolfe at Quebec on 13 September 1759, and, according to local legend in Lincoln, he is believed to have been the officer who assured the general of the French retreat:

> 'See how they run!' one of the officers exclaimed, as the French fled in confusion before the levelled bayonets.
>
> 'Who run?' demanded the mortally wounded Wolfe, opening his eyes like a man aroused from sleep.
>
> 'The enemy, sir,' was the reply. 'They give way everywhere!'

Boardman gained the rank of general. He had four brothers who served in the army - one of whom was killed at the Battle of Falkirk Muir on 17 January 1746, during the Jacobite Rising, and another brother married into the family of the founders of Gonville and Caius College at Cambridge University.

His grandfather was born on 30 September 1758, and was also named Gonville. He had entered the 62nd (Wiltshire) Regiment of Foot, and because of his father's influence he is said to have been appointed staff officer and the regiment's quartermaster before he reached his teens. However, he proved his worth on several occasions. He became a lieutenant-general and distinguished himself with General John Burgoyne in the American War of Independence. He was present at the actions at Trios Riviers, the capture of Mount Independence and Freeman's Farm on 19 September 1777. He is said to have been entrusted with the colours of the 9th (Norfolk) Regiment on them being captured at Saratoga in New York State on 17 October 1777, and he was held a captive of the Convention for three years. The Bromhead baronetcy was created for him in recognition of his military service on 19 February 1806. He was succeeded on his death by his eldest son, later Sir Edward Francis, who was a mathematician

Gonville's father, Major Sir Edmund de Gonville, born on 22 January 1791, served in the Walcherne Expedition of 1809, in the Peninsula campaign, and he fought at Waterloo as a lieutenant in the 54th (Dorset) Regiment, where he lost an eye, and led the 'Forlorn Hope' at the Battle of Cambrai. He succeeded as the 3rd Baron Bromhead on 14 March 1855, and died on 25 October 1870. His gravestone confirms that he fought at Waterloo. As a point of interest, he was born on what would become the day of the Battles of iSandlwana/Rorke's Drift, and died on the anniversary of the Battle of Balaclava. His uncle commanded the 77th (Middlesex) Regiment at the Battle of El Bodon on 25 September 1811, where he led them in a successful uphill assault against French cavalry.

Of his own generation, his eldest brother, Edward, born on 21 March 1832, had fought in the Crimea with the 4th (King's Own) Regiment, and died while serving as a captain with the 76th (West Riding) Regiment at Thyetmyo in Burma, on 9 January 1869. The second son, Benjamin Parnell, was born on 22 October 1838, and succeeded as the 4th Baron Bromhead on 25 October 1870. In 1879 he was a colonel with the Indian Staff Corps, serving with the 22nd (Punjabi) Bengal Native Infantry at Kandahar in the Afghan War, and later served in the Sudan, being one time a commandant with the 32nd Sikh Pioneers. He lost both his hands in action in 1888, and after being appointed CB, he died in 1934. Gonville's older brother, Charles James, born on 15 September 1840, served with the 24th Regiment from 1859 to 1891, including in the Zulu War, and had become a favourite of Garnet Wolseley during the Ashanti campaign of 1874. He was appointed CB, was colonel of the South Wales Borderers regimental district from 1892 to 1897, and died on Christmas eve, 24 December 1922. Benjamin Parnell's daughters (and Gonville's nieces) married into the aristocracy. His oldest daughter, Janetta (Jenny), married Field Marshal William, 1st Baron Birdwood, and his third daughter, Kathleen, married into the family of the 4th Baron Raglan, whose ancestor, the 1st Baron Raglan, was the commander-in-chief of the British Expeditionary force to the Crimea.

On 7 March 1879, the *Daily Telegraph* published a letter from Reverend Henry Calverley develop the rector of Bassingham church. This stated the following:

> Whatever may be the merits or demerits, from a political or military point of view of the Zulu War, England in general, and Lincolnshire in particular, may well be proud of the Bromheads of Thurlby Hall. They are certainly a 'fighting family', soldiers 'to the manner born', and they deserve well of their country. Ensign Boardman Bromhead fought at Quebec against the French in 1759, under General Wolfe, and was the man who told him as he lay dying in the arms of victory: 'They run!' His grandson, Sir Edmund de Gonville Bromhead fought at Waterloo. Of his four sons, three are living and long may they live. The eldest, Captain Bromhead, of the 76th, died at Burmah [*sic*]; the second son, and present baronet, Sir Benjamin Bromhead, of the 22nd Bengal Native Infantry, is now serving with Sir Sam Browne at Kandahar. If he has not fought and won, it is his misfortune and not his fault. The third son, Major Charles Bromhead, of the 24th, is a very distinguished officer, and won glory and his majority in the Ashantee campaign. The fourth son, Lieutenant (now presumably Major) Gonville Bromhead, also of the 24th, has proved himself, though last, not least, of the gallant brotherhood, by his brilliant feat of arms at Rorke's Drift. Of such stuff heroes are made. All honour to the brave, whether alive or dead, who 'count their lives not dear' at the call of duty, and who make the name of England a terror and praise throughout the world. Such men as these, though deed yet speak, and will speak, through future ages. This is rather a warlike trumpet for a minister of peace to blow. But I must take things, not as they ought to be, but as they are. And I am not sure if things were called by their right names, whether the foreign battles of the state militant of the present day are not more useful as well as more creditable than the home battles about doctrine and discipline, conformity or unconformity, which occupy so much of the time and energies of her clerical sister, the church militant.

Speaking at the Lincoln Masonic Hall in 1879, a Colonel Ancott stated:

> The mayor has alluded in his address to the Bromheads as a family of warriors, and he would relate to them an anecdote of the late

> Colonel Bromhead. In the Peninsular War there was fought a very gallant action at El Bodon, in which Her Majesty's 77th Regiment of Foot, together with his (Colonel Ancott's) father's own regiment, the 11th Light Dragoons, succeeded in beating off a force of no fewer than 10,000 Frenchmen. Colonel Bromhead, who commanded before the battle, addressed his regiment in the following short and economic words: 'Men of the 77th, you see the enemy. If you don't kill them they will kill you, and now let's go at them'. They did go at them, and the result was the victory at El Bodon.

A guide for visitors to the church of St Germain in Thurlby, states:

> It would be impossible for the visitor to be unaware of the contribution to the life of the church, the local community and to the nation made by the Bromhead family who have lived at Thurlby Hall since the seventeenth century. The family crest is over the vestry door and on the windows of the north aisle, their distinguished service in their country's armed forces is commemorated in numerous plaques and particularly in the east window in memory of Gonville Bromhead VC, the hero of Rorke's Drift. The initials E. Ff. B. 1842, in so many places show how thorough and extensive was the restoration of St Germains which Sir Edward Bromhead undertook in 1842-43. There are indications everywhere of the family's love for the church and concern for its fabric. The parishioners of Thurlby are very conscious of the debt they owe to the Bromhead family, a debt which can only be repaid with love and respect for its members with loyalty to the church whose continuing witness the family has done much to ensure.

A letter I received from one of Gonville Bromhead's descendants, part of which appears in the Coghill biography, states: '…you refer to Lieutenant Bromhead as "Gonny" taken presumably from Gonville, his first name. He himself pronounced his first and surname as if the "O" was replaced by "U"—Gunville Brumhead—as it were. As told to me by my grannie talking of "Uncle Gunny"'.

Gonville was educated at the Thomas Magnus Grammar School in Newark-on-Trent, where he excelled at various sports. The *Newark Magnus* publication described him as a member of the cricket eleven: 'Gonville Bromhead, afterwards famous as in command at Rorke's Drift, a left-hand medium bowler. Mention of it (Rorke's Drift) could still bring cheers at Magnus gatherings many years afterwards. Bromhead became the fourth old boy to give his name to a House'.

On 20 April 1867 he entered the 24th (2nd Warwickshire) Regiment of Foot, as ensign by purchase, and was trained at Croydon, where he gained popularity among his fellow officers as one who was a helpful senior to new recruits. At nearly six feet tall, and with a powerful frame, he became a champion at any sport he cared to put his hand to. He made a good impression, and an article about him published in the *Hartlepool Mail* of 26 February 1879, stated:

> I was with him for some time at the army tutors at Croydon some twelve years ago, and it is interesting to look back upon him as he appeared to us at the time. About five-feet-ten-inches in height, so well-built that he did not look as tall, he seemed to me to be quite the bean ideal of an English officer. It was our custom of an evening, as soon as 'study' was over, to indulge in bouts of wrestling, boxing and singlestick in the gymnasium outside, and Bromhead was so expert in all of these that he invariably beat everyone opposed to him. With all this he was so kind and genial that the youngsters among us could chaff him and play tricks on him with impunity, and without fear of retaliation. Quiet and most unassuming in his demeanour, he nevertheless often showed friendliness to those who happened to be unpopular. By kindness to newcomers, and in a thousand other ways, the thorough worth and goodness were with him.

He was promoted by selection to the rank of lieutenant on 28 October 1871. Unfortunately he was developing a hearing problem which threatened the progress of his military career. However, in 1878 he was the officer in command of B Company, 2nd Battalion, 24th Regiment, when the unit received orders for active service in South Africa, and they embarked aboard the troopship *Himalaya* at Portsmouth on 1 February 1878, to set sail for the Cape of Good Hope, where he took part in the Ninth Cape Frontier War, and the Zulu War.

For his gallant conduct at the defence of Rorke's Drift, Lieutenant Gonville Bromhead was mentioned in despatches and was awarded the Victoria Cross, which was announced in the *London Gazette* on 2 May 1879. He received the medal from Sir Garnet Wolseley, while he was still on active service at Pine Tree Camp, Utrecht, Transvaal, on 22 August 1879. The official citation for his Victoria Cross stated:

> The lieutenant-general commanding the troops reports that, had it not been for the fine example and excellent behaviour of these

> two officers (Lieutenants Chard and Bromhead) under the most trying circumstances, the defence of Rorke's Drift post would not have been conducted with that intelligence and tenacity which so essentially characterised it. The lieutenant-general adds that its success must, in a great degree, be attributable to the two young officers who exercised the chief command on the occasion in question.

He remained stationed at Rorke's Drift for a while after the battle, where his 'quiet and unassuming demeanour' had not faded with the fame he was beginning to have thrust upon him, and which he found difficult to accept. A contribution to this would almost certainly have been because he, like Major Chard, had already begun to suffer the effects of the jealousy their unwanted hero status would also create. Major Francis Clery, of the 32nd (Cornwall) Light Infantry, observed:

> ...the height of his enjoyment seemed to be to sit all day on a stone on the ground smoking a most uninviting-looking pipe. The only thing that seemed equal to moving him in any way was an allusion to the defence of Rorke's Drift. This used to have a sort of electrical effect upon him, for he would jump up and off he would go, not a word could be got out of him. When I told him he should send me an official report on the affair it seemed to have a most distressing effect on him.

Although his younger brother, Charles, had become a favourite of Sir Garnet Wolseley, it did not stop the general from remarking in his journal of 11 September 1879, 'I have now given away these decorations [the Victoria Cross] to both the officers who took part in the defence of Rorke's Drift, and two duller, more stupid, more uninteresting men or less like gentlemen it has not been my luck to meet for a long time'.

He also received the South Africa Medal with 1877-8-9 clasp. He was promoted captain and brevet-major, dated back to 23 January 1879, and he was twice mentioned in despatches, on 1 March and 15 March 1879. He and Major Chard had the rare distinction of being thanked by the British parliament. Men of B Company who took part in the defence of Rorke's Drift received an illuminated address from the mayor of Durban just before they sailed to Gibraltar in January 1880.

He served at Gibraltar in 1880, and while home on leave in June that year he was invited to Windsor Castle for an audience with Queen Victoria, who gave him a signed photograph. He was guest of honour at several functions, and on 25 June he was invited to Lincoln Masonic Hall, where the mayor presented him with a jewelled sword and an illuminated address. The tenants of Thurlby Hall presented him with a commemorative revolver. In his acceptance speech at the Masonic hall, which was sometimes interrupted by loud cheers, he stated:

> Mr mayor and citizens of this ancient city of Lincoln, I beg to thank you very much for the very kind and flattering address with which you have presented me this day, and also for this magnificent sword, which I assure you will always remain in my family as an heirloom forever. I feel great difficulty in adequately expressing to you my deep sense of the sympathy and kindness with which I have been received since my return to England, but I assure you nothing had given me greater gratification than the splendid reception I have met with this day, especially, as since my boyhood, when I left Thurlby, I have been personally almost a stranger in these parts. I am not vain enough to take this great reception all to myself, and I beg to thank you on behalf of Major Chard, Surgeon-Major Reynolds, Mr Dalton, Mr Dunne and the Reverend Mr Smith, all brave and stalwart men, who were with us on 22 January 1879, and the greater part of whom I am proud to say I still retain in the company which I have the honour to command. I beg to thank you again for the very kind reception which you have given me.

In August 1880 he was posted to Secunderabad in India, and returned to England later that year. On 1 July 1881 the 24th Regiment were re-designated the South Wales Borderers. From 1 October to 5 December 1882, he attended the Hythe School of Musketry, where he gained a 1st Class Extra certificate. On 2 January 1883 he sailed from Portsmouth on the *Serapis*, to join the 2nd Battalion, South Wales Borderers, at Secunderabad. He was promoted to major on 4 April 1883. He took part in the expedition to Upper Burma from 27 October 1886 to 24 May 1888, taking part in the Third Burmese War in November 1885, for which he received the Burma Medal with 1885-9 and 1887-9 clasps.

Major Bromhead never married, and according to Brigadier David Bromhead his main passion was for salmon fishing. He died of enteric fever at Camp Dabhaura, Allahabad, India, on 9 February 1891, aged forty-six, and he was buried at the New Cantonment Cemetery in Allahabad. He left his medals to his brother, Charles, and they are with the regimental museum in Brecon. His name is inscribed on the colour pole of the 24th Regiment, and there is a stained glass memorial window dedicated to him at the church of St Germain. His great-great-nephew, Brigadier David Bromhead, was appointed colonel of the Royal Regiment of Wales in 1994.

Corporal William Wilson Allan VC

The exact date of William's birth is not certain, though it has been recorded to have been some time in February 1844. His name is sometimes spelt 'Allen' but it is 'Allan' on all the census returns, with no suggestion of the middle name of 'Wilson', however, he seems to have added the middle name towards the end of his life, and his grave records his name as W W Allan.

According to the 1851 census he was born at Kyloe near Berwick-upon-Tweed in Northumberland, and was then aged six, being the first born of the family. According to local council researchers at Kyloe, who believe they have located his birth certificate, he was born at Beal in Kyloe Parish, Islandshire, which was then the area known as North Durham.

His father, Thomas (born at Coldstream in Berwickshire on 22 September 1816), was an itinerant agricultural labourer, and his family of four boys and four girls were born in different towns on the Northumberland coast. His mother's name was Eleanor (known as Ellen, formerly Weatherston, born at Berwickshire in 1822). In 1851 the family were living at Belford Moor near Berwick-upon-Tweed.

William was aged fifteen when he enlisted at York on 27 October 1859, and as 1240 Private Allan he was posted to the 2nd Battalion, 24th (2nd Warwickshire) Regiment of Foot at Aldershot. He was slightly built, at five-feet-four-inches tall, but he was a tough Geordie character, and was confined in cells on several occasions in the early 1860s before he settled into army life. He served on Mauritius and, following thirteen years service in the East, he returned to the depot at Brecon on 21 April 1874. His father died at Bedlington, Northumberland, on 17 January 1872, having not known his son would gain the Victoria Cross.

He married Sarah Ann Reeves (born in Brecon) at the Brecon Registry Office on 16 August 1876; his new wife being twelve years younger than him. Her father, Richard, had been a staff-sergeant in the Monmouthshire Militia. Their first two daughters, Helena Letitia and Elizabeth Alice, were born in Brecon in April 1877 and on 11 July 1878 respectively.

William was promoted to lance-corporal on 18 May 1876, to corporal on 6 July 1877, and having gained a second class certificate of education, he became an assistant-schoolmaster. In 1878 he was awarded a prize for 'good shooting and judgement of distance'. Corporal Allen was posted to his battalion on 26 January 1878, and on 2 February he sailed with his unit from Portsmouth on the troopship *Himalaya* for active service in South Africa. He took part in the Cape Frontier War 1878, being promoted to lance-sergeant on 22 May 1878, being reduced to corporal at Pietermaritzburg on 21 October 1878.

Disabled by the injuries he received at Rorke's Drift, he was taken to Helpmekaar, and on 4 February he wrote a letter informing his wife: 'I am getting the better of my wound more rapidly than could be expected…My arm is mending quickly'. He was transported back to England on the *Tamar* and taken to Netley Military Hospital. The Zulu slug had left William's arm partly disabled, but with such a strong constitution he was well enough to attend a victory celebration banquet at Portland Hall in Portsea on 25 October 1879, organised by the people of Portsmouth for the servicemen who had fought in the Zulu campaign.

By 8 November he was serving as provisional staff-sergeant with the 3rd/24th Regiment Militia. His award of Victoria Cross had been announced in the *London Gazette* of 2 May 1879, and on 9 December 1879 he went to Windsor Castle to receive the Victoria Cross from Queen Victoria. He also received the South Africa Medal with 1877-8-9 clasp. On 11 June 1880, William was appointed sergeant at the Colchester depot.

He returned to Brecon for the birth of his first son, Llewellyn Glendower, in July 1880. Grace was born in July 1883, Margaret Mary was born in April 1882 (but she died an infant at Colchester in January 1883) and Gwlydo Annie was born in 1885.

On 13 November 1880, one of Sergeant Allan's fellow defenders of Rorke's Drift, William Partridge (24th Regiment) married his wife's sister, Mary Letitia, known as 'Polly', at the Brecon Registry Office, and Sarah's brother, Richard Reeves, was also serving with the 24th Regiment in 1881. In 1886, William became sergeant, instructor of musketry, to C Company, 4th Volunteer Battalion of the South Wales Borderers, stationed at Monmouth, where he made the family home at 85 Monnow Road, St Mary's Parish, and became a well-known and respected member of the community. Sarah opened a grocery shop next door at number eighty-seven. A child named Jessie was born in 1886, but she died less than two years later. Olive was born in April 1888.

Sarah gave birth to Sybil Jean in January 1890, but a serious influenza epidemic hit the town, and it was thought that William was a victim. However, he was seriously ill with dropsy for seven days, and when further complications developed he deteriorated and died of 'aortic valvular disease of the heart' at his home on 12 March 1890, aged forty-six. He was buried with his baby daughter at Monmouth Cemetery, with military honours provided by the South Wales Borderers, and a stone cross was erected at his grave by the 4th Volunteer Battalion.

Sergeant Allan's sudden death left his wife and children in difficult circumstances, so the mayor of Monmouth set up a benefit appeal to help them. His Victoria Cross is with the South Wales Borderers Museum at Brecon, with an inscribed pocket-watch which was given to the museum by his grandson. It had been presented to Sergeant Allan by the mayor of Brecon while he was serving at the barracks as an instructor. Sarah died at 50 Cinderhill Road in Monmouth in January 1906.

His grave was renovated and a re-dedication service was held on 4 July 2018, during which the regiment displayed his Victoria Cross.

Private Frederick Hitch VC

According to his gravestone, Frederick Hitch was born on 29 November 1856 at 7 Chase Side in Southgate, Edmonton, Middlesex (now Greater London), and was christened at the local Weld Chapel. He was the sixth son, and ninth child of eleven, to John Hitch (born in Hull in 1808) and his wife Sarah (formerly Champness—born at Epping in Essex in 1819). His father was a journeyman boot and shoemaker, and the 1861 census shows the family had moved to 7 Chase Side, and in 1871 to Chase Road.

It seems that Fred had committed some kind of petty crime for which he pleaded guilty at Westminster Police Court. In consequence of this he agreed to enlist into the British army on 7 March 1877, and as 1362 Private Hitch he was posted to the 2nd Battalion, 24th Regiment at Dover on 11 May 1877. His physical description was given as 'five-feet-eight-inches tall, with brown hair, hazel eyes and a fresh complexion'. He was only able to sign an 'X' on his enlistment papers.

He served for a while at Chatham, then his unit received orders for active service in South Africa and sailed to the Cape with the battalion, taking part in the Cape Frontier War, and during the Zulu War he was present at the defence of Rorke's Drift. After the battle he stated:

> I had not had time to form an opinion as to whether the Zulus would take the fort or not. My only wish was—as I believe was that of every other man—to fight as hard as I could, and I did it

> until I was wounded. I crept to the rear, and with the assistance of Private Deakin, tied up my wound as well as I could by tearing off the sleeve of a greatcoat for the purpose. I then knocked about as well as I could, serving the others with ammunition until I became exhausted from loss of blood and fell down unconscious. I did not come to until the morning, just as peep of day, and then found myself in a stable. The Zulus, meanwhile, had retired, but were again advancing to attack us, and they saw the general and his column coming, and again retired.

After spending time under medical care at Durban, Private Hitch was sent home on the *Tamar*. His award of the Victoria Cross was announced in the *London Gazette* on 2 May 1879. On returning to England, he went to Netley Hospital, and on 12 August 1879, Queen Victoria visited him and presented him with the Victoria Cross in person. He also received the South Africa Medal with 1877-8-9 clasp. He had thirty-nine pieces of broken bone taken from his shoulder, and a medical board decided that his arm was permanently disabled. He was discharged unfit for further service on 25 August 1879.

Fred Hitch returned to civilian life in London, and on 5 July 1881 he married Emily Matilda Meurisse (born in Richmond, Surrey, in 1865), who was of German descent, at St Matthew's Church in Bayswater. They had made their home at Porchester Square in Westminster, and had six children. Their three sons all passed-out as drum majors at the Duke of York School. Frederick later joined the Metropolitan Police, and Charles served with the 60th Rifles and the South Wales Borderers.

The 1891 census shows Fred living with his family at 1 Epirus Mews, on Epirus Road in the parish of St John's, Fulham, London, and he was self-employed as a cab proprietor, having bought a taxi cab and two horses and set up a small transport business in south London. While he was working at the Royal United Services Institute in Whitehall, Cecil Rhodes visited and congratulated him on his bravery.

His Victoria Cross was stolen from his coat, the family had to pay for a replacement and Fred had to sign a declaration to return the medal if the original was found. He was presented with the replacement by Lord Roberts in 1908, and later the family located the original VC at an auction and had to buy it back for £85. He wore his Victoria Cross at the coronation of King Edward VII.

He was living in Duke Street in Chiswick when the age of the motor car began to make its mark and he went to work as a taxi driver for the General Motor Cab Company in Chiswick. By 1912 he was living on his own in rented accommodation at 62 Cranbrook Road, Turnham Green in Chiswick. During Christmas 1912 the drivers at his depot went on strike and he spent much of his time on picket duty in bitterly cold weather, which seems to have damaged his health, and, on 6 January 1913, he complained of bad pains in his side. His landlady tried to comfort him, but he died later in the day, aged fifty-six. An inquest found that he had died of pleura-pneumonia and heart failure. His funeral was an impressive affair, attended by John Fielding VC, Frank Bourne DCM, his friend Joseph Farmer, a Boer War holder of the Victoria Cross, and over a thousand London cab drivers. He was buried with military honours provided by the South Wales Borderers at St Nicholas Churchyard, Chiswick Old Cemetery. His monument was paid for by public subscription, one of the donations coming from the family of Major Chard. The inscription reads: 'To the memory of Frederick Hitch VC, born 29 Nov. 1856, died 6 Jan. 1913. This memorial was erected by voluntary subscription to commemorate his heroic action at Rorke's Drift, 22 January 1879'. A blue plaque was erected at the house where he died, which states: 'Private Frederick Hitch VC, 1859-1913, hero of Rorke's Drift, lived and died here'. His Victoria Cross is with the regimental museum in Brecon.

Private Alfred Henry Hook VC

Alfred Hook was born in Churcham, Huntley, near Gloucester, on 6 August 1850, the eldest son of three in the family of six children to Henry Hook (1828-80) and his wife, Helen, Eleanor or Ellen (formerly Higgs—1831-1921). His father was an agricultural labourer, and their home was a house called 'Birdwood', known as 'Hook's Farm'. At the time of the 1861 census they were living in a cottage in Churcham (probably still the house where he was born), where Alfred, aged only ten, and his father, were recorded as working as wood-cutters. All Alfred's siblings had been born in Churcham, except the sixth child, Emily, who was born at Blaisdon in the Forest of Dean, Gloucestershire, in 1863.

While living at Aston Ingham, Newent, Gloucestershire, Alfred met Comfort Jones (born in Newent on 14 August 1849) and they married on 26 December 1870. The 1871 census records them as living in Picklenash in Newent, along with his wife's parents, John and Ann. They had three children born in Newent; Raymond John was born on 29 October 1871, Mary Henrietta on 19 September 1873, and Julia Ann on 16 May 1876.

He had enlisted into the Royal Monmouth Militia at Monmouth on 7 May 1869, and served with the unit until May 1874. He joined the regular army on 13 March 1877, and as 1373 Private 'Henry' Hook he was posted to the 2nd Battalion, 24th Regiment at Monmouth, signing up for six years. He received orders for active service in South Africa and sailed to the Cape with his battalion in February 1878. He took part in the Cape Frontier War, and during the Zulu War he was present at the defence of Rorke's Drift. He left a detailed account of his experiences and the action within the hospital.

Private Henry Hook was mentioned in despatches, and his award of the Victoria Cross was announced in the *London Gazette* on 2 May 1879. On 29 January he was one of the soldiers who transferred to G Company to make up the numbers the unit had lost at iSandlwana; becoming orderly to Major Black. He remained stationed at Rorke's Drift, and on 3 August 1879 he became one of a very few number of men to be decorated with the Victoria Cross at the place where he had earned it, when General Wolseley pinned the medal to his chest. He also received the South Africa Medal with 1877-8-9 clasp.

Henry returned from Gibraltar to discharge from the army at Brecon on 25 June 1880, perhaps because his father was ill, because he died on 29 December 1880. His wife was apparently led to believe that 'Alfred' had been killed in action, which seems to have caused problems as he appears on the 1881 census as a domestic groom in Glendower Street, Monmouth, while Comfort and their children lived with her parents at Mount Pleasant in Newent, Gloucester. Comfort had become a gloveress (person who makes gloves). For the record, the 1891 census states that the family lived at 28 Kilcote Road in Newent. Comfort married David Meyrick in Gloucester on 1 June 1895, and she died in Newent on 11 July 1900.

Henry moved to London, where he lived in lodgings at Sydenham Hill, and gained employment as a general cleaner. He applied for a job at the British Museum, and after being recommended by Major Bromhead and Lord Chelmsford, he was taken on as an 'inside duster' from 26 December 1881. He was later appointed umbrella caretaker in the reading room at the museum, a position he held until his retirement. He became a member of the Loyal St James Lodge of Oddfellows in London; served as a corporal in the Bloomsbury Rifle Volunteers; and was sergeant in the 19th Middlesex RVC from April 1896 to January 1905. He was sergeant instructor of musketry, 1st Volunteer Battalion, Royal Fusiliers, serving the unit for twenty years. A silver-plated memorial trophy bearing his name was presented to the British Museum Rifle Association, to be awarded for services to the association. In the mid-1890s he moved to 4 Cumberland Street, Pimlico.

He met Ada Lettia Taylor (born in London in 1864) at a concert. Although Henry's divorce was not finalised until 25 August 1897, the pair married at St Andrew's Church, Islington, on 10 April 1897. They had two daughters: Victoria Catherine was born in March 1899, and Letitia Jean was born in December 1902. In 1901 they lived at 25 Lesley Street, in the Lower Holloway district of Islington.

Henry had suffered from headaches, which were possibly caused by his wound, and by 1904 his condition had become serious. He was advised to return to his native county in the hope that the air would help combat his condition. He tendered his resignation, which took effect from 31 December 1904, and the museum trustees granted him a pension of £40 a year. He was placed in the care of the Phoenix Lodge of Oddfellows at Gloucester, who recommended a doctor, and his family resided at 2 Osborn Villas, Rosebury Avenue, Gloucester.

Henry Hook died of pulmonary consumption on 12 March 1905, aged fifty-four. His funeral was attended by thousands of people, and twenty-three regiments were represented. He was buried with military honours at St Andrew's Churchyard, Churcham. Fred Hitch attended the funeral with his son, who was one of the bearers. On 28 September 1906, his widow and daughters were present when a memorial cross was unveiled at his grave, and there is a memorial brass plate at Brecon Cathedral. His medals are in the South Wales Borderers Regimental Museum. His grave was renovated in 2008.

Private Robert Jones VC

Born at 5 Ty Newydd, Clytha, Monmouthshire on 19 August 1857, Robert Jones was the fourth of five sons in a family of seven children to Robert Jones, 'a farmer of thirty-three acres,' and his wife, Hannah (formerly Fryer). He was christened at Penrhos in Monmouth. He became a rural worker like his father, the 1871 census stating that at the age of fourteen he was employed at, and living in, the Drybridge Farm, in the St Mary's Parish district of Monmouth.

His father is said to have greatly disapproved when he joined the army at Monmouth on 10 January 1876, and as 716 Private R. Jones he was posted to the 2nd Battalion, 24th Regiment. He was described as being five-feet-seven-inches tall, and having a fresh complexion, grey eyes and brown hair. He received orders for active service in South Africa, and sailed to the Cape with his unit in February 1878. He served in the Cape Frontier War, and during the Zulu War he was present at the defence of Rorke's Drift.

For his conduct at the defence of Rorke's Drift, Private Robert Jones was mentioned in despatches, and his award of the Victoria Cross was announced in the *London Gazette* on 2 May 1879. He received the medal from Lord Wolseley while still on active service at Utrecht in the Transvaal on 11 September 1879. He also received the South Africa Medal with 1877-8-9 clasp. His service in the campaign left him with one bullet and four *assegai* wounds, and he left an account of the part he played in the action at Rorke's Drift.

He served at Gibraltar in 1880, and in India, from where he returned to Britain on 25 November 1881. He transferred to the army reserve, was recalled for service on 2 August 1882, and transferred back to the army reserve on 7 February 1883. He was finally discharged from the army on 26 January 1888.

He married Elizabeth Hopkins at Llantilio, Crosseny, Monmouthshire, on 7 January 1885, and they had five children. Alice Margaret was born in Monmouthshire in 1886, Edith Emily in Peterchurch on 7 October 1888, Robert at Peterchurch in 1892, Lily Rose at Peterchurch on 10 December 1895, and Ellen, known as Nellie was born at Peterchurch in 1898. In 1891 Robert was living at The Lodge in Dorstone, Hereford, while his wife and girls were 'visiting friends' at Ewyas Harold in Hereford. They went to live in the village of Peterchurch, Herefordshire, and Robert gained employment for Major De La Hay, a retired officer, at the nearby Crossways House. The family home was at Rose Cottage, on Rose Farm, and they also acquired some land in the village of St Margaret's. Robert had been wounded close to his eyes and sometimes suffered severe pains in his head.

In August 1898 he collapsed, and, although he recovered, his wife noticed a change in his character. On 6 September he was seen to be acting strangely before he went to work, and when he arrived he asked to borrow the major's gun and two cartridges and went into the garden, presumably to shoot birds. The gun was heard to go off, and he was found dead with the back of his head blown away. An inquest found that he had committed suicide while of unsound mind. He was aged forty-one. Two days later he was given a modest military funeral, and members of his old regiment attended as he was buried in St Peter's Churchyard. Robert Jones was known to be a good father, and he was a talented amateur poet. A poem of his is preserved at the regimental museum. His is the only Victoria Cross of the seven gained by the 24th Regiment at Rorke's Drift which remains in private hands, as part of the collection owned by Lord Ashcroft.

Private William Jones VC

Two individuals named William Jones were born in Bristol in 1839, and his family descendants believe him to be the one born on 16 August 1839, at 5 Lucas Street, Castle Precinct. He was the second son of four in the family of five children to a stonemason named William Jones (born in 1806 at Cwmcarvan in Monmouthshire), and his wife, Mary Ann (late Martin, formerly Lancastle—born in 1816 at Llanon in Carmarthenshire). The Wesleyan Methodist Chapel at Coleford, in the Forest of Dean, Gloucestershire, records the baptism of William and James Jones on 22 March 1840, and the 1851 census records a family living in East Dean, near Ross-on-Wye, which may be them. William served an apprenticeship as a shoemaker before entering the army, and there are records of a shoemaker named Jones who lived in Cowell Street in Evesham, Worcestershire, who may have been William.

He enlisted at Birmingham on 21 December 1858, and as 593 Private W. Jones he was posted to the 2nd Battalion, 24th Regiment. He was described as being five-feet-five-inches tall, with a sallow complexion, dark brown eyes and brown hair. While serving at Mauritius he was promoted to corporal on 1 September 1859, but he was reduced to private on 5 September 1860. He re-engaged at Rangoon on 10 January 1868, to complete twenty-one years service, and he also served in India.

He married Elizabeth Goddard at the Wesleyan Methodist Chapel in Farnham, Hampshire, on 25 May 1875. He was posted to Dover, where a child named William was born on 15 November 1876, who was sent to live with his grandparents in Farnham.

He received orders for active service in South Africa and sailed with his battalion to the Cape in February 1878, taking part in the Cape Frontier War. His wife went with him, but she died of tuberculosis on 11 October 1878. During the Zulu War he was present at the defence of Rorke's Drift.

For his service during the Zulu War, Private William Jones was mentioned in despatches, and his award of the Victoria Cross was announced in the *London Gazette* on 2 May 1879. He also received the South Africa Medal with 1877-8-9 clasp. He was decorated by Queen

Victoria at Windsor Castle on 13 January 1880. He was examined by a medical board at Pietermaritzburg on 3 September 1879, which found that he was suffering from chronic rheumatism. He was sent to Netley Hospital, and on 2 February 1880 he was discharged as 'unfit for further service due to chronic rheumatism of the joints'. He was in possession of three good conduct badges.

His intended place of residence was 174 Lupin Street in the Aston district of Birmingham, and by the time of the 1881 Census he was named as a warehouseman visiting Charles and Elizabeth Goddard at Court 3, 6 Love Lane, Duddeston, Aston, Birmingham. A child named Albert Ulundi (Frodsham) was born there on 12 May 1881, and Elizabeth (Frodsham) was born on 19 June 1883 at 7 Holt Street, Duddeston, Aston, Birmingham. Albert's unusual name suggests that he may have been fathered by William, and he and Elizabeth are the only two children who had their names changed to Jones. By the time of the 1891 Census the family home was 8 Luxton Street, Duddeston, Aston, Birmingham. Charles had moved out of the house and William was recorded as a boarder.

He moved to Rutland Street, Chorlton-on-Medlock in Manchester, and by 1901 he lived at 7 Ash Street, Miles Platting. He toured with Buffalo Bill's Wild West Show when it came to Lancashire, and he appeared at Hamilton's Pansterorama in Rochdale to recite his account of the defence. However, he could not get regular employment because of his health, and he was forced to pawn his VC to provide for his family. It is now with the regimental museum. William was aged sixty-one when he married Elizabeth at St Augustine's Church in Newton Heath, Manchester, on 16 July 1901.

In 1912 they were living at 72 Sanderson Street, Collyhurst, Manchester, when William was found wandering the streets in an 'impoverished' condition and his wife had to collect him from Bridge Street Workhouse in Salford. He died at his daughter's home, 6 Brompton Street, Ardwick, Manchester, on 15 April 1913 aged seventy-three, and he was buried with military honours at Philips Park Cemetery, Manchester. A ceremony was held at the cemetery in 2007 to commemorate the unveiling of a new headstone at his grave.

Private John Williams (Fielding) VC

John Fielding was born in Merthyr Road, Abergavenny, Monmouthshire, on 25 September 1857. He was the second son of nine in the family of ten children to Michael Fielding, and his wife, Margaret (formerly Godsil). His parents were both born at Cork in Ireland in 1836. The family settled at 3 Penywain Cottages, Llantarnam, Cwmbran, when John was five. His father was a gardener, and John went to work as a labourer at the Patent Nut and Bolt Factory in Cwmbran in 1865.

He entered the Royal Monmouth Militia in 1877, but when he decided to join the regular army his family disapproved and tried to stop him, so he used the name John Williams to enlist into the 24th Regiment at Monmouth, on 22 May 1877, along with Joseph Williams from Newport, who was killed in action fighting alongside John in the hospital at Rorke's Drift. 1393 Private John Williams was posted to the 2nd Battalion at Dover. He was just less than five-feet-six-inches tall, with a fresh complexion, blue eyes and light-brown hair. His religion was Church of England.

He received orders for active service in South Africa, and sailed to the Cape in February 1878. He was charged at King William's Town on 20 April 1878 with quitting barracks improperly, admonished. He took part in the Cape Frontier War, and during the Zulu War he was present at the defence of Rorke's Drift. The official citation for the award of the Victoria Cross to Private John Williams appeared in the *London Gazette* for 2 May 1879.

He was granted good conduct pay from 23 May 1879, but the trauma of the events at Rorke's Drift seem to have affected him badly, and he was charged with being absent from duty at Pietermaritzburg on 25 October 1879, for which he was severely reprimanded (admonished). He went to Gibraltar, where he was charged with being drunk on 13 February 1880, returning to barracks at 4.30 p.m. He received his Victoria Cross from Major-General Anderson at the Almeda Parade Ground in Gibraltar on 1 March 1880. He arrived in India on 12 August 1880, where he was charged at Secunderabad with being in bed at 7.00 a.m. on 18 August 1881, against orders. He was charged at Secunderabad for committing a nuisance in the water room on 1 May 1882, being confined to barracks for five days. His good conduct pay was increased to two pence a day from 23 May 1883, and he obtained a fourth class certificate of education. He returned from India on 30 November 1883.

He transferred to the army reserve at Brecon on 13 December 1888, his character being described as very good, and his intended place of residence was 3 Stercus Row, Cwmbran, Monmouthshire, his next-of-kin being his father, of 4 Abbey Row, Llantarnam. He was at some time a sergeant with the 3rd Volunteer Battalion of the South Wales

Borderers. He attested for general service infantry at Newport on 23 May 1889, and discharged on termination of his engagement on 22 May 1893, becoming attached to the civilian staff at Brecon Barracks.

He went back to work at the Nut and Bolt Factory, and he met Elizabeth Murphy (born in Cwmbran in 1859), who already had a daughter, named Annie. They married at St Alban's Catholic Church in Pontypool, on 15 April 1884, and together they had three sons and two daughters. The 1891 and 1901 censuses show them living at 43 Morgan John Street, Llantarnam, while the 1911 census shows them living at 146 Pritchard Terrace, Llantarnam, Cwmbran. He was appointed recruiting officer at the barracks during the Great War, where he suffered a double tragedy. His wife died on 29 May 1914, and later that year he received the tragic news that their eldest son, Tom, had been killed in action at Mons while serving with the South Wales Borderers.

He was present at a garden party held by King George V and Queen Mary at Buckingham Palace on 26 June 1920, to commemorate all holders of the Victoria Cross, and he attended a VC dinner in the House of Lords on 9 November 1929, which was hosted by the Prince of Wales. He led a quiet life in Llantarnam Road, Cwmbran. Described as 'a rather tall, charming man', he retired from Brecon Barracks on 20 May 1920, and left the Nut and Bolt Factory in 1922. He eventually went to live with his married daughter, Margaret, at 28 Cocker Avenue, Cwmbran.

On 24 November 1932, the last surviving Zulu War VC was visiting his daughter, Elizabeth, at Tycoch, Cwmbran. While he was there he suffered heart failure and died in the early hours of 25 November 1932. He was aged seventy-five. His funeral cortege was half-a-mile long, including a place of honour for survivors of the Zulu War, and there were floral tributes from the families of Fred Hitch and Harry Hook. He was buried with military honours provided by the South Wales Borderers, who erected a memorial at his grave in St Michael of All Angels Churchyard in Llantarnam.

Surgeon James Henry Reynolds VC

James Henry Reynolds was born at Kingstown (now Dun Laughaire), Ireland, on 3 February 1844, the son of Laurence Reynolds, a merchant and justice of the peace, of Dalyston House, Granard, County Longford. He had an older brother named Thomas James. James was educated at Castle Knock and at Trinity College, Dublin, from where he graduated as a bachelor of medicine and bachelor of surgery in 1867.

Prior to the Crimean War, medical officers and orderlies were 'regimental' in that medical officers were appointed to each regiment and it was their duty to provide a hospital and keep an eye on the continuing health of the troops in the regiment, not just at the theatre of war. However, during the Crimean campaign the Medical Staff Corps was established, which became the Army Hospital Corps (men only) in the following year, and later was officered from the Army Medical Department.

Doctor Reynolds entered the Medical Staff Corps as assistant-surgeon on 31 March 1868, and in this capacity he was appointed to the 36th (Herefordshire) Regiment on 24 March 1869. He received a commendation for his efficient service during an outbreak of cholera in the regiment in India.

In 1873, a co-ordinated medical service was set up, and a qualifying doctor needed to be single, aged over twenty-one, and much more trained and qualified. Having been placed on the medical staff in 1870, Doctor Reynolds was appointed surgeon in the Army Medical Service in 1873.

When the 1st Battalion, 24th Regiment sailed to South Africa in 1874, he went with them as part of the medical team. He took part in the campaign in Griqualand West in 1875, and during the Ninth Cape Frontier War he was stationed at the Impetu depot with the 24th Regiment when the garrison was besieged for several weeks until relief came in January 1878. He was appointed for service with the British troops preparing for hostilities against the Zulus, and on 22 January 1879 he was on medical duties at Rorke's Drift. He was helped by a servant named William Pearce, who was aged about twenty-seven and was born at Devonport in Plymouth.

His award of the Victoria Cross was announced in the *London Gazette* of 17 June 1879, and he was promoted to surgeon-major, dated 23 January 1879. He remained at Rorke's Drift after the battle, and Henry Harford wrote:

> I shall not easily forget one particular night when Doctor Reynolds and I met in the dark having literally been washed out of our sleeping place, and mooched about, endeavouring to find a more sheltered spot. Suddenly we hit on the idea of lying down under the eaves of B Company's [storehouse] roof, so coiled ourselves up in our soaking-wet blankets, thanking our stars that at all events there would be no river running under us, when presently swish came about half a ton of water clean on top of us—B Company were emptying their tarpaulin!

He was at the decisive Battle of Ulundi to witness the defeat of the Zulus, and he arrived back in England on board the *Eagle* on 2 October 1879. For his service he was awarded the South Africa Medal with 1877-8-9 clasp. In July 1879, he was awarded the British Medical Association's gold medal, and he was elected Honorary Fellow of the Royal College of Physicians, Ireland, and Honorary Doctor of Law, Dublin. On 17 October 1879, he and John Chard were guests of honour at a dinner held at the Wanderers Club, Pall Mall, London, 'in recognition of their splendid defence of Rorke's Drift'.

In 1880 he was appointed Senior Medical Officer for the expedition to aid Captain Charles Boycott during the Irish Land War, and while stationed at Richmond Barracks in Dublin he married Elizabeth Mary McCormick, the daughter of a medical doctor named George McCormick, at Glenealy Church in County Wicklow on 22 September 1880. They lived at 5 Usher's Island in Dublin, where a son named Percival was born on 9 January 1884. His wife was aged only thirty when she died on 8 December 1886. In 1891 he was living at Cheriton Cliffs, St Paul's Parish, Sandgate, at Hythe in Kent, with his four children: George, Percy, Henry and Lily, who had all been born in Ireland. He also had a daughter named Elizabeth.

He was promoted to lieutenant-colonel on 1 April 1887 and to brigade-surgeon lieutenant-colonel on 25 December 1892. He retired on 8 January 1896, and while on the retired list he was employed as senior medical officer at the Royal Army Clothing Factory at Pimlico in London. He retired this post in May 1905. A keen sportsman, he was a member of the Army and Navy Club from 1890 until his death. On 9 November 1929, he and John Fielding were guests of honour as the two senior Victoria Cross holders at a dinner hosted by the Prince of Wales in the Royal Gallery at the House of Lords.

The 1901 census records him as living alone at 156 Cambridge Street in Belgravia, London, and he was living at the Rubens Hotel in Westminster when he became ill and was admitted to the Empire Nursing Home in Victoria, London. He died of pleurisy and influenza on 4 March 1932 aged eighty-eight, and he was buried in St Mary's Roman Catholic Cemetery, Kensal Rise, London. The granite cross memorial which marks his grave became blackened and had subsided badly, so it was cleaned and re-set in 1991. His medals are with the Royal Army Medical Corps Museum in Aldershot.

At the time of the death of Doctor Reynolds, Walter G. Spencer sent some personal recollections of him, which were published in the *British Medical Journal*:

> When Colonel Reynolds was in charge of the Pimlico Clothing Department, he frequently sent workers to Westminster Hospital for treatment, and later he came to me about his health, the last time at the beginning of 1929. Then a cancer, for which a grave operation would previously have been called for, disappeared in about ten days under radium. Colonel Reynolds was thus able to walk at the head of the VCs at the thanksgiving ceremony and to be present at the dinner in the House of Lords. Our conversations often returned to Rorke's Drift, and from notes I jotted down I have picked out a few of his reminiscences, which I have not noticed in print.
>
> There were thirty-six patients in the hospital, most in different stages of typhoid fever. No preparations had been made for the defence of the station. Reynolds was senior officer, having been already six years in South Africa; Bromhead and Chard were young subalterns just come out from England; Dalton, an army non-commissioned officer, who had re-joined, had had experience in methods of defence employed by the Boers. When fugitives from iSandlwana reached Rorke's Drift it was first proposed to evacuate the place, but Reynolds declared that to be impossible. Even if the convoy could cross the river the ascent of the opposite bank was so long and steep that the Zulus would certainly catch it up. It was Dalton who arranged the defence with mealie bags.
>
> When the Zulus came into view, there appeared horsemen in scarlet and the cry was that the cavalry were returning; but Reynolds pointed out that the riders were not rising in their saddles, but sat on the horses as the natives did. Coming nearer, the Zulu *impi* drew up and ceremoniously took snuff, heralding a charge to the uttermost. A few Zulus got into the garden and into the hospital before two patients in bed could be got within the laager, and a third lost his head, took a wrong turning, and was also killed. The remaining thirty-three cases were saved and survived the subsequent stench.

A number of items which Surgeon Reynolds had used at Rorke's Drift were auctioned at Spinks in 2001. They included two Gladstone bags engraved with his initials, a travelling wooden medicine chest containing unused ointment tubes and glass bottles, and two leather pocket cases containing the surgical instruments he used in the field. The lot included his revolver, an eighteenth century pocket-watch he had been given by his grandfather, a silver medal which had been presented to him by the Royal Welsh Fusiliers and dress miniatures of his Victoria Cross and South Africa campaign medal.

In 1884 the Army Medical Corps once more became the Medical Staff Corps, and in 1898 it was amalgamated with the officers of the medical department to form the Royal Army Medical Corps. It has the distinction of being the first administrative corps to be granted the title 'Royal'. The modern Corps is responsible for all medical, surgical, hygienic and sanitary arrangements of the army, and its officers act as expert advisers to commands on all matters connected with the health and physical welfare of the troops. Its establishment and equipment are so arranged as to meet the varying needs of service in any part of Britain and its overseas possessions.

Commissary James Langley Dalton VC

James Langley Dalton was born in 1831 in the parish of St Andrews at Holborn, London. He gave up his job as a clerk in a stationers' shop to enlist into the army at Victoria, London, on 20 November 1849, being just under six feet tall, with a fresh complexion, hazel eyes and red hair, and as 965 Private Dalton he was posted to the 85th King's Light Infantry (Buck's Volunteers) at Waterford in Ireland. The 1851 census lists him as a soldier of the 85th Regiment stationed at Fulwood Barracks in Preston, and he was later stationed at Hull and Portsmouth. In 1853 the battalion embarked for service at Mauritius, where he was promoted to corporal on 1 July 1853, and drew his first entitlement to good conduct pay on 21 December 1854. He left the island three years later, having been promoted to sergeant on 7 September 1855. In 1856 he sailed with his regiment to the Cape, taking part in the Eighth Cape Frontier War. He re-engaged at Pembroke Docks on 21 December 1859 for a further eleven years service.

He transferred to the Commissariat Staff Corps at Aldershot on 31 March 1862, being appointed colour-sergeant on 1 June 1863. While stationed in Aldershot until 1867, he attended the Hythe School of Musketry in 1864, and on 7 February 1866 he was appointed clerk and master-sergeant. His last tour of overseas duty was in Canada from 1868 to 1871, and he served during General Wolseley's Red River Expedition. The reorganisation of the Commissariat saw him transferred to the Army Service Corps on 1 April 1870, as second class staff sergeant, and on 1 July he was promoted to first class staff sergeant—the equivalent of

This picture is not chronologically accurate, but it gives a good visual impression of the desperate situation in the British camp at iSandlwana as Lieutenants Coghill and Melvill attempt to save the Queen's Colour of their battalion.

Nevill Coghill was the son of an Irish landowner. He excelled at outdoor activities, and was especially competent on the back of a horse. He was appointed lieutenant in 1875, and met his death just three days before his 27th birthday.

Teignmouth Melvill was born in London to parents who hailed from Cornwall. His family served with distinction in India, his father being a former officer in the Bengal Army. He was appointed lieutenant in 1868, and was married with two sons when he was killed in action during the Zulu War.

A soldier of the 24th Regiment as he may have looked while on active service in South Africa. (John Anderson)

Samuel Wassall was born in Birmingham in 1856. He had worked in the local dye factory before he enlisted into the British Army in 1874. He was the first soldier of the 80th (Staffordshire) Regiment to be awarded the Victoria Cross. He was married and had nine children when he worked at the Barrow-in-Furness shipyard, and was one of only three surviving Zulu War VCs when he died in 1927.

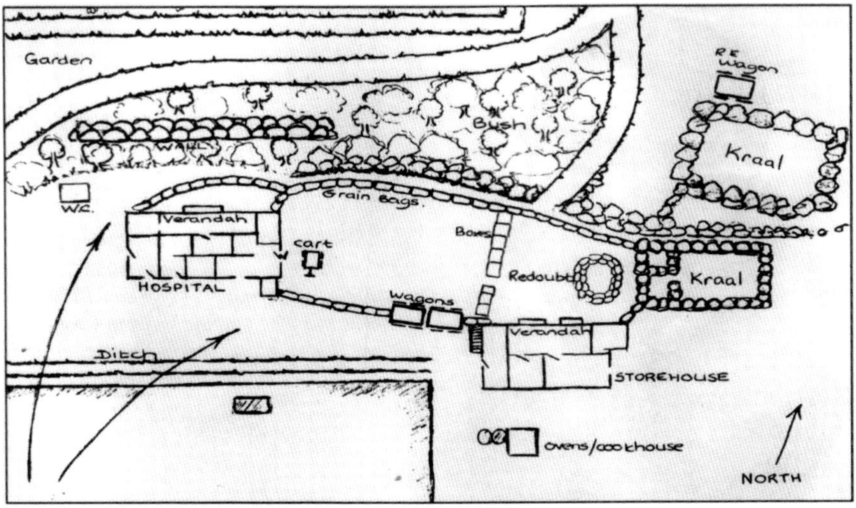

At Rorke's Drift, a wall of grain bags three units high was constructed. This enclosed the front of the hospital and ran along the ledge of the rocky terrace to the stone wall of the kraal. It also stretched from the far end of the storehouse down to the edge of these rocks. Two wagons were utilised to form part of the defensive wall connecting the right hand front corner of the storehouse with the left hand back corner of the hospital. The arrows indicate the initial Zulu attack. (Tracey Bancroft)

John Chard was a West Country man who was commissioned as lieutenant in the Royal Engineers in 1868. Though he became known as 'The Hero of Rorke's Drift', he was of a very modest disposition and did not take full advantage of his fame. He never married and died, aged just 50, in 1897.

A member of a highly-distinguished military family from Lincolnshire, Gonville Bromhead was commissioned as lieutenant in the 24th Regiment in 1867. After service in Burma he died, unmarried, in India in 1891.

An Irishman who became an assistant-surgeon in the Medical Staff Corps in 1868, James Reynolds was attached to the 1st Battalion, 24th Regiment for active service in South Africa. Only John Williams of the Zulu War VCs survived him when he died in London in 1932.

James Langley Dalton was born in London and joined the army in 1849. He was in South Africa when the Zulu War broke out. On joining the Commissariat he went on active service. His campaign experience was of great value after news of the Zulu advance on Rorke's Drift was announced. He later prospected for gold in South Africa, where he died in 1884.

A modern depiction of the defence of Rorke's Drift at the height of the fighting. (Geoff Dickson)

This warrior of the uDhloko regiment, following the usual practice on campaign, has jettisoned much of his ceremonial dress and retains only the otterskin headband and cowtail arm and leg decorations. Reflecting his married status he wears the headring, and also a charm necklace made up of small wooden blocks and pouches of animal skin. (Richard Scollins, with information provided by Ian James Knight)

Six men of the 24th Regiment were instructed to barricade the hospital and defend the patients as best they could. Knowing they had little chance of escape, they fought back the warriors until most of the patients had been evacuated. Four of the six hospital defenders were awarded the Victoria Cross for their valour, and the other two, Privates Joseph Williams and Robert Cole, were deprived of the medal because they were killed. (Geoff Dickson)

The men who defended the garrison at Rorke's Drift expected no mercy from the Zulus, and they fought with great gallantry, vowing to sell their lives dearly. Some of the men who were wounded helped at the ramparts by distributing ammunition and giving shouts of encouragement. They held back the ferocious onslaughts stubbornly, and their steadfast determination disheartened the warriors and forced them to give up the fight. (Geoff Dickson)

Anthony Booth was born in Nottingham in 1846. He joined the 80th (Staffordshire) Regiment in 1864, and was appointed sergeant in 1870. He was a married man with five surviving children when he went to the Cape on active service. Several of his sons were serving with the Staffordshires when he died in the West Midlands in 1899.

A sketch depicting the carnage on the Devil's Pass at the eastern end of Hlobane Mountain as the British force tried desperately to escape from the ferocious Zulu warriors. Those who did not were slaughtered without mercy.

Redvers Buller was born in the West Country. The headmaster at Eton once described him as 'very solid and sturdy, with a will of his own'. Lord Wolseley said he was 'the bravest man I have ever known'.

Colonel Buller behaved with the greatest gallantry during the retreat from Hlobane, for which he was awarded the Victoria Cross. He saved so many lives that Colonel Wood declared: 'He had won it a dozen times.'

The son of a Dublin vicar, William Knox Leet served with distinction in the Indian Mutiny. Having been appointed Companion of the Bath (CB) and honorary major-general, he died in Kent in 1898.

As Captain Campbell lies dead, Lieutenant Lysons and Private Fowler race forward to attack the caves at the southern face of Hlobane Mountain in an attempt to dislodge a party of Zulus. Colonel Wood described the action as 'the bravest deed I ever saw performed in my life'.

Henry Lysons was one of twins born to a senior officer who had fought in the Crimea. He later saw active service with the Nile Expedition and in Burma. He died in London in 1907.

Edmund Fowler came from Waterford in Ireland. Having been ordered to forfeit his Victoria Cross for a minor offence, Queen Victoria subsequently refused to deprive him of his medal. He was married and had six children when he died in Colchester in 1926.

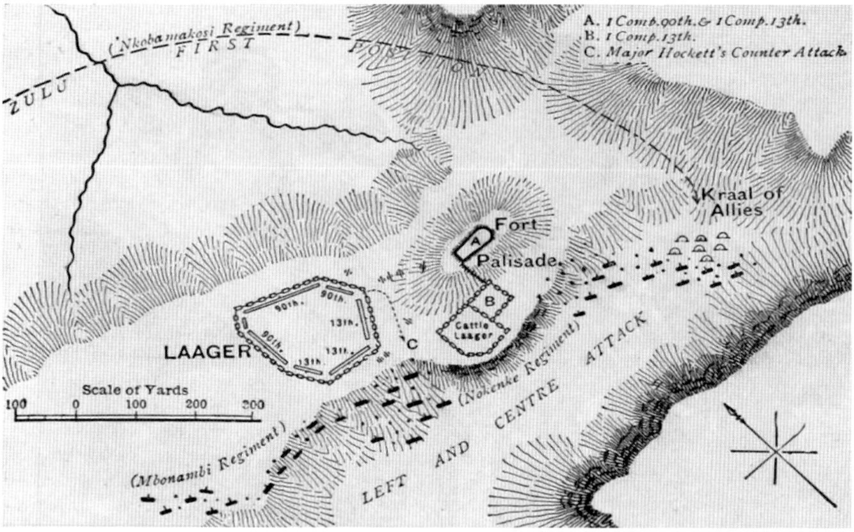

Map showing the disposition of British troops at Khambula and how the battle developed.

British troops pour devastating fire at the Zulus from the ridge which ran along the defensive position on Khambula Hill.

Edward Browne was the son of an officer in the Durham Light Infantry; he had a brother who became a general with the Cornwall Light Infantry. He was educated at the Royal Military Academy at Sandhurst and became an officer with the 24th Regiment in 1871. He died in Switzerland in 1907.

With Zulu warriors almost on them, Captain Beresford would not take no for an answer, having ridden back to rescue Sergeant John Fitzmaurice of the 24th Regiment. He dragged his stricken comrade up into the saddle and got him away from the immediate danger.

William Beresford was born in Ireland, the son of a vicar who became the 4th Marques of Waterford. He fought in Afghanistan prior to the Zulu War, and after a successful career in horse-racing he died at Dorking in 1900.

Cecil D'Arcy was one of nine children born in New Zealand to an officer in the British Army who was of Irish descent. He was believed to be the first holder of the Victoria Cross for the Zulu War to die, but there is some uncertainty concerning the circumstances of his death.

Edmund O'Toole (right) and Cecil D'Arcy. Once believed to have been born in South Africa, Edmund was a Dubliner who was once described as a 'rip-roaring Irishman'. He and Cecil D'Arcy joined the Frontier Light Horse on its establishment in 1877. The circumstances of his death are not certain.

Sketches from a newspaper of the day depicting the Zulu War Victoria Cross actions of Surgeon Reynolds, Lieutenant Browne, Private Wassall, Major Leet and Colonel Buller.

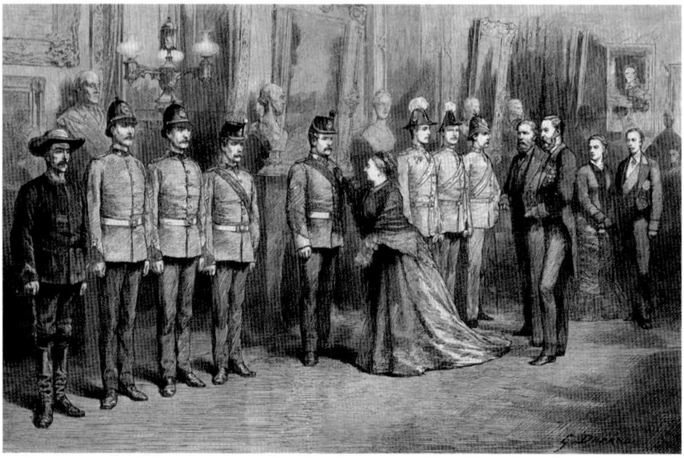

At Windsor Castle on 9 December 1879, Queen Victoria presented gallantry medals to five men for service in the Zulu War. They were Trooper Richard Brown DCM, Frontier Light Horse (far left); Private William Roy DCM, 1st/24th Regiment (second left); Private John Power DCM, 1st/24th Regiment (third left); Corporal William Allan, 2nd/24th Regiment, being presented with the Victoria Cross; and Lieutenant-Colonel William Knox Leet, 13th Light Infantry, waiting at the end of the line for his presentation of Victoria Cross.

Veteran VC holders of the South Wales Borderers pictured during a reunion in 1898, six of them having gained the award during the Zulu War. Standing from left to right are Robert Jones, Harry Hook and William Jones. Seated from left to right are David Bell (Andaman Islands in 1867), Edward Browne, Fred Hitch and John Fielding.

a warrant officer. He was discharged in London on 28 November 1871, having received three good conduct badges, and he was awarded the Long Service Good Conduct Medal. Remarks on his discharge papers state 'his conduct has been very good'.

By 1877 he was in South Africa serving as a senior officer. On 13 December 1877, he was appointed to British forces for the Ninth Cape Frontier War, for which he was mentioned in despatches: 'Mr Dalton, acting assistant commissary, has been most energetic. The sole officer at Ibeka in that department, under great difficulties he increased the supplies, and provided three columns in their advances, and the stations in Galekaland, with the utmost regularity'.

He and Louis Byrne rode through pouring rain on New Year's Day 1879 to join the British forces at Helpmekaar, and then they moved up to Rorke's Drift. James Dalton was highly praised for the part he played in the action at Rorke's Drift, and he is mentioned in several accounts by fellow defenders, praising his valour and initiative.

Private Hook stated: 'Mr Dalton came up and said if we left the Drift every man was certain to be killed. He had formerly been a sergeant-major in a line regiment and was one of the bravest men that ever lived'. Mr Dunne recorded: 'Dalton the lionhearted, as brave a soldier as ever lived, had joined us, and hearing the terrible news said, "Now, we must make a defence!" It was his suggestion which decided us to form a breastwork of bags of grain, boxes of biscuits, and everything that would help to stop a bullet or keep out a man'. Doctor Reynolds reported: 'My first move was to consult with Lieutenant Bromhead, and Commissary Dalton, Lieutenant Chard not having as yet joined us from the pontoon. We quickly decided that, with barricades well placed around our position, a stand could best be made where we were. At this period, Mr Dalton's energies were invaluable'. Lieutenant Chard reported:

> There was a short, but desperate, struggle during which Mr Dalton shot a Zulu who was in the act of stabbing a corporal [Roland Miller] of the Army Hospital Corps, the muzzle of whose rifle he had seized, and with Lieutenant Bromhead and many of the men behaved with great gallantry; Mr Dalton dropping a man each time he fired his rifle. While firing from behind the biscuit boxes, Mr Dalton, who had been using his rifle with deadly effect, and by his quickness and coolness had been the means of saving many men's lives, was shot through the body. I was standing near him at the time, and he handed me his rifle so coolly that I had no idea until afterwards that

> he had been wounded so severely. He waited quite quietly for me to take the cartridges he had left out of his pockets. We put him inside our mealie sack redoubt, building it up around him.

Reverend Smith stated:

> Mr Dalton, who is a tall man, was continually going along the barricades, fearlessly exposing himself and cheering the men, and using his own rifle most effectively. A Zulu ran up near the barricade. Mr Dalton called out 'Pot that fellow!' and himself aimed over the parapet at another, when his rifle dropped and he turned round, quite pale, and said that he had been shot. The doctor was by his side at once, and found that a bullet had passed quite through above the right shoulder. Unable any longer to use his rifle, he did not cease to direct the fire of the men who were near him.

Henry Harford recorded: 'Mr James Dalton, who in the absence of Lieutenant Chard, devised all the rapid arrangements for the defence, as well as working like a Trojan himself with the men at the barricades and did much gallant work during the night. I noticed that directly Mr Smith or Mr Dalton showed themselves they received an ovation from the men, which was unmistakable'. Private Hitch stated: 'Mr Dalton was very active up till he was wounded'. Corporal Lyons noted: 'Mr Dalton deserved any amount of praise'.

He was sent to recuperate at Pietermaritzburg for six months. The medical records of Surgeon Blair-Brown are interesting to note:

> James Dalton was hit in the right shoulder. The bullet entered about half-an-inch above the middle of the clavicle, and made its escape posteriorly at the lower border of the trapezious muscle. The course taken was curious, regularly running round the shoulder and down the back, escaping all the important structures. The wounds, like all those received at Rorke's Drift, were wide and open and sloughing when seen by me on 26 January. After the slough came away the usual tenax was applied. I had no antiseptic to use. I thought of quinine, which I knew was a wonderful preserver in animal tissue, and used a solution of that, experimenting in this case. It seemed to answer, as the wounds got well after being injected several times with it.

When the 2nd Battalion marched into Pietermaritzburg on 16 October 1879, it was recorded in the *Natal Witness*:

> The spectators in Church Street could not make out why one company of the noble 24th suddenly raised a deafening cheer when coming to the clubhouse. The fact was that B Company, the gallant defenders of Rorke's Drift, under Major Bromhead VC, had recognised amongst the spectators Assistant Commissary Dalton, one of the leaders on that night. May we ask why Mr Dalton has not yet received the Victoria Cross?

Evidence of the reason for this was stated in document WO32 7386, dated 18 October 1879, which states: 'I think we are giving the VC very freely I think, but probably Mr Dalton has as good a claim as the others who have got the Cross for Rorke's Drift defence. I don't think there is a case for Mr Dunne'.

Consequently, Walter Dunne was overlooked, but the award to Mr Dalton was announced in the *London Gazette* on 17 November 1879, and he received the medal from Major-General Hugh Clifford VC, during a parade of the troops at Fort Napier in Pietermaritzburg on 16 January 1880, 'amid surroundings well calculated to make it impressive to participators and spectators alike'. He also received the South Africa Medal with 1877-8-9 clasp. For his gallantry, Dalton had been awarded a permanent commission as sub-assistant commissary on 21 November 1879, back-dated to his temporary appointment in December 1877, and he became senior commissariat officer at Fort Napier. He was promoted to assistant-commissary from 13 December 1879. He sailed to England in February 1880.

Little is known about the last years of his life. The 1881 census states that he was living in lodgings at 17 Cottage Grove, Lambeth, London, giving his age as forty-six. A man named Robert Dalton is listed as being a visitor at the address. He eventually returned to South Africa, making his living as a gold prospector. He owned shares in the Little Bess Mine at Barberton during the Transvaal gold rush days of 1884-86. He decided to spend the Christmas of 1886 with his old friend, former Sergeant John Sherwood Williams, at the Grosvenor Hotel in Port Elizabeth, Cape Province. After spending the day of 7 January 1887 confined to his bed, he died suddenly in his room during the night. He was in his fifty-fourth year, and had remained unmarried. He was buried in the Russell Road Roman Catholic Cemetery in Port Elizabeth, and a stone memorial was erected 'by his old comrade Sergeant John Williams and friends of Natal'. The centenary was celebrated with a wreath-laying ceremony at his grave. The Royal Corps of Transport purchased his medals in 1986, and they are now with the Royal Logistic Corps Museum at Aldershot. When the new military installation was established near Abingdon in Oxfordshire in 1992 they were named Dalton Barracks after him.

The Corps of Wagoners, formed in 1794, had a short existence, and in 1799 the Royal Wagon Train was formed to perform transport duties. The Corps went through Wellington's campaigns in the Peninsula, was at Waterloo, and was disbanded in 1833. The Land Transport Corps was formed at the time of the Crimean War in 1855 and was re-named the Military Train in the following year. In 1869 the commissaries of the Commissariat and the officers of the Military Train were amalgamated into the Control Department, and in the following year the other ranks of the Military Train were re-designated as The Army Service Corps (ASC), officered by the Control Department. In 1877 the Control Department was divided into the Commissariat and Transport Department and the Ordnance Store Department, and in 1888 they were amalgamated to form the Army Service Corps.

The Corps has a distinguished history, having been represented in almost every campaign fought by the British army. The ASC received the prefix 'Royal' for service in the Great War, which in turn amalgamated into the Royal Corps of Transport in 1965. The Royal Logistic Corps was formed on 5 April 1993 by the amalgamation of five British army corps, including The Royal Corps of Transport and the Royal Army Ordnance Corps. The combined services have five battle honours and five holders of the Victoria Cross.

Corporal Frederick Schiess VC

Ferdinand Christian Schiess, usually known as Frederich, was born at Bergedorf, Canton Berne, Switzerland, on 7 April 1856, the son of Niclaus Schiess, who worked as a stone cutter, and his wife Anna (formerly Ruchti). His father was known locally as 'Bernese Schiess'. Their parents having died while they were young, Ferdinand, and his sister, Anna Marie, were brought - up at the Municipal Orphanage at Herisau in Canton Apenzell. 'Friederich', as he became known, left the orphanage at the age of fifteen. The Franco-Prussian War began in 1870, so he joined General Bourbaki's French Legions. In 1877 he boarded the *Adele* at Hamburg bound for South Africa, arriving at East London on 21 August 1877. He was a strong, stocky young man, and was able to find work as a general labourer.

He served with distinction as a volunteer in the Cape Frontier War, and when colonial forces were being mustered for the campaign against the Zulus, Colonel Anthony Durnford, of the Royal Engineers, appointed him a corporal in the 2nd Battalion, 3rd Regiment, Natal Native Contingent, under Commandant Robert Lonsdale.

Commandant George Hamilton-Browne, an Irish colonial adventurer of the 3rd Natal Native Contingent, which was Schiess's unit, stated:

> [They were] a motley crowd, a few of them old soldiers and ex-clerks, the majority of them runaway sailors, ex-navvies, and East London boatmen. They were an awfully tough crowd, but they looked a hard-fighting lot and though their language was strong, and they were evidently very rough, they looked very ready...

This unit was intended to be used as scouts for the advancing British army. On the outbreak of hostilities there had been no time to train the men in the use of firearms and, due to loyalty fears expressed by some Natal colonists, no guns were issued to the ordinary natives. Only the African officers and ten NCOs from each company received Enfield percussion rifles. All other ranks were required to carry their traditional weapons of spears and shields. They had no uniform and remained dressed in their traditional native attire. The only item which distinguished them from Zulu warriors was a red rag, known as a *pugree*, wrapped around their forehead. Lieutenant Chard reported:

> Corporal Schiess, Natal Native Contingent, who was a patient in the hospital with a wound in the foot, which caused him great pain, behaved with the greatest coolness and gallantry throughout the attack, and at this time [the retreat to the biscuit boxes] creeping out a short distance along the wall we had abandoned, and slowly raised himself, to get a shot at some of the enemy who had been particularly annoying, his hat was blown off by a shot from a Zulu on the other side of the wall. He immediately jumped up, bayoneted the Zulu, and shot a second, and bayoneted a third who came to their assistance, and then returned to his place.

Reverend Smith stated:

> One fellow fired at Corporal Schiess, of the Natal Native Contingent, the charge blowing his hat off. He instantly jumped upon the parapet and bayoneted the man, regained his place and shot

> another, and then, repeating his former exploit, climbed upon the sacks and bayoneted a third. A bullet struck him on the instep early in the fight, but he would not allow that his wound was sufficient reason for leaving his post, yet he has suffered most acutely from it since.

Private Hitch noted:

> There was a certain space of about nine yards where the barricade was uncompleted. It was, of course, the weakest link in the chain, and the Zulus were not long in discovering this fact. In this position eight of us, Bromhead, Nichols [Nicholson], Fagan, Cole, Dalton, Schiess, Williams and myself—made a stand, and it was here, I think, that the hardest work was done.

Henry Harford stated: 'Some of the men of the 24th told me that he fought like a tiger. At one time, when some Zulus actually managed to clutch hold of his bayonet, he got it out of their hands, and springing over the parapet bayoneted some six or seven straight away'.

Captain William Penn-Symons recorded: 'Corporal Schiess, they said, "fought like a tiger". He could not restrain himself, but more than once dashed over the barricade, bayoneted a Zulu, and got back in again'.

Surgeon Reynolds was a first-hand witness to the fighting at the compound in front of the hospital veranda when it was at its fiercest, and later stated: 'It would be difficult to pick out the heroes from our garrison, but Corporal Schiess, of the Natal Native Contingent, (a Swede by birth) came under my notice as the most deserving of praise and recommendation'.

Eventually, Major Chard was asked to provide a statement concerning Schiess's bravery, which he did in a letter dated 22 October 1879. The letter formed the basis of his Victoria Cross citation:

> I have the honour in accordance with instructions from the field marshal, commander-in-chief, to forward for your approval this my application for the decoration of the Victoria Cross on behalf of Corporal Schiess, late Natal Native Contingent, in recognition of his gallant conduct on 22-23 Jany last at Rorke's Drift.
>
> 'This man, who had been wounded in the attack on Sihayo's Kraal a few days before, was a patient at Rorke's Drift on 22 Jany 1879, and in spite of his wound (in the foot) he particularly attracted my notice by his activity and devoted gallantry throughout the

> defence. Amongst many acts of his I may mention one I myself witnessed—after we had retired to our inner line of defence. The Zulus occupied the wall of mealie bags we had abandoned. Corporal Schiess, without any order, crept out along this wall a few feet, to dislodge one in particular of the enemy who was shooting better than usual; on his raising himself to get a shot, the Zulu who was close to him on the other side of the wall, fired knocking off his hat. Cpl Schiess immediately jumped on the wall and bayoneted the Zulu, and in less time than I take to write it, shot a second and bayoneted a third, and then came back to the cover of the inner defence again.

Corporal Schiess became the first man serving with South African forces under British command to be awarded the Victoria Cross, when his VC citation, the last for the defence of Rorke's Drift, appeared in the *London Gazette* of 29 November 1879: 'For conspicuous gallantry in the defence of Rorke's Drift post on the night of 22 January 1879, when, in spite of his having been wounded in the foot a few days previously, greatly distinguished himself when the Garrison were repulsing, with the bayonet, a series of desperate assaults made by the Zulus, and displayed great activity and devoted gallantry throughout the defence'.

Frederich suffered most acutely from his wounded foot after the defence, but he served throughout the Zulu War, and he was with the British square at Ulundi on 4 July 1879, to witness the final defeat of the Zulu army. For his services in the campaign he also received the South Africa Medal with 1877-8-9 clasp. When the Natal Native Contingent was disbanded he joined Lonsdale's Horse on 24 January 1880. He received his Victoria Cross from Sir Garnet Wolseley at a special parade of the troops in garrison in Pietermaritzburg, on 3 February 1880.

When he left Lonsdale's Horse he went back to civilian life and gained employment in the telegraph office at Durban. However, by 1884 he was unemployed and had become destitute. He spent most of his time writing neat and legible letters, desperately trying to gain some kind of government work in Natal, the colony he had fought so bravely to defend. Towards the end of the year he was found in tragic circumstances on the streets of Cape Town suffering from the effects of exposure to the elements and malnutrition. The Royal Navy offered him a trip to England on the *Serapis*, the cost of his rations being paid for by a public fund. Sadly, his health deteriorated and he died on board ship off the coast of Angola, West Africa. He was only twenty-eight years old. The ship's log recorded: 'Sunday, 14 December 1884,

10.20 a.m. Departed this life Mr F. C. Schiess VC, aged twenty-eight. 5.10 p.m. Stopped. Committed to the deep the remains of the late Mr Schiess VC. 5.15 p.m. Proceeded. He was buried about 1,376 kilometres north-east of St Helena in the South Atlantic Ocean. (Latitude 13.00 south - Longitude 07.24 west)'. His Victoria Cross is believed to have been found on his person, and is now at the National Army Museum, and there is a bronze plaque dedicated to him at the Rorke's Drift Memorial Museum in Natal.

A strange note appears at the back of a page in Captain Penn-Symons' report held at the Brecon Museum, which states: 'I saw Corp. Schiess in Nov. 1891, in Allahabad, India. He had been working in a jeweller's shop, and was just going to Australia. Being afraid to lose his Victoria Cross, he has sent it on ahead by registered post to his destination'.

The 'personalia' column in the *Natal Witness* for 2 November 1899, states: 'Cpl Schiess, Natal Native Forces, was at Rorke's Drift in January 1879. P. G. Crow asks "Where is he now?"'

Two days later came this response: 'A correspondent writes that he remembers reading years ago both in the *Witness* and the *Advertiser* of Corporal Schiess (of Rorke's Drift fame) dying in India destitute.'

A far more detailed account was published forty-eight hours later:

> I see information is asked on the whereabouts of the late Corporal Schiess. Immediately after the Zulu War he joined the Telegraph Service as a linesman and was stationed at Durban. He left after being decorated with the VC. He went through the Basuto War later, and returned to Durban invalided and destitute. He was (if memory serves me correctly) sent to England in one of HM transports and died either at Netley or Haslar Hospital. The Hon. Mr Jameson was, I think the means of his being sent home. I have a good photo given me by Schiess. Should anyone care for a copy I will get it re-taken.

Chapter 5

The iNtombe River Massacre

The setbacks suffered by the central column and the right flank coastal column, under Colonel Charles Pearson, which was being besieged by Zulu forces at the fort of the Eshowe mission station, brought the campaign to a halt and reinforcements were requested from Britain. During this time the only free column was the most northerly, on the left of the invasion force, under Colonel Evelyn Wood VC.

The news of the disaster at iSandlwana was received by Colonel Wood from a mounted native on 24 January: '...just as we were driving before us the abaQulusi tribe, which we had surprised between the Zungwini range and the northern side of the Hlobane Mountain'. Wood was forced to retire to Fort Thinta and consider what had become an uncertain situation. For the time being his column was ordered to reconnoitre the area of the headwaters of the White Mfolosi River, near present-day Vryheid. He eventually decided to move his force to a stronger position, and by the end of the month he had established a redoubt and wagon laager on a narrow high ridge 'where water and firewood, which covered the southern slopes of that range of hills, were plentiful'. The area was known as Khambula Hill to the British, but locally it was called Ngaba ka Hawana (Hawana's Stronghold).

Colonel Wood had proved his prowess as a fighting man, having gained the Victoria Cross during the Indian Rebellion of 1857. He was said to have been remarkably accident-prone—he was attacked by a tiger, was once trampled by a giraffe, and accidently took an overdose of morphine—but he was a highly respected officer who knew how to get the best out of his men.

Colour-Sergeant Anthony Booth and a detachment of the 80th Regiment, under Major Charles Tucker, were sent to garrison Luneburg, where it arrived on 9 February. Two days later Booth reverted to sergeant. The garrison at Luneburg was supplied by wagons from Derby and the sergeant spent much of his time with these convoys. Twenty-four wagons left Derby early in March fully-loaded with crates containing supplies of food, various weapons and ammunition—and apparently a good supply of gin. Torrential rain had swollen the rivers and waterlogged the already muddy roads, making it difficult for the passage of heavy wagons. The tracks from Derby to Luneburg ran by Myer's Mission Station, which had been burned out by local natives on the day before the British invasion, and through the drift across the iNtombe River and into disputed territory close to the Tafelburg Mountains on the north side of the water, which contained caves that formed the stronghold of a renegade Zulu chief named Mbilini. He was known to be an aggressive warrior, but being an exiled Swazi prince he was also believed to be less resentful towards the British invasion force. The wagons became bogged down just north of the drift and Major Tucker became concerned for the safety of the convoy. He sent a detachment of the 80th Regiment to bring the wagons in, but this escort was recalled and it returned to Luneburg with all the men, having had to abandon the wagons and all the supplies.

On the morning of 7 March, Captain David Moriarty and a company of the 80th Regiment rode out of Luneburg, with Sergeant Booth acting as quartermaster in charge of the commissariat wagon and equipment, such as beams and barrels, for constructing a raft. They found the wagons scattered along the track north of the river, and they had already been plundered by Mbilini's natives. In dreadful conditions they managed to collect the wagons together at Myer's Drift. On 10 March, Lieutenant Lindopp and Sergeant Booth supervised the building of the raft, and by the evening of the following day they had managed to ferry two wagons back across the river to the south bank. Lieutenant Henry Harward then arrived from Luneburg, thus becoming the senior officer on the south side of the river in charge of thirty-four men.

That evening Sergeant Booth was preparing rations when some natives came into the camp to sell mealies (probably stolen from the wagons two days earlier) and one of the white conductors said that he recognised one as Mbilini. Sergeant Booth was suspicious of this, so he crossed the river to mount the guard for the night, and while he was there he reported what he had been told. Captain Moriarty dismissed the claim and is said to have questioned the sergeant's keenness and replied in a jocular way, 'you're as bad as your pals said of you. You would shoot your own brother!' With that the sergeant returned to his wagon. A total of seventy-one men remained on the north bank, and the wagons were situated in a 'V' shape, with the apex facing away from the embankment. There were gaps between the wagons and Major Tucker warned Moriarty that the defences were not secure. However, no action was taken and the camp settled down for the night.

At 04.30 hours the sound of a rifle shot was heard from the north and Harward asked Sergeant Booth to warn the men on the other side of the river. He instructed a sentry to inform Moriarty of the situation, to which Moriarty sent back orders that the men on the south bank were to dress and remain in their tents. Booth returned to his wagon, put on his ammunition belt and checked his rifle for use. He was feeling too uneasy to go back to sleep so he decided to have a smoke. About thirty minutes later a second shot rang out, followed by anxious shouts from the sentries, and looking out from the wagon Sergeant Booth was alarmed to see the camp alive with Zulu warriors moving in on the tents across the river. They showed no mercy as they attacked the soldiers as they were lying in their beds or cut them down as they stumbled from their tents. As the dreadful slaughter continued a few half-naked unarmed men staggered towards the river in an attempt to get away from the wrath of the frenzied warriors.

Captain Moriarty was among the first to come out of his tent, shouting: 'Guards, turn out!' He soon found himself surrounded by several warriors. He shot three of his assailants, and took up an *assegai* from one of the Zulus he had shot with which to defend himself. He stabbed and thrust the *assegai* with such ferocious bravery that the warriors backed-off and kept their distance. However, a spear came flying through the air and hit him in the chest, and after he was hit by a bullet he fell to the ground and is said to have shouted: 'I'm done. Fire away boys. Death or glory!'

The soldiers on the south bank had retained their arms and when the Zulus began to shoot at them they were able to return fire. Sergeant Booth had chosen the commissariat wagon as a rallying point after the first alarm, so he and a few men scrambled underneath it, using animal carcasses for protection. As they continued to fire, Lieutenant Harward called out to them, 'Fire away lads, I shall be ready in a minute'. He told them to fall back to an old burned-out mission building about four hundred paces to the rear. Then to their surprise he mounted and rode away in the direction of Luneburg and abandoned them to their fate.

Sergeant Booth ordered eight men to accompany him to the edge of the river where some men were in a most perilous situation. As they tried to swim across, warriors on the far bank took shots or threw spears at them each time their heads surfaced the water, so they were forced to hold their breath and try to stay below the surface as they struggled forward. As they reached the south embankment they tried desperately to scramble up the embankment under enemy fire in an exhausted state. They were shocked and distressed, and completely naked, so Booth told them to run on ahead, formed his men into a defensive square, and covered the retreat with volley fire. Zulus tried to outflank them at Myer's Mission Station, but the sergeant kept his composure and ordered his men to keep firing as they retired. Many Zulus came after them, but they managed to reach another building near Raby's Farm, from where Sergeant Booth, Corporal Burgess and five other private soldiers kept the warriors at a distance. One particularly strong volley is said to have frightened the Zulus to such an extent that they gave up the chase, and not wanting to be deprived of any plunder they returned to the river. Had it not been for Sergeant Booth's coolness and leadership not a man would have survived.

Lieutenant Harward had reached Luneburg by 06.30 and reported the incident to Major Tucker, who got together a relief force of 150 men and rushed to the scene. They reached Sergeant Booth and his men at the mission station, and as they prepared to carry on down to the river, Sergeant Booth expressed a desire to go with them, but Major Tucker decided that he had seen enough horror for one day and would not allow him to do so. They found the camp destroyed and seventy-nine men had been terribly cut up.

Sergeant Anthony Clarke Booth VC

Anthony Clarke Booth was born in what is now Hucknall Road at Carrington, near Nottingham, on 21 April 1846. The 1851 census states he was the son of William Booth (born at Basford in Nottingham on 27 July 1817 and died at Sherwood in Basford on 4 April 1881), a lace manufacturer, and his wife, Sarah (formerly Clarke—born in Nottingham in 1811 and died in Basford in October 1879). The family home was at number 3 Club Row, Bulwell Lane in Carrington, Basford, Nottingham. He had an older brother named Herbert Clarke, and three sisters named Mary, Sarah and Lucy, and Sarah's mother and brother (Elizabeth and Thomas) also lived at the address. The 1861 census records them as having moved to 167 of the same lane, and Emily had been added to the family.

Anthony worked as a tailor, but he had a cousin serving with the Royal Scots Greys, and listening to his stories prompted him to join the army. He attempted to enlist into the Royal Marine Light Infantry at Nottingham in 1864, but during his medical in Derby he was suspected of having a heart murmur and he was rejected. While on a trip to Sheffield on 28 October of the same year he tried again and was accepted for the 80th Regiment (Staffordshire Volunteers). He was five-feet-six-inches tall, being of exemplary character. 919 Private Booth joined his new regiment at Cork in Ireland on 10 November, where he remained for three months. Returning to England he served at Chatham and in Devon, being promoted to corporal on 1 July 1865. On 1 September he was confined in cells and was reduced to the rank of private.

The 80th Regiment (Staffordshire Volunteers) was raised by Field Marshal Lord Henry William Paget, the First Marquess of Anglesey, in response to the threat posed by the French Revolution on 9 December 1793. The unit was largely recruited from the Staffordshire Militia and comprised men living on the estates of Paget's father, the Earl of Uxbridge. It served in operations in Flanders in 1794, in Egypt in 1801, the Sikh Wars in the Punjab of 1845-46 and 1848-49, in Burma in 1852 and in the Indian Mutiny of 1857-58.

He married Lucy (born in Cork, Ireland in 1847, died at Brierley Hill in Staffordshire on 11 June 1912), the daughter of a shoemaker named Matthew O'Brien (or O'Brion), at St Stephen's Church in Stoke Damerel, Devonport, on 18 September 1866. During two years of home service, Herbert was born at Portland on 12 July 1867, and Anthony was born at Fleetwood on 15 September 1868. On returning to Ireland in 1869 he was promoted to corporal on 20 April, and re-engaged at Belfast on 5 September 1869, to complete twenty-one years. He was appointed sergeant on 1 January 1870. William was born in Belfast on 21 November 1870.

On 12 January 1872, he embarked on the troopship *Orantes* for overseas duty at the Straits Settlement in Malaya, arriving at Singapore on 17 March. He was appointed acting barrack sergeant on 27 November, attached to the commissariat department at the Hong Kong station, returning to Singapore on 15 February 1876. Florence was born on 17 August 1873, and Henry 'Harry' Charles was born on 3 October 1875, while he was serving at Hong Kong.

On 2 November 1875, the governor of Perak in Malaysia had been murdered, and Sergeant Booth was one of forty men sent to Perak to reinforce soldiers of the 80th Regiment who were already there dealing with an uprising (including Private Wassall) and his unit defended a stockade at Rassa. He was awarded the Indian General Service Medal with Perak clasp. He returned to the Hong Kong station for a short while.

Sergeant Booth sailed with the regimental headquarters bound for Mauritius, but when measles broke out among the children on board the ship they were diverted to the Cape, arriving at East London on 11 March 1877, where they were refused permission to land for a while because of the sickness. At least one of their children seems to have been affected by the sickness. A daughter named Lucy was born on 10 February 1877, but she died on 14 March 1879, while Sergeant Booth was on active duty at Luneburg.

The 80th Regiment reached Pretoria on 13 March 1878, where they were attached to the brigade being prepared by Colonel Hugh Rowlands VC for an expedition against Sekhukhune. The Pedi and the Boers had disputes over land boundaries along the Eastern Transvaal border and several confrontations had occurred. The brigade also consisted of the 1st Battalion, 13th Light Infantry, and 400 mounted volunteers. They moved to Fort Weber and were ready to assault Sekhukhune's mountain stronghold by 4 October. However, a drought ground the operation to a halt through lack of water and pasture for the transport animals. When sickness began to hit them it was decided to postpone the campaign until a more favourable time and they withdrew.

When hostilities with the Zulus became imminent he left his family at Pietermaritzburg and moved to Derby near the border with Zululand, where Colonel Rowlands was preparing a reserve column in readiness for the invasion, with orders to protect the settlements around Luneburg. Colonel Rowlands went to Pretoria to keep an eye on the Boers and his force came under the direct command of Colonel Wood.

At a parade of the troops on 13 March, he and his men were complimented on their bravery, and he was promoted to colour-sergeant and appointed acting pay sergeant. On the following day he wrote a letter to his family in which he enquired about the health of his daughter Lucy. He expressed some hopeful assurance that she may not have been as ill as was thought. Unfortunately, Lucy died on the very day he wrote the letter.

The 80th Regiment left Luneburg on 9 April to join Evelyn Wood's Flying Column, and Colour-Sergeant Booth was present during the Battle of Ulundi on 4 July. In October he took part in the short, decisive attack on Sekhukhune's stronghold, during which the chief was captured. Lord Wolseley ordered another special parade, during which Colour-Sergeant Booth was presented with a nickel-silver revolver, a knife and a gun belt with a pouch of ammunition by the drivers he had rescued at the iNtombe River. By the end of the year he had been re-united with his immediate family. His mother died on 3 December 1879, so he returned to England aboard the *Orantes* to be reunited with his family.

For his gallantry at the iNtombe River, Sergeant Booth was mentioned in despatches and he was recommended to receive the Distinguished Conduct Medal. Controversy concerning Harward's conduct followed, which delayed the award. However, on 23 February 1880 the *London Gazette* announced that Sergeant Booth had been awarded the Victoria Cross, and he was decorated by Queen Victoria at Windsor Castle on 26 June 1880. He also received the South Africa Medal with 1878-9 clasp.

When Lord Chelmsford was informed of the massacre at the iNtombe River he was furious. Lieutenant Harward was court-martialled in a trial that began on 20 February 1880 and lasted for a week. Harward was accused of abandoning his men in the face of an enemy and not having laagered the camp to form a suitable defence against enemy attack. He was acquitted, having put forward a defence, in which he pointed out that he only had two wagons and therefore could not laager them. He stated that he was the only man who had a horse and had he not ridden for help the probability was that the whole force would have been slaughtered, not just Moriarty's men on the north bank.

When General Garnet Wolseley heard of Harward's acquittal he refused to accept the findings, and not being one to mince his words he was as forthright in his views in the same way as he had been concerning the case of Lieutenants Melvill and Coghill, and several other officers who escaped from iSandlwana. He stated:

> Had I accepted the verdict it would have been a tacit acknowledgement that I concurred in what appears to be a monstrous theory, viz, that a regimental officer, who is the only officer present with a party of soldiers actually and seriously engaged with the enemy, can, under any pretext whatever, be justified in deserting them, and by so doing, leaving them to their fate. The more helpless a position in which an officer finds his men, the more it is his bounden

> duty to stay and share their fortune, whether for good or ill. It is because the British officer has always done so that he possesses the influence he does in the ranks of our army. The soldier has learnt to feel that, come what may, he can in the direst moment of danger look with implicit faith to his officer, knowing that he will never desert him under any possible circumstances. It is to this faith of the British soldier in his officers that we owe most of the gallant deeds recorded in our military annals, and it is because the verdict of this court martial strikes at the root of his faith, that I feel it necessary to mark officially my emphatic dissent from the theory upon which the verdict has been found.

The Duke of Cambridge approved of Wolseley's remarks and ordered them to be read to every regiment in Her Majesty's service. Consequently, Harward resigned his commission in May 1880, and with his career ruined he disappeared from the public eye.

Two letters Sergeant Booth wrote to his family are still in the possession of his family. One of them, written to his wife from Luneburg on 14 March 1879, states:

> My dear wife and children.
>
> You must please excuse me not answering your last letter that I received about eight days since. I know you will be thankful for the most miraculous escape I have had—and I know you and our children will be proud of your husband and father when you will see in papers and the account of the Battle of iNtombe River.
>
> We left Luneburg on the morning of 7 March to escort a convoy of wagons about some twenty-four in number. We arrived at the iNtombe River some six miles from Luneburg on the road to Derby about 11.00 a.m. The river was very high and we could not cross it only on a raft that me and Mr Lindopp and some of the men constructed, the rains coming down heavens which continued for four days successively. I was acting quartermaster-sergeant for the 103 men, Captain Moriarty, Lieutenant Johnson, Lieutenant Lindopp and Doctor Cobbin, also a lot of volunteers and [native] drivers. In all that we engaged in the battle 154 men and officers, and all told only about forty-one men and some natives arrived at Luneburg to tell the tale. Mr Lindopp had gone to Luneburg the night before the battle. Lieutenant Johnson and one man called Lieutenant Harward came out to relieve us. That would leave 152 men all told at the iNtombe River at about 4.30 a.m. on 12 March 1879.

I was awoke by hearing a shot fired in the direction of the mountains. I should have told you we were under Mbilini's cave—a notorious chieftain. Lieutenant Harward called for me and told me to alarm the camp on the other side of the river, for there was me and Lieutenant Harward and thirty-three men on one side of the river, and the remainder on the other side. I called out for the sentry on the other side to alarm the camp. He did not answer me, but a man named Tucker came to the river side, and I told him to tell Captain Moriarty that a shot had been fired and to alarm the camp. He sent word back that the men was to get dressed but to remain in their tents.

I was in the commissariat wagon taking charge of the goods. I went in the wagon again and bit my pipe and looked at my watch. It was a quarter to five. I put on my ammunition belt, and me and another man was smoking in the wagon when about five o'clock I heard another shot fired and someone shout 'Sergeant Johnson'. I looked out of the wagon, and I shall never forget the sight I saw. The day was just breaking, and there was about five thousand Zulus on the other side [of the river]. They were close to the tents, and shouted their war cry of *'Usuthu!'* They fired a volley into us on this side of the river, then they commenced *assegaing* the men as they lay in their tents.

I rallied my party by the wagon and poured heavy fire into them as fast as we could. Some of the men coming out from the other side of the river and coming across to us. Crawford was one of them. He was the only man out of his tent that got across alive. Captain Moriarty and Doctor Cobbin were murdered in their tents, and most of the men also.

I commanded the party on this side, as Lieutenant Harward saddled his horse and galloped away, leaving us to do the best we could. When I saw all our men across, about fifteen in number, and all as naked as they were born, I sent them on in front and we retired firing at them. There was hundreds of the kaffirs crossing the river to try to cut us off, but we made good our retreat to a mission station, and expected to be outflanked there, but we fought our way to within a mile of Luneburg. The distance we had to run and fight was nearly five miles, so you can guess how we were situated. We arrived at Luneburg about fifteen minutes past seven, losing nine on my side and forty-six on the other side was buried, and all the remainder were *assegaied* in the river. A party went out to bury them on the same day, but they have all been and took them up again (I mean the kaffirs, and skinned them). So we are ordered out again to go and bury them. We go directly. I am one of them.

I am acting pay-sergeant of the company now. There was a parade. And I and my small party was highly complimented on the bravery we exhibited in saving as many lives as we did, and bring them in with such little loss of life on my side. I am mentioned in despatches to the general and to Colonel Wood. There is also a letter sent to the editor of the *Natal Argus*. I will send you one when I get it.

Now, dear wife, I hope you and our children are all well. I hope Lucy is better and that she was not so far gone as you thought.

With fondest love to you and all the chicks. I remain trusting God to spare me from all evil, and grant me life to see you all again.

I remain your loving husband: A. Booth

PS: Remember me to all enquiring friends.

I received a letter from Florence Bennett, and another from Bill and Andrew, with some Christmas cards for all the children. I received them the day before I left for the iNtombe River. I could not find it when I returned. Sergeant Else got my colours—and he was tried—and reduced. The next day he was restored. I may get Frederick's colours? A. B.

A letter written by Mr Josiah Sussens, of the Transvaal Rifle Volunteers, concerning his escape from iNtombe, which was published in the *Transvaal Argus*, stated:

…I made for Meyer's Station as fast as I could, and overtook one soldier on the road who was shot dead just as I got to him. I overtook two others shortly after, who were also shot. Getting further on, I fell in with Sergeant Booth and about a dozen men, who were keeping up a retreating fire and fighting very pluckily. I rested for a few minutes with them, during which time I espied the Zulus coming round the hill to intercept us. I informed Sergeant Booth of this, and he kept up a steady fire upon them, and made the enemy retire back into the hills.

I cannot speak too highly of the conduct of Sergeant Booth on this occasion; he fought most pluckily, and lost four of his small band here. It was entirely owing to their doing so well that any of us managed to get through it all. The Zulus would have entirely surrounded us, and not a soul could have escaped. Seventeen loaders and drivers were killed altogether, amongst them being Whittington, Campbell and Goss. As I got in camp I met Major Tucker going out with his men to relief.

> Eight of us managed to get into Luneburg, and perhaps it would not be out of place if I were to state how I was received. Arriving in a state of nudity, with the exception of a soldier's overcoat got from a native on the road, I applied to the authorities for blankets to sleep under, but was refused. They said they had none. Eight of us only had two blankets between the lot. To add to our annoyance, two wounded Zulus were brought in (one was on my own cartel and were put in a nice tent and covered with blankets, whilst we had to take our chance as best we could underneath the wagons. Only a very few of us survivors had any clothes on when we arrived, and we managed to get along as best we could. A shirt from one soldier, trousers from a second, boots from a third, and so on. A sale of clothing took place afterwards, when we were allowed to buy a few things. And so we got on!

A History of the South Staffordshire Regiment, states:

> On 5 April 1879, a party of mounted men of the 80th Regiment, under Captain Prior and Lieutenant Ussher, intercepted a party of Zulus. Among them was Sihayo's son, who was killed, another being the celebrated chief, Mbilini, who was one of the party, and was shot by Captain Prior, and mortally wounded, but he managed to escape, dying on his way to his cave in the Hlobane Mountain, but the news of his death was not confirmed until 23rd by the general commanding the 4th Column. It was the Chief Mbilini who led the *impi* which cut up the company of the 80th at iNtombi Drift, and it was an act of retributive justice that an officer of the 80th Regiment should have killed him.

Anthony reverted to sergeant on 19 October 1881, and after the army establishment reforms he transferred to the South Staffordshire Regiment. Andrew was born in Dublin on 17 May 1881, and Albert Edward was born at Tralee in Kerry on 10 June 1883. He remained in Ireland until September 1883, being awarded the Long Service Good Conduct Medal on 1 July 1883, which gave him a gratuity of £5. At Lichfield on 1 October 1883, he gave notice of his desire to stay in military service and he was promoted to colour-sergeant on 15 March 1884. On 16 May 1888, he transferred to the 1st Volunteer Battalion, South Staffordshire Regiment at Brierley Hill, Dudley (now in the West Midlands), as colour-sergeant and sergeant instructor. He held a certificate of second class education. The 1891 census records that he was living at 19 Hall Street in the parish of Kingswinford, Brierley Hill, with his wife, Lucy, and four children, although he had seven surviving children, so it is presumed that his three eldest sons were serving abroad with the Staffordshires.

Colour-Sergeant Booth discharged from the army at Lichfield on 30 April 1898. He died of rheumatic fever and jaundice in his home at 19 William Street, Brierley Hill, on 8 December 1899, aged fifty-three. He was buried with military honours provided by his old regiment at St Michael's Roman Catholic Church in Brierley Hill. Anthony was serving as drill instructor with the Brierley Hill Volunteers, and three other sons were serving with the regiment in India at the time of his death. Eight of his grandchildren served in the Great War, and two of them were killed in action. His son, Andrew, lived until 1959, when he died at West Bromwich. An article in a local newspaper recorded 'the letters VC live on in his family for his grandson…has them as his initials'.

His medals and a personal revolver of his are displayed at the regimental museum in Lichfield, Staffordshire, and there is a memorial plaque at the regimental chapel in Lichfield.

In 1881, the 80th Regiment amalgamated with the 38th (1st Staffordshire) Regiment to form the South Staffordshire Regiment. It became the Staffordshire Regiment (Prince of Wales's) in 1957, and is now the 3rd Battalion of the Mercian Regiment.

Chapter 6

Hlobane Mountain

The main threat to Wood's operations in the region came from the notorious abaQulusi Zulus, about a thousand marauding warriors, whose stronghold was an almost impregnable natural fortress at a flat-topped feature called Hlobane Mountain, which rose 400 feet from the plain around it and was surrounded by a line of almost vertical, and therefore inaccessible, cliffs. The mountain was skirted to the east by the Zungwini Range, and the Ntendeka Plateau to the west, which was connected to the main complex by a steep ridge, and was where the Zulus were known to graze their cattle.

Colonel Redvers Buller, of the 60th Rifles, Wood's right-hand man, brought the Frontier Light Horse to join the column. Buller was fearless, and knew the importance of aggression in battle. He was a dynamic and tenacious commander, and his men were devoted to him. They did vital work in scouting and protecting supply columns, raiding Zulu *kraals* and rounding up livestock to supplement the commissariat. The iNtombe massacre caused even more unease in the area, so Colonel Buller continued to harass the Zulus, and even led a force into the Tafelburg Mountains to hunt down Mbilini, but the Zulu chief had retired to the stronghold at Hlobane, where most of the Zulus in the area were now concentrated.

Lord Chelmsford decided to take a force to relieve the British column which was besieged at Eshowe, so he asked Colonel Wood to create a diversion. Colonel Wood planned to attack Hlobane, and directed a two-pronged offensive of mounted troops against the stronghold on the stormy night of 27 March 1879. One section of 640 men, under Colonel Russell (of the 12th Lancers), who had led the mounted troops to the relief of Rorke's Drift on the morning after the defence, moved to the

Ntendeka Plateau to the western end of the complex with orders to gain the summit up a very steep pass. This force included Lieutenant Edward Browne, of the 24th Regiment, who commanded eighty men of the Mounted Infantry. Colonel Buller took the other section to ascend the eastern end of the mountain and drive the enemy into the path of Russell's force. Buller's force of 675 men was accompanied by Major William Knox Leet, of the 13th Light Infantry, who had transferred to the base camp at Khambula in February 1879, taking command of the 1st Battalion of Wood's Irregulars, a unit of locally-recruited natives. Major Leet wrenched his knee out of joint during a tug-of-war contest held in the camp, and because of his injury Colonel Wood suggested he should stay behind when the troops moved out. However, he decided that he would be able to cope with the injury as long as he remained mounted. Among the men of the Frontier Light Horse were Lieutenant Cecil D'Arcy and Sergeant Edmund O'Toole.

Colonel Buller's column moved to the eastern end of the mountain, and on reaching the pass they dismounted and made their way up towards the summit, which they reached before dawn, and remounted. Everything was going to plan as Buller led his troops across the plateau, engaging the Zulus and dispersing them, while rounding up cattle as he progressed. Major Leet had been sent on ahead with Major Edmund John Tremlett, of the Royal Artillery, to inspect the pass at the western end of the mountain. They met Lieutenant Browne and his mounted force scouting ahead of Russell's column, who informed them that the pass down to Ntendeka would be very hazardous for mounted troops to negotiate. Major Leet and his men returned to Buller to report what they had been told, and Major Leet added that he had also been informed that the safest way to get down the pass was to keep to the right hand side.

However, as they continued westward, some men, including Lieutenant D'Arcy, saw what they first thought was the dark shadow of a cloud moving towards them from the south-east. On realising that the sky was not cloudy, Colonel Buller looked through his field glasses and saw that it was a large Zulu *impi* moving towards Hlobane. Pointing towards them, Lieutenant D'Arcy exclaimed to his commander 'it's all up with us this time, colonel!'

The approach of such a large army of warriors encouraged the abaQulusi into a determined counter-offensive, forcing Buller to order a general withdrawal. He continued the journey westward across Hlobane with his men, and arrived at the top of the steep pass which led down to the Ntendeka. It was a hazardous descent for mounted troops, especially in a state of panic. He ordered Lieutenant Everitt, of the Frontier Light Horse, to form a rearguard, and when they came under heavy enemy fire, Trooper Hartley fell out of his saddle. Sergeant O'Toole kept his nerve and helped his comrade back onto his horse so he was able to get to the top of the pass. As the troops struggled down the hill in awful confusion, the enemy bombarded them with rocks and spears, before closing in on them in desperate hand-to-hand fighting. It was at this point that Colonel Buller showed great horsemanship and outstanding personal courage.

Lieutenant D'Arcy helped to keep the Zulus at bay until four of his men had been killed, and they had begun to fall back with warriors massing around them. Everitt's horse was stabbed, and he had fought to a state of exhaustion. Several warriors were about to move in for the kill when Colonel Buller rode up and pulled him away from the immediate danger, and sent him on his way down the pass. Returning to the fray, Buller covered the retreat of three horsemen, continuing to return on one perilous mission after another to try to rescue stranded men, saving the lives of Captain Arthur Blaine and Trooper Randall, of the Frontier Light Horse. At about this time, Corporal William Dommett Vinnicombe and Trooper Richard Brown, both of the Frontier Light Horse, shared their horses with other men at a perilous time when to be dismounted meant certain death. They were awarded the Distinguished Conduct Medal for their gallantry.

Lieutenant D'Arcy had made sure that all the troops had begun to descend the pass before he started to do so himself. A heavy boulder came bounding down the slope and severed his horse's leg as it smashed into it. He was forced to destroy the animal with his pistol on the spot, and he was removing the girdle and saddle when another horse knocked him down as it rushed by and nearly crushed him. He got to his feet, and on hearing anguished cries and fearful screams for mercy he saw frenzied Zulus getting in among the panic-stricken fugitives and stabbing at them with their spears. Realising the desperate situation, he jumped down to a lower level, and although he was burdened by cumbersome boots and heavy kit he struggled on as fast as he could. The Zulus came after him for about three hundred paces, and they were tracking him down and getting perilously close, when a trooper of his unit caught him a loose horse. He scrambled up onto its back and quickly rode on.

He had not gone far when he came upon another trooper of his unit who had sustained a serious leg wound and could not go any further on foot. Cecil dismounted and helped the man onto his horse, spurred it on, and continued himself on foot. He was beginning to get very tired and once again he was in great peril of being caught by warriors, when Colonel Buller rode up and told him to mount up behind him. The lieutenant tried, but he was too weary and he pleaded emotionally with Buller to leave him and save himself, but Buller told him not to be a fool. With warriors almost upon them he made one last desperate effort to climb onto the horse and on succeeding he was carried down to the Ntendeka Plateau. Lieutenant Blaine met them with tears in his eyes, because he thought Cecil had been killed. He eventually reached Khambula doubled up in pain behind Major Tremlett.

Unfortunately, only Major Leet and two other men took the advice on keeping to the right of the pass, they being Lieutenant Duncombe of Wood's Irregulars, who was mounted, and Lieutenant Metcalfe-Smith, who was on foot. On reaching the pass, Major Leet saw that the side of the hill was very steep, and congested with large boulders in all directions. In spite of this, he eased his horse over the crest of the hill and began to guide it down the perilous slope, slithering and recovering in a desperate effort to stay mounted. As he did so, large numbers of Zulus appeared on the crest of a hill, and on seeing them they opened fire and began to pursue them, shouting angrily. About halfway down they realised they had gone in the wrong direction and found themselves looking over a dangerous precipice. They had no choice but to go back almost into the path of the attacking warriors, and fortunately they managed to get back on the right track.

By this time the Zulus were getting perilously close, firing and throwing their *assegais*, and to his alarm his horse was shot and fell and he was forced to hobble on his injured knee as best he could. A horse which was carrying ammunition cantered near, so he grabbed hold of its tail and brought it to a standstill, cut the straps of the pack with his knife and scrambled onto its back. This horse was also shot from under him and he had to get a third mount, which had no bridle. Lieutenant Duncombe's horse became exhausted to a standstill, so he got off and started to run, turning now and then to fire at his pursuers, and he managed to kill three of them. Unfortunately, he was eventually caught and stabbed to death. Many men gave up all hope of escape and shot themselves.

Lieutenant Smith was completely exhausted and sat down contemplating taking his own life, when Major Leet rode up and told him to grab hold of his saddle. However, the officer was so done for and the ground so rocky that he could hardly keep up, and he shouted to the major that it was no use. He was at the point of being speared when Major Leet, having remained in extreme danger, dragged his comrade up behind him, and with this double burden he spurred his horse on under heavy enemy fire. They came in sight of Colonel Buller's column coming down the mountain to their left, and with renewed hope they struggled down to the bottom of the pass where the terrain was less rocky, and although a large enemy force came in sight moving up the valley below them to try to cut them off, in a last desperate effort the horse raced across Ntendeka, and brought them to the comparative safety of Colonel Buller's men.

Lieutenant Browne received a misinterpreted order which sent his mounted troops away from Hlobane to the west, thus escaping the terrible disaster which befell the British force. The men who got back to Khambula had to push their bodies to absolute exhaustion to get away and survive the debacle. Fifteen officers and seventy-nine men had lost their lives. Sergeant O'Toole was among the first to respond when Colonel Buller requested volunteers to return to hostile territory to brave the terrible weather and the danger of marauding Zulus to search the mountains for any sign of surviving stragglers. The place where this dreadful massacre took place came to be known as the 'Devil's Pass'.

Lieutenant Blaine left an account on 31 March 1879, which highlighted the confusion as the British scrambled desperately down the hill:

> It was just possible for men to go down with horse in single file; but the kaffirs were behind us in hundreds, and everyone was so anxious to get down that we got all jammed up. Then an awful confusion took place. The kaffirs got in amongst us and *assegaied* our fellows. We could not hit them even with our carbines, for we were too jammed up. The officers could not use their swords. A lot of us got down, and then we rallied our fellows and made a stand for a time. We retired fighting. The Zulus were the whole time within a hundred yards behind us, sometimes even closer. They did not fire much, but were evidently trying to *assegai*. We lost no end of horses, and men jumped up behind others. But, both Buller and myself were riding one for some time. D'Arcy's horse fell down the *krantz* and broke his leg, so he was dismounted, but we soon put him up behind us. The Hlobane retreat was a most awful affair. Never do I wish to see another day like it.

> We retired well, but I shall never forget the kaffirs getting in amongst us and *assegaing* our poor fellows. Some of the cries for mercy from the poor fellows brought tears to our eyes. We lost over a hundred officers and men. No men ever fought more pluckily than the Zulus, they are brave men indeed.

Trooper George Mossop, of the Frontier Light Horse, left an account which expressed the dreadful horror and hopelessness of the situation, in which he stated:

> Many glancing sights had I seen that day with the Zulus with some of our men, who had fallen into their hands—dead or alive. I do not know! It is not good to write about such sights; all I can say is that it was a horror! Perhaps the man at my side had seen that which induced him to act in the way he did. I knew him well, but will not mention his name.
>
> 'Do you think there is any chance of pushing through?' I asked him. I was obliged to shout to make myself heard. The din was terrific.
>
> 'Not a hope!' he replied, and placing the muzzle of his carbine in his mouth he pulled the trigger. A lot of his brains or other soft stuff splashed on my neck.
>
> It was the last straw! I gave one yell, let go of the bridle of my pony, and bounded down into the pass. My feet landed fairly on the smooth rump of a dead horse, slid from under me, coming to rest on my back upon a dead Zulu. On I scrambled, down over dead horse, men, and rocks, until I reached the jam of horsemen. Madly, blindly, recklessly, I fought—my only thought to get away from all these horrors.

Colonel Wood set out from the camp at Khambula to join Colonel Russell at the Ntendeka Plateau. At three o'clock on the following morning he changed direction and travelled eastward along the southern slopes of Hlobane to locate Colonel Buller's column. His personal staff went with him, including Lieutenant Henry Lysons, of the 90th Light Infantry, and Private Edmund Fowler, who was one of eight men of the 90th Light Infantry who formed an escort. They met Colonel Frederick Weatherley, commanding the Border Horse, and were proceeding up the mountain pass following Buller's tracks when they came under fire from Zulus hiding in caves above them. Colonel Wood's horse was hit and as it fell to the ground it rolled onto him and trapped him. Several men were killed, and the wounded lay in great peril from the enemy firing. The

Border Horse was ordered to dislodge the enemy, but there was a delay in their advance.

Captain Ronald Campbell, of the Coldstream Guards, became agitated and retorted at them, drew his sword and charged forward. Lieutenant Lysons asked for permission to go with him and he advanced with Private Fowler and two other men of the escort. They scaled a low wall and ran forward in a most determined manner along a track about seventy paces long and two paces wide, with a sheer rock face four metres high on one side. They scrambled between boulders and crawled over fallen rocks on the slope of a hill to get at the enemy warriors who were causing the casualties. Captain Campbell arrived at the cave first, where he was hit in the head by a slug fired at close range and he fell dead. Lysons and Fowler were just behind him, and leaping over his body they sprang forward firing into the cave. They each killed a Zulu, but their leader, Mbilini, was able to escape along a subterranean passageway. Lieutenant Lysons remained at the mouth of the cave to keep a look out for enemy snipers, while the three privates picked up Captain Campbell's body and carried it down the pass.

Lieutenant-Colonel Redvers Henry Buller VC

Redvers Henry Buller was born at Downes House in Crediton, near Exeter, on 7 December 1839. The Buller family had been prominent in Cornwall for over 200 years before coming into residence at Downes House in 1739. He was the second of seven sons in the family of eleven children to James Wentworth Buller MP (born at Downes House on 1 October 1798), and Charlotte Juliana Jane Howard Molyneaux (born at Westminster in London on 8 February 1809), the daughter of Lord Henry Howard, who was a niece of the 12th Duke of Norfolk. His father succeeded to Downes in 1827, and he was Liberal Member of Parliament for Exeter from 1830 to 1835, and for North Devon from 1857 until his death in 1865.

The 1851 census has him living at 11 Louisa Terrace at Littleham in Exmouth, where he was being educated. All the family were Harrovian by tradition, so Redvers attended that school, but following a difference of opinion with the authorities he was transferred to Eton, where he gained a reputation for his daring and sense of adventure, being particularly good at rowing and horsemanship. The headmaster described him as 'very solid and sturdy, with a will of his own'.

On 13 December 1855, he arrived at Exeter railway station and was met by his forty-four-year-old blood-stained mother who had suffered a haemorrhage. He attended to her in the waiting room for two days before she died in his arms. His oldest sister, Julia, died on 11 May 1856. A third traumatic event occurred when he was up a tree near Downes, lopping off branches and he cut his leg so severely that the doctor told him that he would die if he did not have the limb amputated. Redvers declared that he would rather die with two legs than live with one and refused to allow it. It was the correct decision, because the wound eventually healed, though he was less agile than he had been.

On 23 May 1858, he was commissioned as ensign in the 60th Rifles. He joined the 2nd Battalion at Winchester and sailed to India in 1860. They were posted for active service in China, where a force landed at Pehtang for what became known as the Opium War. He took part in the storming of the Taku Forts on 15 August 1860, after which the Allied force occupied Pekin. He was awarded the China Medal with Taku Forts and Pekin clasps, but he did not believe the war was justified and he was reluctant to wear the medal. He was sailing home on the *Simoon* when it ran into a hurricane and nearly sank.

The 60th Rifles became The King's Royal Rifle Corps in 1830, and no other British regiment of the line has more battle honours. The unit was raised in 1755 in North America as the 62nd Royal Americans, and became the 60th Rifles in 1757. It fought under General James Wolfe at Quebec in 1759; at Martinique in 1762; in all the battles of the Peninsula campaign; at Multan and Gujerat in the Sikh Wars; in South Africa, 1851-53; at the storming of the Taku Forts in 1860, during the Second China War; and units were fighting in Afghanistan and Zululand in 1879-80.

Redvers was promoted to lieutenant on 9 December 1862, and joined the 4th Battalion at Quebec in Canada, commanded by Colonel Robert Hawley, who Redvers said had taught him all he knew about being a soldier. In 1867 he became a look-out officer visiting frontier stations in Western Canada. During this time he met Lord Wolseley, and he returned to Quebec in the summer of 1869 a well-trained and experienced young man. He was promoted to captain on 28 May 1870. Later that year he joined Wolseley at Thunder Bay, where he was assembling a force to deal with a rebellion in the Red River Colony. Buller soon caught his commander's eye as he took part in hazardous white water boat journeys between Lake Superior and Fort Garry. When they reached the trouble spot the rebels had departed and Wolseley considered him 'an able friend, and valued comrade'.

He was at the Staff College in August 1873, when Wolseley requested his services for the Ashanti Expedition, and he joined the force as chief intelligence officer. He landed on 2 October 1873, and during the campaign Captain Buller was at the forefront of the troops trying to defeat the rebel forces before the March rains arrived. At Essaman on 14 October the force of an enemy bullet was stopped by a compass in his pocket. Ashanti forces were defeated at Amoaful on 31 January 1874, and after being slightly wounded at Ordashu, he took part in the capture of Kumasi on 5 February. He was appointed to the quartermaster-general's staff and became a prize agent. He was struck down with fever and returned home. For his service he received the Ashanti Medal. He was promoted to brevet-major on 31 March 1874, was appointed CB, and he became DAAG on 1 April 1874. His brother died on 13 October 1874 and he came into the residency at Downes House. He became Lord of the Manor at Cowick and Hayes Barton.

In January 1878 he became special service officer to Lord Chelmsford, commander-in-chief of the British forces in South Africa, where he arrived on 4 March. On 22 April he was placed in command of the Frontier Light Horse, and with Buller as their driving force they became a highly effective colonial unit. He took part in the Cape Frontier War, for which he was twice mentioned in despatches, and Chelmsford stated that the success of the campaign was due to Buller's 'dogged perseverance'.

Lieutenant D'Arcy stated that Buller 'behaved like a tiger drunk with blood'. It was said of both Buller and Wood that 'few understand savage warfare better'. He was present at Ulundi for the final defeat of the Zulus. Wood considered him 'my right-hand man. Careful of his men's lives. Reckless of his own. Untiring and unflinching in the performance of his duties. We owed much of our success to his brilliant leadership of the mounted men'.

For his conduct at Hlobane, the *London Gazette* of 11 June 1879 announced that he had been awarded the Victoria Cross. Wood stated that he 'had won it a dozen times'. He received the medal from Lord Wolseley at St Paul's Camp in Zululand on 16 July 1879, along with Major Chard and Doctor Reynolds. He had been in the saddle more than any other man, so much so that he eventually broke down from the effects of exposure and fatigue. As a result he was sent home on medical grounds.

He arrived home on 28 August, and he was welcomed with a banquet held in his honour at the Victoria Hall in Exeter. He and Colonel Wood were invited to Balmoral for an audience with Queen Victoria.

He was appointed ADC to the queen on 27 September, which carried the rank of colonel, and he was appointed CMG on 19 December. He was given a majority in the 60th Rifles on 13 March 1880, being appointed AA and QMG for Scotland and then Aldershot.

He was appointed chief-of-staff to General Wood, who was in South Africa again to deal with the Transvaal Boers, and Buller arrived there on 26 February 1881. However, the fighting was almost over, with the British suffering a humiliating defeat at Majuba Hill, and the conflict left a bad taste in the mouths of the British authorities for two decades.

On 10 August 1882, Redvers married Lady Jane Charlotte Howard, who was the widow of one of his cousins. She had four children from her previous marriage. Their daughter, Audrey Charlotte Georgina, was born in July 1883.

When General Gordon became besieged in Khartoum by Mahdi forces, General Buller joined Lord Wolseley as his chief-of-staff at Cairo on 16 August 1884, setting off on the Nile Expedition in October 1884, in an effort to try to relieve him. Following the battle of Abu Klea on 17 January 1885, he was sent forward to command the Desert Column with orders to capture the town of Metemmeh. However, the warning of the approach of a large Sudanese force caused him to fall back to the town of Korti, a manoeuvre he performed with great skill and averted a possible disaster. He was twice mentioned in despatches and received an additional clasp.

He returned to England in October 1885 and was appointed Knight Commander of the Bath (KCB), and on 1 November 1885 he became deputy adjutant-general at Horse Guards. He went to Ireland in a civilian capacity in August 1886 to restore order as special commissioner at County Kerry. He reorganised the constabulary with his usual vigour, being appointed under-secretary for Ireland in 1886. He was called to the Privy Council, but his sympathy with the Irish peasantry was not considered acceptable to some ministers. On 15 October 1887, he returned to military duties as quartermaster-general, where he applied his usual enthusiasm to his new post. Using the lessons he had learned while on active service, he restructured the supply and transport system in 1888, which resulted in a fully military Army Service Corps.

On 1 October 1890 he took over from Lord Wolseley as adjutant-general, an office he held until 30 September 1897. On 1 April 1891 he was promoted to lieutenant-general, receiving a special award for distinguished service on 10 March 1892, and he was appointed KGCB on 26 May 1894. He became honorary-colonel in the Devonshire Regiment, and colonel-commandant in his old regiment, which had become the King's Royal Rifle Corps. He desired to become the commander-in-chief of the British army, and he was in line for the post when there was a change of government and he was disappointed when the appointment went to Lord Wolseley instead. He was given command of the troops at Aldershot on 9 October 1898. On 29 March 1899, he and Evelyn Wood were among twenty-three veterans who attended the 20th Khambula anniversary dinner held in London.

General Buller's previous experience warranted his being appointed commander-in-chief in South Africa during the Boer War. He was aware that the theatre of war suited the Boers and he fully expected a difficult campaign. On 11 October 1899 the Boers invaded Natal with 23,000 commandos. Buller arrived at the end of the month with 70,000 troops to find that Ladysmith, Kimberley and Mafeking were under siege. He decided to split his troops, sending one column to Kimberley, while he led 18,000 men to Ladysmith. This decision was questioned, and his campaign became hindered by political and media interference.

His reputation had preceded him, and when the Boer commander, General Joubert, learned who was leading the British relief force, he urgently addressed his men: 'I have to tell you that we have now to face the bravest and finest general in the world, who is accompanied by an army of men who will go through fire and water for him. For those of you who fought in the previous struggle with the English I need not have to say that I speak of General Buller'.

On 15 December 1899 the British reached the railway station at Colenso, where a strong Boer force had entrenched on the far side of the river. Twelve British guns were deployed in positions in open ground, where they came under devastating fire. Buller requested a desire to get the guns away and in the desperate struggle his men suffered 1,200 casualties and received seven Victoria Crosses. Buller received a shrapnel wound, and stated later 'I do not believe any living man could have got those guns away'. With further reverses suffered by the other column at Magersfontein and Stormburg, in what became known as 'Black Week', an irate Ladysmith civilian was prompted to remark 'we are an army of lions led by donkeys'.

Buller admitted that his force was not strong enough to achieve his objective, and Field Marshal Lord Roberts was sent out with reinforcements. After a defeat on Spion Kop, the British eventually gained the initiative and relieved the besieged towns, finally entering the Boer capital of Pretoria on 5 June 1900. Buller led the Natal Field

Force in a guerrilla war against Boer commando units, and they entered the enemy strongpoint of Lydenburg on 7 September 1900. Lord Roberts thanked General Buller for his services, for which he received the Queen's Medal with six clasps and a commemorative sword. On his return to England, he was presented with a jewelled sword of honour, and he was made a freeman of Southampton, Exeter and Plymouth. He was a special guest of Queen Victoria at Windsor Castle on 17 November 1900, being appointed GCMG.

The 1st Army Corps was created on 1 October 1901, and General Buller was, controversially, given command. He was eventually forced to resign. The people of Exeter protested, and to show support they commissioned a statue to be placed in the town to honour his name. It was unveiled on 5 September 1905, and bears the inscription 'he saved Natal'. He remained on active service for another five years, but he spent the rest of his life as a retired country gentleman in Devon. Both he and his wife gave much of their time to civic duties and philanthropy. Georgina helped to nurse the wounded during the Boer War and the Great War, for which she was appointed DCBE and received the Royal Red Cross.

Sir Redvers Buller died at Downes House on 2 June 1908, aged sixty-eight. He was buried with military honours in the family grave at Crediton church. General Botha sent a tribute to his old adversary. Memorial services were held at Aldershot and on St Michael's Mount in Cornwall. Memorials were placed at Crediton church, at Exeter Cathedral and Winchester Cathedral, where Buller is depicted as a bronze recumbent figure bearing the inscription 'a great leader—beloved of his men'. Viscount Wolseley regarded him as 'the bravest man I have ever known'.

Major William Knox Leet VC

William Knox Leet was born at Dalkey, a seaside resort and a southern suburb of Dublin, on 3 November 1833. He was the son of the Reverend Edward Leet (born in Dublin in 1800, died on 8 June 1878), rector of St Patrick's Parish Church in Dalkey, who took the unusual step of changing his middle name to 'St Patrick'. His mother was Sarah (formerly Knox—born in 1797, died 14 February 1866 in Dublin). His grandfather, Ambrose Leet (1769-1850), was vice-president of the inland office of the Dublin post office and published the popular *A Directory of Noted Places in Ireland* in 1814. Ambrose's uncle was sheriff of Dublin, who is remembered in local circles for having a street fight with Arthur Guinness, the founder of the brewery. He had an older brother named Henry.

William entered the 13th (1st Somersetshire) Light Infantry as ensign on 4 July 1855, being posted to the 1st Battalion, and he was promoted to lieutenant on 1 February 1856. He served with distinction during the Indian Mutiny, both with his battalion under Lord Mark Kerr, and as staff officer with various columns of troops during the Central India and Trans-Gogra operations. He was orderly officer to Major John William Cox, of his regiment, being twice mentioned in his general orders. He was present at the engagements at Betwah Road in Amorah on 25 April 1858, after which Major Cox reported 'Lieutenant Leet was conspicuous for the steadiness and zeal with which he carried and explained my orders to the skirmishers on several occasions under heavy fire'. He took part in the fighting at Nuggar in Amorah on 29 April and 9 June 1858, and Major Cox again mentioned his service, 'Lt Leet acted as staff officer to my entire satisfaction'. He took part in the actions at Tirboot, Toolespore; and at Nepaul Terai in Bootwall on two occasions. He acted as aide-de-camp to the 13th Light Infantry, and for his service he received the Indian Mutiny Medal with Central India clasp.

The 13th (1st Somersetshire) Light Infantry was one of nine regiments raised by King James II when he expanded the size of his army in response to the Monmouth Rebellion. On 20 June 1685, the 7th Earl of Huntingdon was issued with a warrant allowing him to raise a regiment, and he became colonel of the Earl of Huntingdon's Regiment of Foot. The Earl of Peterborough converted it temporarily into a regiment of dragoons in 1706, during which time it saw much service at Gibraltar and fought at Dettingen. It fought at Culloden, with which action the unique practice of the sergeants of the regiment wearing their sashes over the left shoulder is traditionally associated, the officers having all become casualties. It changed its name to that of each new commander until 1751, when it was numbered 13th, to which the 1st Somersetshire was added in 1782, being converted to light infantry in 1822. It saw service in all the major conflicts the British army was involved in during the Victorian era. For distinguished service in Afghanistan in 1842 it was granted the mural crown superscribed 'Jellalabad'. It fought in the Crimean War and the Indian Mutiny, where it gained its first two Victoria Crosses.

On his return to England, William was appointed adjutant of his regiment on 2 August 1858, a post he retained until 20 June 1864. He was promoted to captain on 4 November 1864, and on 30 September

1871 he was appointed musket instructor to the 10th Depot Battalion at Hythe. On 1 July 1872 he became deputy assistant adjutant general and quartermaster at Cork, continuing in this appointment until 30 September 1877. He was a keen tennis player, the sport for which he won a cup at the All England Lawn Tennis Club at Wimbledon. He married Charlotte Elizabeth Anne, daughter of Thomas Sherlock, of Bandon, County Cork. They had sons named Bertie Fielding (born at Youghatt in Ireland on 29 April 1873) and Dudley Knox (born at Stoke Damerel in July 1881).

The 13th Light Infantry sailed for active service in South Africa in April 1877, and five months later Captain Leet arrived in the colony to join his battalion, being promoted to brevet-major on 1 October 1877, and to major on 1 May 1878. He took part in the aborted advance on Sekhukhune's stronghold in October 1878, before moving to Utrecht on 13 December 1878 to join Colonel Wood's column. When the advance into Zululand began, Major Leet was placed in charge of the depot at Balte Spruit. He took part in the subsequent operations with the Flying Column, and he was in the square at Ulundi.

When it was suggested that Major Leet's gallantry in rescuing Lieutenant Smith should be recognised it seems that Colonel Wood refused to forward the recommendation. However, Major Leet certainly felt badly done by and he promptly wrote a letter from Khambula, dated 6 April 1879, to an anonymous officer friend of his at the War Office:

> My dear colonel:
>
> Before this reaches you the news of our big fights here will have reached you, and the despatches and newspaper accounts will have furnished you with the particulars. Thank God I have yet escaped unhurt while so many good men have been killed. These Zulus are certainly terrible fellows—the finest specimens of humanity and the bravest men I have ever seen. Our work is still cut out for us and many a fine soldier will be lost before the war is over. I enclose copies of my reports. They will I feel sure interest you, and the general will probably like to look over them. I have I believe been fortunate enough to be mentioned in the official despatches. They all say here that I ought to get the VC for saving young Smith's life at the risk of my own, but Colonel Wood being a VC man himself it is said (I do not know with what foundation) does not care to increase the number more than he can help. It is also said that there is an objection to recommending field officers, but that seems absurd. I do not at all know myself whether I deserve it, but if I do it seems

very hard that I should not get it. The statement from young Smith was sent to Colonel Wood. Do you think I deserve it? If so, can you assist me in the matter? You have connections with the press, and in that way (of course without compromising me in any way) you might bring public opinion to bear. I think it likely that the 'specials' of the '*Times*' and '*Standard*' will report my case, and if so you could easily work it without compromising me. Remember I only ask you to do this if you think I thoroughly deserve it otherwise I would not have it at any price. I feel quite sure I can entirely depend on you in this matter to act judiciously. I would of course give my eyes for a VC if outsiders think I deserve it and it would be a grievous blow to me if I deserve and do not get it.

I am very sincerely yours,
W. Knox-Leet

The letter had the desired effect, and for his gallant conduct at Hlobane Mountain, Major Leet was awarded the Victoria Cross, which was announced in the *London Gazette* of 17 June 1879. Having been promoted to brevet lieutenant-colonel on 29 November 1879, on 9 December he was invited to Windsor Castle to be presented with the Victoria Cross from the sovereign. Of his action at Hlobane, Major Leet later stated:

I began the descent accompanied by Lieutenant Duncombe, 2nd Battalion, Wood's Irregulars, who was on horseback and Lieutenant Smith, Frontier Light Horse, who was on foot, his horse having been shot. We had only gone down a very short distance when large numbers of Zulus appeared on the crest of the hill, and seeing us at once opened fire and pursued us with loud shouts. The side of the hill was extremely steep, and very irregular, with large boulders in all directions, and when we had got down about halfway we found we had taken the wrong direction and were over a precipice. There was nothing for it but to turn back in the face of the pursuers and join the right direction again if possible. Fortunately we succeeded, but by this time the Zulus in large numbers were within a few yards of us, firing and throwing their *assegais*. Lieutenant Duncombe finding his horse done up got off, and as he ran along occasionally turned to fire. I saw him in this way shoot three men within fifteen yards of him. At this time Lieutenant Smith became completely exhausted and sat down, and it was apparent that if I left him he must be *assegaid* in another minute. I therefore made him get up and run along holding on to the pack saddle, but the ground was so rocky and he was so done up that he could not come on, and I therefore stopped and managed with great difficulty to get

> him up behind me, the pack saddle having no stirrups. My horse at this time was almost exhausted, and the ground even rougher and steeper than higher up, and the Zulus having *assegaid* poor Lieutenant Duncombe were all but on us. At the same time we saw large numbers of the enemy coming up the valley under us from the right and running hard with the intention of cutting us off from Colonel Buller's men, who were coming down the end of the mountain over to our left, and for whom we were making. The ground now became better, less rough, and my horse making a final effort brought us to within a couple of hundred yards of Colonel Buller's men, and to comparative safety.

Major Metcalfe-Smith presented him with a silver cup in gratitude for saving his life, and later wrote:

> I am most anxious to bring to notice, that, in the retreat from the Hlobane Mountain on 28th, Major Leet, of the 13th Light Infantry, who was quite a stranger to me, saved my life, with almost the certainty of losing his own life in doing so. We were going along the top of the mountain, pursued by the Zulus, when Major Leet said to Colonel Buller that the best way to get the men down was by the right side; and the colonel said it was, and called out so to the men. However, everyone but Major Leet, myself, and one other man, kept on to the front of the mountain; while we began to descend on the right. Major Leet and the other man were on horseback, but I was on foot, my horse having been shot. When we had got down a little way a great many Zulus rushed after us, and were catching us up very quickly. The side of the mountain was dreadfully steep and rugged, and there was no pathway at all. They were firing and throwing their *assegais* at us while they rushed upon us. The third man (Lieutenant Duncombe, of Wood's Irregulars) was killed about halfway down.
>
> While I was running by myself and trying to get away from the Zulus, who were rapidly catching me up, I turned round and shot one with my revolver. I was then quite exhausted and out of breath, and intended to sit down and give up all chance of saving my life, as the Zulus were within a few yards of me. But, Major Leet persisted in waiting for me, and called to me to catch hold of the pack-saddle he was riding, which I did. Major Leet then finding that I could not keep beside the horse, I was so done up and the hill so steep, insisted (though I told him it was no use) in stopping and dragging me up behind him on the horse, which was also greatly exhausted. By good luck he escaped from the bullets and *assegais* of

> the Zulus, and got near the colonel's men, coming down from the end of the mountain. Had it not been for Major Leet, nothing could have saved me, and I owe him the deepest gratitude, which I shall feet as long as I live.

In 1881, William was living with his wife and sons at the Raglan Barracks at St Aubyn in Stoke Damerel, Devonport. He was promoted to lieutenant-colonel on 1 July 1881, when the 13th became the Somerset Light Infantry, and he was appointed officer commanding the 1st Battalion on 1 May 1883. He became colonel of the 2nd Battalion on 29 November 1883, commanding the unit during an expedition to Mandalay in Burma. He received the Indian General Service Medal with Burma 1885-87 clasp. He retired from the army on 1 May 1887.

His wife died at Ashford in Kent in 1891, and the 1891 census records him living at a house called 'Springmore' at 291 Ailsa Road in All Saint's, Isleworth, Middlesex, with a housekeeper and a servant. Having been appointed Companion of the Bath (CB) and honorary major-general, his last will and testament was drawn up at a house called 'Sunnyside' (also in Ailsa Road), St Margaret's Parish, Twickenham, on 13 January 1896; he left a large sum of money to Henry Knox Leet, a retired Royal Navy captain. He died at Grove House in Great Chart, near Ashford in Kent, on 29 June 1898, aged sixty-five. At his own request he received a private funeral, as he was buried in the churchyard of St Mary the Virgin in Great Chart. He left his medals and mementos, including the silver cup, to his sons. The centenary of the Zulu War was commemorated by a special display in the Somerset and County Museum in Taunton, where his Victoria Cross and other decorations are held. His headstone was restored in 1992, and he is named on the Burma War Memorial in Taunton.

In 1881, the 13th Light Infantry became The Prince Albert's Light Infantry (Somersetshire Regiment). The title changed to The Somersetshire Light Infantry (Prince Albert's) in 1920, and in 1959 The Somersetshire Light Infantry merged with The Duke of Cornwall's Light Infantry to form The Somerset and Cornwall Light Infantry. In 1968 it amalgamated with the light infantry regiments of Yorkshire, Shropshire and Durham to form The Light Infantry, and in 2007 was merged with the regiments of Devon and Dorset, Gloucestershire, Berkshire and Wiltshire and the Royal Green Jackets to form The Rifles.

Lieutenant Henry Lysons VC

The Lysons family was prominent in Gloucestershire from the seventeenth century onwards, having connections with the parishes of Rodmarton and Cherington, and a family seat at Hempsted Court in Gloucester, which they had built in the late seventeenth century.

Henry Lysons was born at Morden, in the borough of Merton near Wimbledon, Surrey, on 13 July 1858. He was the twin of Arthur, who were the sons of General Sir Daniel Lysons GCB (born at Rodmarton in Gloucestershire in 1816), of the 1st Royal Dragoons, and his first wife, Harriet Sophia (formerly Bridges, born in 1822). Henry's grandfather was the Reverend Daniel Lysons (1762-1834), who had succeeded to the family estates at Rodmarton in 1804. His father is said to have been the first man to reach the shore in the Crimea in September 1854, and he brought the 1st Brigade of the Light Division out of the final action at Sebastopol, which was the failed assault on the Great Redan on 8 September 1855. He wrote a book about his experiences in the campaign. The twins were baptised at St Lawrence's Church in Morden on 29 August 1858.

Henry had an older brother named Daniel Charles William, born at Dover in September 1857, a brother named Charles was born at Morden on 8 April 1860, and Frederick Bridges was born at Epsom in Surrey in July 1861. A daughter named Harriet Josepha was born in Canada in 1862, but the family suffered a triple tragedy within a year and three months when young Arthur died at Morden on 11 February 1863, little Harriet died at Montreal in Canada on 20 May 1863, and Harriet Sophia died in Montreal on 15 May 1864.

Henry served with the 1st Staffordshire Militia, and entered the 90th Light Infantry (Perthshire Volunteers), becoming ensign on 11 May 1878. His brother, Daniel, had entered the 60th Rifles in 1877. He sailed for active service in South Africa as aide-de-camp to Colonel Wood, taking part in the Cape Frontier War. He arrived at Utrecht in September 1878, and took part in the invasion of Zululand with the 4th Column on 6 January 1879.

Lieutenant Lysons was later among the party of troops sent out to recover the body of the prince imperial on 1 June, and he was in the square at Ulundi to witness the final defeat of the Zulu army on 4 July.

For their gallant conduct at Hlobane, Lieutenant Lysons and Private Fowler were awarded the Victoria Cross, which was announced in the *London Gazette* for 7 April 1882; over three years after their deed. Henry was serving at Fort William in Bengal, India, at the time, and he received the medal from Colonel Craig, officer commanding at Cawnpore, on 18 August 1882. He had also received the South Africa Medal with 1877-8-9 clasp.

Henry was promoted to full lieutenant on 15 December 1879, and served as adjutant with the 90th Light Infantry from 21 June 1880 until 19 November 1882. He sailed for active service in north-east Africa, being employed under Lord Wolseley with the Expeditionary Force at Cairo from 26 February 1884 to 4 October 1885, during which time he joined the Nile Expedition for the failed attempt to relieve General Gordon at Khartoum. For his service he received the Egypt Medal with a clasp, and the Khedives Bronze Star. His brother, Charles, died while serving with the Royal Welsh Fusiliers at Kalha in Burma on 15 April 1886.

He subsequently served as aide-de-camp to General Dunne, officer commanding the 2nd Infantry Brigade at Aldershot, from 1 February 1886 to 31 March 1887, being promoted to captain on 23 June 1886. He was appointed garrison-adjutant at Dublin from 1 June 1887 to 31 January 1889. He was specially selected to attend the Staff College at Sandhurst, where he passed the final exam in 1890. He returned to Aldershot as aide-de-camp (extra) to the general officer commanding from 22 June 1891 to 8 October 1893. On 15 November 1895 he was appointed deputy-assistant adjutant-general of the Western Command on the staff of Lord Wolseley, a position he vacated on 14 November 1898. He had transferred as major in the Royal Fusiliers on 6 April 1898.

He met Vanda Louise de Bretton Treffrey while she was living with her grandmother at Wentworth House in John Street, Hampstead Heath, and they married at St Fimbarrus Church in Fowey, Cornwall, on 6 October 1897. Vanda had been born at St Austell in Cornwall in March 1874, and was therefore sixteen years younger than him. Her family home was in the village of Place, near Fowey, and she was the daughter of Charles Treffrey, who was a justice of the peace and high sheriff of Cornwall. They are said to have had a son named Henry Daniel, but there is no mention of him in any official documentation. Henry's father was a constable at the Tower of London when he died at 22 Warwick Square in Westminster, London, on 29 January 1898, leaving a large sum of money to Henry's step-mother.

On 29 March 1899 he was one of twenty-three veterans who attended the Khambula 20th anniversary banquet held in London, which was presided over by Evelyn Wood. On 12 December 1900, he was promoted to lieutenant-colonel, commanding the 1st Battalion, Bedfordshire Regiment, and he was appointed Companion of the Bath (CB) on 10 February 1904. He became colonel on 23 July 1904, being appointed assistant quartermaster-general of the eastern command headquarters at Naina Tal in Madras Province in India. He retired onto half-pay on 10 January 1906, and returned to England.

Henry Lysons died at Claessens House, 3 Mandeville Place, in Marylebone, London, on 24 July 1907, two weeks after his forty-ninth birthday. He was buried privately at St Peter's Churchyard in Rodmarton, where a basic headstone marks the plot. Vanda was living at Whitehall Old Cleave in Washford, Somerset, and died at 15 Henrietta Street in Cavendish Street, London, on 18 April 1924, and is buried with Henry.

The medals of Colonel Lysons are held at the Cameronians (Scottish Rifles) Regimental Museum in Hamilton.

The 90th Regiment of Foot was raised by Thomas Graham, later Lord Lynedoch, in 1794, and served in the Egyptian campaign of 1801. It distinguished itself in the Crimea, gaining its first two Victoria Crosses, and during the Indian Mutiny, particularly during the Second Relief of Lucknow in November 1857, and gained a further six Victoria Crosses for the campaign. The 90th Light Infantry became the Cameronians (Scottish Rifles) in 1881, and was sadly disbanded on 14 May 1968 to avoid amalgamation. The unit retains a regimental museum in Hamilton.

Private Edmund John Fowler VC

Edmund John Fowler was born at Crooke, Passage East, east of Waterford in Ireland in 1861, the son of John and Bridget Fowler. He left his job as a trade servant to enlist into the 90th Light Infantry (Perthshire Volunteers), at Waterford, on 19 March 1877, as 1317 Private Fowler, and he joined the regiment at Limerick. Private Fowler sailed for active service in South Africa, where he took part in the Cape Frontier War and the invasion of Zululand.

The announcement of the award of Victoria Cross to Private Fowler, which appeared in the *London Gazette* for 7 April 1882, states:

> During the assault on Hlobane Mountain, Sir Evelyn Wood ordered the dislodgement of certain Zulus (who were causing the troops much loss) from strong natural caves commanding the position in which some of the wounded were lying. Some delay occurred in the execution of the orders issued. Captain The Honourable Ronald

> Campbell, Coldstream Guards, followed by Lieutenant Lysons and Private Fowler, ran forward in a most determined manner and advanced over a mass of fallen boulders and between walls of rock which led to a cave in which the enemy were hidden. It being impossible for two men to walk abreast, the assailants were consequently obliged to keep their single file, and as Captain Campbell was leading he arrived first at the mouth of the cave from which the Zulus were firing, and there he met his death. Lieutenant Lysons and Private Fowler, who were following close behind him, immediately dashed at the cave from which led several subterranean passages, and firing into the chasm below, succeeded in forcing the occupants to vacate their stronghold. Lieutenant Lysons remained at the cave's mouth for some minutes after the attack, during which Captain Campbell's body was carried down the slopes.

Private Fowler took part in the Flying Column's advance on Ulundi, and in the battle which took place there on 4 July. For his service he received the South Africa Medal with 1877-8-9 clasp, and three years after his gallant deed, the *London Gazette* of 7 April 1882 announced that he and Lieutenant Lysons had been awarded the Victoria Cross. Having been promoted to corporal on 10 April 1882, he received the medal from Queen Victoria at Windsor Castle on 13 May 1882. Colonel Wood requested a Victoria Cross memorandum in respect of Captain Ronald Campbell, but nothing came of it and efforts since have also failed.

Under the heading 'One of the Bravest Deeds I Ever Saw,' Evelyn Wood wrote the following account in *Pearson's Magazine* for February 1896:

> It having been decided to invade Zululand, three main columns, right, centre and left, moved across the border; but the incident with which I am now concerned took place in the operations of the left or northern column, which was under my command. On 22 January 1879, the centre column was overwhelmed at a place called iSandlwana—the Little Hand—nearly every man, in all some 1,500, being destroyed.
>
> The news of the disaster, carried by a mounted native, reached us on 24 January, just as we were driving before us the Amaqulisi tribe, which we had surprised between the Zungi range and the northern side of the Hlobane Mountain. We pursued the enemy for a mile or two, and I then moved the column back over the Umvelosi River, and proceeded to one of the lower features of the Ngaba-ka-Hawane mountains, where water, and firewood which covered the

southern slopes of that range of hills, were plentiful. The infantry remained in this position, called Khambula, till the final advance on Ulundi, the mounted men, under Colonel Redvers Buller CB, being constantly employed in making raids, which were carried far into the enemy's country.

Ronald Campbell, second son of Lord Cawdor, born at Stackpool Court, Pembroke, in December 1848, was educated at Eton, and joined the Coldstream Guards in 1866. He was adjutant of the 1st Battalion from 1872 to 1878, when, having been nominated as a 'special service officer' for duty in South Africa, he reported himself to me, as the officer commanding the troops at Utrecht in the Transvaal, shortly before Christmas.

I gave Captain Campbell charge of the adjutant-general's duties, and, as he messed with me, I saw a great deal of him and became greatly attached to him. A tall, powerful, well-made man, with strikingly handsome features, he showed towards me, his commanding officer, the greatest consideration and devotion in small matters of everyday life, while on 28 March he manifested them in their highest aspects.

About twelve miles from the ridge on which Khambula camp was pitched, the elevated table-land comes to an end with a steep fall to the southward. Three miles further south, a hill named Hlobane stands up 1,200 feet above the adjoining country. It is about four miles in length and one and a half miles in breadth. It is absolutely precipitous on the northern side, and also on the upper part of its southern face, and can be climbed only with great difficulty at the eastern and western ends, the former end being the easier of approach.

Colonel Buller and I had often discussed the practicability of taking this stronghold of the abaQuilisi tribe. Early in the month of March he had been upon a ridge which lies 150 feet under the western crest of the mountain, from which he had carried off a great many of the enemy's cattle. It was impossible to tell the exact number of the fighting men on the mountains, but we estimated them at from 800 to 1,000.

About this time the commander-in-chief was preparing to advance to relieve Eshowe, and hearing that his force was to be strongly opposed, he suggested to me that I should make some movement to attract the attention of the Zulus from the southern side of Zululand. We believed it would be possible to take the Hlobane, and my only anxiety was lest while engaged thereon, the Zulus on it might be strongly reinforced from the southward. This indeed actually occurred.

Early on 27 March, Colonel Buller left Khambula with a force of 400 mounted men and thirty natives, and after marching some thirty miles, bivouacked at dusk about five miles south-east of the mountain, changing his position, however, twice during the night in order to guard against being surprised while dismounted.

I had no intention of taking part in the attack, but with an escort of eight men of the 90th Light Infantry and seven natives, one being Umtonga, a half-brother of Cetshwayo's, I left Khambula late in the afternoon, and bivouacked under the western end of the mountain. The party, besides the escort, consisted of Captain The Honourable Ronald Campbell, Mr Lloyd, political agent, who had shown marked courage in leading friendly natives in an expedition against Sekhukhune, and Lieutenant Lysons (90th Light Infantry) aide-de-camp.

Starting at 3.30 a.m. on the 28th, we rode under the southern face of the mountain, hoping to arrive in time to see Colonel Buller ascend its eastern point. We failed to overtake him, for he had left his bivouac, ten miles further to the eastward, at 3.30 a.m. and ascending a steep path, hardly passable for single men when mounted, he led his force up a gully at the break of day, under cover of the morning mist, surprising the Zulus, a few of whom only could fire before he, at the head of his men, gained the summit. When we came in sight of the eastern angle of the mountain, the rear of Buller's column was just gaining the summit, and at this time we met a party of Irregulars who had got off the track, and were marching westward.

Hearing the firing, I directed them to turn round and follow Colonel Buller, and, moving faster myself, passed onto the front with my escort, accompanied by half-a-dozen of the Irregulars, we soon came under a shower of bullets from the front and both flanks, poured in by men behind huge rocks. Turning towards the foe, we wandered still further from Colonel Buller's track, which we had in the first instance followed, but which we had lost on getting to a place where there was only bare rock, without even enough soil to take the imprint of horse' feet. We continued to advance towards the fire directed on us, and presently arrived at a part of the mountain where further progress on horseback was impossible.

Dismounting the men, we left the horses in the charge of two or three soldiers and the natives, and proceeded to climb the steep face of the mountain. I had retained my horse, endeavouring to make it follow me, while Captain Campbell, walking behind, drove it on. While thus engaged, Mr Lloyd, who was climbing alongside on my left, touched me with his elbow, saying: 'That man won't hit us in the face, anyhow,' and raising my eyes I saw about forty yards above us, a Zulu who was bearing down the sights of his gun, which was apparently directed it at the middle of my body. While Lloyd was handing out our revolvers the man fired. He fell, saying: 'I'm hit,' and to my enquiry, 'Badly?' he replied, 'Yes, I fear, very badly'.

Letting go my horse I lifted him from the ground, when Captain Campbell, a much stronger man, relieved me and carried him down the hill to where we had left the horses, while I ascended to the rock whence the Zulu had fired. He had, however, disappeared, and almost immediately afterwards another Zulu fired from underneath some large boulders of granite, killing my horse stone dead, the animal's head striking me as he fell and knocking me down.

Captain Campbell now re-joined me, still some seventy feet from the summit, and agreeing that it was impossible to get much further up the precipitous rock to our front, we retraced our steps to the little ledge where we had left the horses.

Some thousands of years before the date of which I am writing, irregular masses of rock must have fallen from the precipitous sides of Hlobane and these lie piled in confusion about the base of the cliffs, forming caves, some of which are big enough to hold several men. As all the effective fire seemed to come from one of these caves, I directed the Irregulars who had now arrived to advance and storm it. The order was taken by Captain Campbell, who returned saying that the officer in command thought that it was impossible to force the passage through the rocks. This view the officer endeavoured to impress on me, but I realised that while the Zulus held the position it would be difficult, if not impossible, to remove some wounded who were lying near the ledge, and I repeated the order for an attempt to be made.

Captain Campbell had seen the entrance to the Zulu stronghold, and fully recognised the risk to the leading man who should try to enter it. He took the second order, and being again met by objections, shouted: 'Then I will do it myself,' and, jumping over a low wall, he ran up to the entrance to the cave, being followed by Lieutenant Lysons and three 90th Light Infantry men of my mounted escort. One of these, Bugler Walkinshaw, I called back, as I wanted him to attend to Mr Lloyd, who was now dying.

Captain Campbell moved along rock faces that were about eight feet or ten feet high, and moving over great boulders of rock. No one was seen in the passage, but the north side of the mountain above them was lined with Zulus with firearms. Their bullets, however, all passed over the little band, which was protected by the walls of the passage, and Captain Campbell, climbing over the rocks in the most determined manner, led it on for thirty yards to where the passage came to an end.

He and those following him all knew that though no Zulus were in sight, yet their guns were covering the party, and, as all officers of experience are aware, the unseen is the most appalling form of danger. Captain Campbell, determined to secure the safe removal of the wounded, never hesitated a moment, and, while peering down into a cave at his feet, he was shot in the head.

Lieutenant Lysons and Private Fowler passed his body, and firing into the cave killed one of its occupants, the others creeping away by a subterranean passage, to reappear higher up the mountain. The resistance, however, at this point terminated, and the Irregular Horse, regaining Buller's track, reached the top of the mountain without further casualty.

Ronald Campbell gave his life indeed, but attained the object, for he cleared the cave of some good Zulu marksmen, who, secure under cover in their apparently impregnable position, made advance or retreat or the removal of the wounded almost impossible.

How Colonel Redvers Buller cleared the summit of the mountain, seizing all the abaQulisi cattle, and eventually, on the main Zulu army coming into sight, had to retire down the near precipitous face of the mountain, belongs to another story. He covered the retreat, and after bringing three men out of a crowd of Zulus, returned again into the fight to keep back the oncoming wave of black men, and thus allow the footmen to escape. Buller, in holding the ridge, the only avenue of escape, indeed emulated 'Horatius who kept the bridge in the brave days of old'.

While the cave was being cleared by Captain Campbell's party, seeing that Mr Lloyd was dying, I remembered that I had a prayer book in the wallet of the saddle on my horse lying dead some sixty or seventy feet above me, and calling Bugler Walkinshaw, desired him to climb up the mountain, and at any risk to bring back the prayer book, which had been lent to me by Captain Campbell, it being the property of his wife. I told Walkinshaw that if he was not fired upon heavily he might also bring the saddle, which was underneath the horse as it lay dead with all four feet in the air. The bugler, although he was under heavy fire, succeeded in bringing away the saddle without being touched.

I now attempted to put the dead bodies of our friends on one of the ponies, but the Zulu bullets striking around on the rocks, made the animal so unsteady that it was impossible for me to arrange the bodies on the pack-saddle.

The men were taking cover, for though the Zulu fire was indifferent, it had already hit fourteen of the twenty-six horses left on the ledge. Bugler Walkinshaw, coming forward, asked me

> to hold the pony, when he soon adjusted the mournful loads, and then we moved down the hill to where we could obtain soil enough to bury the bodies, and I read the burial service from the prayer book over my two friends. If Ronald Campbell had lived he would have received the Victoria Cross, as Lieutenant Lysons and Private Fowler did; Bugler Walkinshaw received the Distinguished Service Medal.
>
> Fourteen months later, Captain Campbell's widow visited the spot with me in order to place a headstone over her late husband's grave. The memorial was carried up the mountain by some of the tribe engaged in the fight.

Edmund purchased his discharge from the army at Netley on 29 January 1880, but on 14 February 1882 he entered the 2nd Battalion, Royal Irish Regiment at Chatham for active service with the British Expeditionary Force in North-East Africa. He took part in the Sudan operation and with the Nile Expedition in its unsuccessful attempt to relieve General Gordon in Khartoum. He was promoted to sergeant on 24 December 1882. He was in Egypt until 18 February 1883, and for his service he received the Egypt Medal, 1882-89, with The Nile, 1884-85 clasp, and the Khedives Bronze Star (1882 Egypt).

He married Mary McGuire, of Stratham in Donegal, Ireland, in Hampshire in July 1883, soon afterwards being posted to Naini Tal in India on 11 September 1883, where he suffered a bout of enteric fever and began to develop serious problems with varicose veins. He was recommended for a change of climate and returned home on 2 November 1884.

During his home service which followed he suffered an unfortunate fall from grace when he was found guilty of embezzlement. He forfeited his good conduct pay and was in cells from 15 to 23 January 1887, and on the following day he was court-martialled at Devonport, being reduced to the ranks and ordered to forfeit his Victoria Cross and other medals. However, Queen Victoria refused to deprive him of his awards and everything was restored to him on 26 April, when it was also decided that his detention was punishment enough.

While he was stationed at Woodlands Barracks in Plymouth, Mary was born in 1888, and Catherine was born in 1890. William John was born at Enfield Lock in 1892, Margaret was born at Birr in Ireland in 1895, and Patrick was born at Hamilton in Scotland in 1897. William John entered the Royal Army Ordnance Corps, and both Catherine and Margaret went into teaching.

Having reached the rank of colour-sergeant on 11 May 1898, he was eventually medically discharged from army service on 13 February 1900, the cause being stated as 'severe leg ulcers and varicose veins,' which was considered to have been aggravated by service and climate.

Edmund settled at the garrison town of Colchester in Essex. The sixth and last child, Annie, was born in Colchester in 1900, where the 1901 census records him as a publican at the Live and Let Live public house situated at 19 Stanwell Street in St Giles, Colchester. The place where he and Annie were born is given as Scotland.

The 1911 census records the family as living at 11 Priory Street in Colchester, where he is described as a master greengrocer. It seems that he found it difficult to look after his large family just with the shop takings, because he had taken in a lodger in the name of an actress called Violet Ida Hunter, who worked at the Theatre Royal in Colchester, and he auctioned his medals at Sotheby's in 1906, retaining a set of miniature duplicates for wearing.

When his shop was damaged by fire in 1910 he went back into the pub business and became the landlord of the Cups Hotel Tap public house. He was a well-known personality in the town and he was on the local council. He attended the Victoria Cross dinner party as guest of King George V and Queen Alexandra at Buckingham Palace on 26 June 1920, and in the same year he was present during the memorial service at the Cenotaph in Whitehall.

Edmund died at Brerechurch Road in St Giles, Colchester, on 26 March 1926 aged sixty-five, and he was buried with military honours in Colchester Cemetery. Mary died at Colchester on 1 March 1942, and William John died at Gillingham in 1965.

His headstone was rededicated in April 2001, and a plaque was unveiled at his old home on 7 November 2008, in a service attended by some of his descendants. A replica Victoria Cross was on display at Colchester Castle from 7 November 2008 to February 2009 as a tribute to Sergeant Fowler during an exhibition to honour Colchester's two Victoria Cross recipients; the other being James Colvin, who gained the medal for valour on the North-West Frontier of India in 1897. Sergeant Fowler's medals can be seen at the regimental museum in Hamilton.

Bugler Alexander Walkinshaw was awarded the Distinguished Conduct Medal for his conduct in assisting Mr Lloyd at Hlobane Mountain. He remained in Evelyn Wood's employ for much of his life, and he is mentioned a number of times in Wood's memoirs. He was born in about 1855 in Falkirk, the oldest son of six in the family of eleven children to an engine driver named Alexander Walkinshaw (1836-1909), and his wife, Robina Jane Lee (formerly Fordyce, 1836-1916). The 1861 census has the family living at Perth Burgh in Falkirk.

He entered the 90th Light Infantry as 104 Bugler Walkinshaw, and became Sir Evelyn Wood's batman, who he respected and admired. He received the Distinguished Conduct Medal from Queen Victoria at Windsor Castle on 13 May 1882.

He met Empress Eugenie's maid, Euphemie Felcite Rottre (also spelt Rottreau – born in about 1860), in South Africa when they were visiting the death place of Empress Eugenie's son, The Prince Imperial, in 1880. The couple were living at The Scarletts in Colchester, when they married on 15 June 1887. She was a house maid aged thirty, and was the daughter of a clerk named Auguste Rottre. They came into the employ of Evelyn Wood, who had a home in Old Harlow, Essex. Alexander and Euphemie were so dedicated to their employer that they named their only son, 'Evelyn' George Alexander. Evelyn was born in about 1888, at Indre-et-Loire in France, which was where his mother was native; and several members of the family have also been named Evelyn down the years.

Alexander was a butler employed as part of Wood's domestic staff in 1891, where he, his wife and son, are shown as part of the Lieutenant-General's large household in the District Headquarters at Farnborough. The 1901 census records the couple living at 131-133 Cleveland Street in the parish of Holy Trinity, St Marylebone, London, and the 1911 census shows him living in the parish of Christ Church in St Marylebone, London, as a butler on an army pension. His wife is not mentioned. His family descendants have some images of him, and they say he had five medals. They were probably his Distinguished Conduct Medal, South Africa Medal with 1879 clasp, Long Service and Good Conduct Medal, Egypt Medal and the Khedives Bronze Star.

On the Sunday before his death, Sir Evelyn Wood is said to have stated to Alexander: 'I expect to die this afternoon, and I wish to thank you for having risked your life to save mine, not once or twice but many times, and I thank you with all my heart. Alexander attended the funeral at Aldershot as a bearer on 6 December 1919. Sir Evelyn also bequeathed a sum of money to him.

In February 1920, several newspapers reported that Alexander, then aged 65, was apparently planning to go to America, but he eventually settled in France. He died in 1927, in the commune of Neuvy-le-Roi, Indre-et-Loire department of central France.

Chapter 7

Khambula Hill

The British expected the newly-arrived Zulu army to attack the camp at Khambula on the following day. They had been badly mauled at Hlobane and morale was low, but this time they were ready and in compact formation behind fortifications up on a ridge, in an area covering about the size of seven football pitches, with grassland sloping away from it on most sides and a steep-sided ravine to the south. The main position was a wagon laager placed on the high ground, to be manned by several companies each of the 13th and 90th Light Infantry, with the wagons closely parked end-to-end in a rectangle and secured with chains, with additional fortifications created when heaps of stony soil was built up and an entrenchment was dug. About a hundred paces to the east of the wagons they had constructed a stone and earthwork redoubt built on a knoll, about the size of two tennis courts, where one company each of the 13th and 90th Light Infantry would be stationed, with two artillery guns placed in position. A palisade of wooden stakes connected the redoubt with two stone-walled cattle *kraals* on the southern lip of the ridge, one of which was to be manned by a company of the 13th under the command of Captain William Cox. The remaining field pieces of the 11th/7th Brigade, Royal Artillery situated in the open ground between these two main fortifications, and comprised of four 7-pounder field guns, two mule-borne guns positioned in the redoubt area, and several rocket troughs. The total British force was 1,200 imperial infantry and 800 irregular troops, grimly determined to erase the previous defeats, and exact revenge for their comrades.

A mist shrouded the area on the morning of 29 March, and an early patrol of Transvaal Rangers brought in a Zulu defector, who told them that the camp was to be attacked at midday. The patrol also reported that the Zulu army could be seen moving towards Khambula in five columns, but it seemed that they had not yet started to create their chest and horns formation. The commanding officers knew that the men could get to their battle stations very quickly, and as the Zulus were still five miles away Colonel Wood gave the order that they should have their dinner. When the time came the order rang out for the soldiers of the two regiments to assemble at their positions and prepare to face the enemy. Ammunition reserves were set up in convenient places along the rear of the defence lines. The battle began at about 1.30 p.m.

The Zulu leaders had been ordered to avoid a direct assault on British fortifications, so the right horn, consisting mainly of Cetshwayo's iNgobamakhosi Regiment of twenty-four year olds, circled round from the north and paused north-east of the British defences, yelling their war cry and banging their shields, it would seem to try to lure the British force to come out into the open. However, Colonel Wood could see an opportunity to prevent the Zulus from forming their deadly 'chest' and 'horns' formation, and he sent Colonel Buller out with about a hundred mounted men to provoke the warriors into making a premature attack before the other sections of the Zulu army to the south were in place. Buller's men rode towards the enemy, and when they got in range they dismounted and fired a volley into the mass of warriors to sting them into action. The move had the desired effect and warriors poured forward, with increasing speed. The British fell back, stopping occasionally to fire a volley at the enemy, but the sudden noise of rifle fire and yelling natives terrified the horses, and they became restless and difficult to mount, leaving a number of men stranded as the fast-moving Zulus raced forward throwing *assegais*, apparently jeering loudly at the British as they came at them: 'Don't run away, Johnnie, we want to speak to you. We're the boys from iSandlwana!'

It is difficult to imagine how fearful this situation must have been. Nevertheless, Lieutenant Browne rode back to rescue troopers of his squadron who had got into difficulties and would otherwise have fallen into the enemy's frightful grasp. On looking around he saw that Colonel Russell's horse had shied violently and he was struggling to mount it within a few short strides of the leading lines of enemy warriors. He galloped back under heavy fire, took hold of the horse's reins and steadied the beast so that the colonel could remount, but before Russell could get his foot in the stirrup or take hold of the reins the horse bolted again, carrying him right across and perilously close to the oncoming wave of iNgobamakhosi warriors. Lieutenant Browne galloped after him, and with Troop Sergeant-Major Learda, a baSotho of the Edendale Troop, Natal Native Horse, who had rallied a few men, he helped the officer to mount and snatched him from the jaws of certain death.

Trooper Elliot, of the Frontier Light Horse, became stranded because he could not get his horse to keep still for him to mount, and when Sergeant O'Toole saw his plight he rode back to offer assistance. He was praised for his selfless courage on this occasion. Private John Power, of the Mounted Infantry, was also noted for his bravery on this occasion, having already been recorded for gallantry during the 1878 Cape Frontier War, and he had been one of the few troops of the 1st/24th Regiment who had escaped from iSandlwana. His bravery at Ulundi was also brought to the attention of senior officers, and for his gallant conduct on three occasions he was awarded the Distinguished Conduct Medal. TSM Learda also received the Distinguished Conduct Medal.

As soon as the mounted men got back to the camp, troops of the two regiments of light infantry along the north face opened devastating rifle fire. Lieutenant Nicholson's 7-pounder Royal Artillery guns fired shrapnel and case at the fierce warriors attacking from the north region. Cetshwayo is reported to have said that 'it was only with the greatest difficulty that his [iNgobamakhosi] men could be forced to face the guns. One round of case killed ten herd-men of his regiment, in addition to wounding others'. The firing was so fierce and the guns became so hot that water had to be poured over them to allow the breaches to be served. The storm of fire destroyed the right horn as a threat to the camp, and the few hundred surviving warriors retreated. Lieutenant Nicholson was shot through the body and fell mortally wounded, and command of the two guns there passed to acting Sergeant Edward Quigley. Quigley's great energy and zeal in the unfamiliar role of section commander gained him a Distinguished Conduct Medal.

With this right section neutralised, Wood was free to deploy a significant number of the troops and guns from their elevated positions in the redoubt against the chest section, led by the uNkenke warriors, on the right of which was the uNdi corps, which had been defeated at Rorke's Drift. As the battle raged, the uNdi corps rushed the cattle *kraal* being defended by Captain Cox and his men. Wave upon wave of Zulus rushed forward, and Cox and his men fought hard to hold on to the position, meeting the warriors with the point of the bayonet, but Cox was shot through the leg, four of his men were killed and seven wounded. Realising that his men were suffering too many casualties,

Wood sent a runner to order Cox to evacuate the position. The order was given to fall back, and as the soldiers retreated, the uNkenke were flushed with success as they took over the cattle *kraal* and began to fire at the wagon laager.

Lieutenant Lysons and two companies of his regiment were defending the line of communication between the laager and the redoubt. As the cattle *kraal* was being evacuated, a soldier of the 13th Light Infantry was shot down and lay out in the open at the mercy of enemy fire, and the danger of warriors running at him to try to stab him to death. Lysons and three fellow officers ran out and rescued the stricken man just as a party of warriors was about to attack him and cut him to pieces. At about the same time, a Swazi trooper of Wood's Irregulars was wounded and fell down. As he lay in mortal danger from enemy fire, Private Albert Page, of the 13th Light Infantry, dashed out across the bullet-swept open ground, picked him up, and carried him back to comparative safety behind the wagons. For his bravery he was awarded the Distinguished Conduct Medal.

The 90th Light Infantry were stationed mainly at the northern section of the wagon laager. Private Fowler was lying in a ditch next to Colonel Wood when he was having trouble with his rifle. He said to his commanding officer in his Irish accent, 'would you kindly take a shot at that chief, sir? It's a quarter of an hour I'm shooting at him, and I can't seem to hit him at all'. Colonel Wood adjusted the sight lower and put the weapon to his shoulder, but the barrel was overheated and the rifle fired before he took aim. However, he hit the chief, and he killed two more Zulus who had moved up to take his place by aiming at the ground in front of them. After the battle the colonel and Private Fowler checked the distance and found it to be about two hundred paces.

The left horn, led by the uMbonambi Regiment, had disappeared from view as it moved into the valley below the southern ridge of the camp, where its impetus was slowed down by marshy ground. Colonel Wood ordered Major Robert Henry Hackett, of the 90th, to take two companies to the edge of the hill and fire down into them to impede them even further. This action had to be abandoned in the face of heavy Zulu rifle fire to their flank from the cattle laager and a hill to the west of the camp. Hackett received a bullet in the head which blinded him, and one of his subalterns was mortally injured. The left horn of the *impi* eventually climbed the south face of the hill, out of sight of the British troops, until they reached the crest, and as they stormed into sight they were met by a heavy fire from the 13th Light Infantry positioned behind the wagons at the south of the laager.

In addition to the murderous rifle fire, Wood told Major Tremlett to reposition his four 7-pounders so that they could be used to maximum effect against the left horn of the enemy. Major Leet was in command of three infantry companies positioned in the south section of the wagon laager, which was facing the Zulu 'chest' attack. He controlled the volley fire and directed the fire of the field guns, being mentioned in despatches for his conduct.

The left horn and the chest continued to attempt attacks on the camp at various points around the perimeter, but they had failed to implement the chest and horns formation effectively, and they were driven back by the heavy fire from over a thousand rifles and the guns of the Royal Artillery. A correspondent present at the battle wrote: 'But still on they came with the ferocity of tigers, never halting, never wavering, never flinching or hesitating for a moment. Say what people may about its being animal ferocity rather than manly bravery, but no soldier in the world could have been more daring than were the Zulus that day'.

At 5.30 p.m. under such devastating fire-power the Zulu spirit was broken, the onslaught faltered and warriors began to fall back. Two companies of soldiers attacked the warriors in the *kraal* and with jabbing bayonets and bullets they drove the Zulus out. Wood ordered companies of infantry to move forward to fire into the withdrawing Zulu regiments, and then sent Buller's mounted men in pursuit of the increasingly disordered Zulu retreat. With images of what he had witnessed at Hlobane still haunting his mind, Captain D'Arcy is reported to have shouted 'no quarter boys, and remember yesterday!' Lieutenant Browne and Sergeant O'Toole were also among these men. It was reported that the horsemen mercilessly cut down and killed hundreds of fleeing Zulus during a pursuit that continued over many miles. It was said that British foot patrols sought out warriors lying wounded around the camp and killed many of them. The reports caused great controversy in Britain, and letters of protest were sent to the War Office demanding an investigation. However, Colonel Wood denied all the accusations and stated that after the battle his men were too occupied with burying the 785 Zulu bodies found around the vicinity of the camp. Wood's force suffered eighty-three casualties, and it is believed that 3,000 Zulus were either killed in the battle or died of wounds. The fighting had lasted for four hours, the longest battle during the campaign.

Several men left reports of the ill-treatment of warriors after the battle, using words such as 'murdering' and 'slaughter', and the following details came in a letter from Private John Snook written exactly two months after the battle, noting that most of his times and figures are inaccurate, which was published in a West Country newspaper under the heading 'A Tiverton Soldier Under Fire at the Zulu Wars':

> I must tell you of our glorious victory at Kambula Hill on 29 March. The enemy comprised some 25,000 to 30,000 armed men advanced on our camp. We opened fire on them about 1 p.m. and kept up a tremendous fire with our four guns of artillery, and our infantry, composed of the 13th Light Infantry and the 90th Light Infantry, and some colonial volunteers, making our force up to about four-thousand all told. We kept up the fire until 6.20 p.m. when it was commencing to get dark, and the black fellows commenced to retire. We are the only column that has given them 'a proper lamb-basting' as yet. We lost on our side three three officers, one non-commissioned officer, and twenty-three privates killed; and wounded—four officers, two non-commissioned officers, one bugler, and twelve privates. I think we got pretty well considering the number against us, and that we were fighting against our own rifles and ammunition, which they captured from the poor 24th Regiment at Isandula. We took a great number of the rifles back again. It was a narrow escape with me. The captain of my company on my right and a man from Taunton on my left both got wounded in the leg. When the defeated Zulus commenced their retreat at about 5.30 p.m. they were pursued by Buller and his men.
>
> Then we let our mounted men out of the laager wagons, and I can tell you some murdering went on. They followed them up for about nine miles and killed about 700. I only wish it had been a cavalry regiment from home, in which case not one would have got away. As it was, some escaped into the night, it being too dark to follow them further.
>
> On 30 March, about eight miles from camp, we found about five hundred wounded, most of them mortally, and begging us for mercy's sake not to kill them; but they got no chance after what they had done to our comrades at Isandula.

An officer of Wood's Irregulars wrote:

> Towards the end of the pursuit, they were so tired and exhausted that they couldn't move out of a walk, some scarcely looked round and seemed to wish to die without seeing the shot fired. Some

> turned around and walked to meet their death without offering resistance; some threw themselves down on their faces and waited for their despatch by *assegai* or bullet, some got into antbear holes, reeds, or long grass and tried to evade detection, but very few succeeded in this. It was indeed a slaughter.

Colonel Wood referred to the battle as 'a close run thing,' but Khambula proved to be a turning point of the war. At the other end of the country a few days later, on 2 April 1879, Zulu warriors investing Colonel Pearson's column at Eshowe were broken and scattered at the Battle of Gingindlovu, and their total casualties at Hlobane, Khambula and Gingindlovu numbered nearly three thousand dead and perhaps as many wounded. Cetshwayo's warriors were losing heart, and the king himself stated that holding back the British was like 'warding off a falling tree'. The British command had learned much from the early setbacks, and they began to realise that the campaign was turning in their favour. Their determination to avenge the defeat at iSandlwana and other heavy losses turned into an iron resolve when Napoleon, the popular prince imperial of France, was killed in an ambush during a scouting mission on 1 June 1879.

A memorial stone commemorating the Zulu fallen erected at Khambula states: 'The names of the brave defenders of the old Zulu order, who died during this battle are lost to history. Some 1,500 warriors, representing the regiments above, and under the command of Ntshingwayo kaMahole perished here'. The regiments named on the monument are the uMcijo, uMbonambi, uNkenke, uThulwana, Indlondlo, Inluyyengwe, uDududu, iMbube, iSangqu and iNgobamakhosi.

Lieutenant Edward Stevenson Browne VC

Edward Stevenson Browne was born at Park Terrace, St Andrew the Great, Cambridge, on 23 December 1852. He was the son of Salway Browne (born at Hatfield Broad Oak in Essex on 28 October 1819), and his wife, Elizabeth (formerly Stevenson—born in Quebec, Canada, on 26 August 1826). His father was a student at Cambridge University when Edward was born, and served as an officer in the 26th Regiment (Durham Light Infantry). He had an older brother named William Barrington (born in Southampton in July 1849), who became a general with the Duke of Cornwall's Light Infantry, and two younger siblings named Henry Fitzwilliam (born at Southampton in April 1854), and

Louise Constance (born at Tockington in Gloucestershire in July 1856). His father having died at Oaklease, Almondbury in Gloucestershire on 24 July 1859, the 1871 census has them living at 13 Regent Street in East Teignmouth, Devon.

Edward was educated at the Royal Military Academy Sandhurst from 2 August 1869 to 31 December 1870, being commissioned as ensign in the 24th (2nd Warwickshire) Regiment of Foot on 23 September 1871. He was posted to the 1st Battalion and was promoted to lieutenant on 28 October 1871. On 6 January 1872, he sailed with his battalion from Liverpool to Malta, then to Gibraltar on the *Jumna* two months later. In 1874 he sailed to South Africa, taking part in the Griqualand West campaign of 1875.

On 21 April 1877 he was one of a detachment of the 24th Regiment which was formed into the 1st Squadron, Imperial Mounted Infantry. They were under the command of Lieutenant Frederick Carrington, and became known as 'Carrington's Horse'. Based at Utrecht in the Transvaal, the unit was assigned to escort Sir Theophilus Shepstone, the Natal secretary for native affairs, on his missions to meet native representatives to negotiate land boundary disputes. Lieutenant Browne dealt with correspondence, prepared despatches, and was assigned for regular trips to the Orange Free State to buy horses, working tirelessly to break them in and prepare them for use with the mounted troops. On 24 May 1877 he was with the unit when it was photographed at Pretoria during Queen Victoria's birthday parade. On 16 November 1877, Lieutenant Carrington went to the Cape, where he formed the Frontier Light Horse, and Lieutenant Browne was brought back from one of his expeditions to buy horses in Christiana to take over command. He led them in the difficult bush skirmishes against local native tribes in the Cape Frontier War of 1877-78. In September 1878, Lieutenant-Colonel John Russell, 12th Lancers, took over from him, and although the new commander's style of leadership was not popular with the unit, Lieutenant Browne stayed on as second-in-command, and took part in the aborted campaign against Chief Sekhukhune in October 1878.

The Mounted Infantry eventually joined the central column at Rorke's Drift, and when the British crossed the Buffalo River into Zululand on 11 January 1879, Lieutenant Browne was asked to form an escort to accompany Lord Chelmsford when he travelled north for a rendezvous with Colonel Wood. On the following day, Lieutenant Browne led the 1st Mounted Infantry when it took part in the first skirmish with the Zulus at Sihayo's Kraal. They arrived at iSandlwana on 20 January, and on the following morning Lieutenant Browne was asked to take a small mounted unit to patrol the hills to the east of the British camp. They saw several contingents of Zulus on distant hills, and when a party of warriors tried to outflank them and cut them off, they exchanged shots and two Zulus were hit. Lieutenant Browne reported what had happened, unaware that he had come into contact with a scouting party from the massive main Zulu *impi* which was hiding nearby.

On 22 January he left iSandlwana with Lord Chelmsford's force, later returning to the devastated camp, and spent an uneasy night among the carnage. He was with the mounted troops which relieved Rorke's Drift on the morning of 23 January. After a period of inactivity, the Mounted Infantry moved north, joining Colonel Wood's 4th Column in the base camp at Khambula Hill on 14 March. Lieutenant Browne took part in a number of scouting missions under the command of Colonel Buller.

During the advance on Ulundi, Lieutenant Browne commanded the 1st Squadron, Mounted Infantry, in a dangerous reconnaissance across the White Mfolozi River on 3 July 1879, and on the following day he was present in the British square which advanced on Ulundi for the final defeat of the Zulus. He took part in the second campaign against Sekhukhune in October 1879.

On 17 June 1879, the *London Gazette* announced that Lieutenant Browne had been awarded the Victoria Cross. The citation states that his act of valour was at Hlobane, but the date given is the 29th, which was the day of the Battle at Khambula and not Hlobane. The citation reads: 'For his gallant conduct, on 29 March 1879, when the Mounted Infantry were being driven in by the enemy at Inhlobana, in galloping back and twice assisting on his horse (under heavy fire and within a few yards of the enemy) one of the mounted men, who must otherwise have fallen into the enemy's hands'.

He received the Victoria Cross from Lord Wolseley while still on active service at Pine Tree Camp, Utrecht, on 22 August 1879. He also received the South Africa Medal with 1877-8-9 clasp, and he was mentioned in despatches for the Hlobane /Khambula operations. He did not leave an account of his service in South Africa.

On 6 November 1879, he married Amelia Wright in Edinburgh, and they had two sons and two daughters: Edward Dennis was born at Gosport in Hampshire on 28 August 1880; Ethel Winifred was born at Abergavenny in Monmouthshire on 13 November 1881; Maurice was born at Abergavenny on 13 December 1884; and Ella Moxton was born at Dublin on 9 February 1889. Maurice commanded the 2nd Battalion, Middlesex Regiment during the Great War. He achieved the rank of colonel in 1942, and was appointed CBE, MC, JP and DL. He retired in 1952, and died on 21 December 1961.

Promoted to captain on 19 May 1880, Edward was adjutant to the 3rd Battalion, Monmouth Rifle Volunteers from 19 September 1881 to 18 September 1886, during which time he was promoted to major on 2 November 1885. The 24th Regiment was re-designated the South Wales Borderers in 1881, and he sailed to India with the unit, becoming deputy assistant adjutant-general, musketry, at Bengal from 3 November 1891 to 7 July 1892. He was promoted to lieutenant-colonel on 8 April 1893. He returned to Britain, and on 8 April 1897 he was appointed colonel, officer commanding, 24th Regimental District at Brecon. In June 1897, he received Queen Victoria's Diamond Jubilee Medal, and on 29 March 1899, he attended a banquet held at the Prince's Restaurant in London to commemorate the twentieth anniversary of the Battle of Khambula. From 4 March 1900 to 6 September 1902, he was assistant adjutant-general, North Eastern District. On 7 September 1902, he became general officer commanding the 5th Army Corps at York, with the rank of temporary brigadier-general. On 3 December 1902, he became honorary colonel, 2nd Volunteer Battalion, West Yorkshire Regiment, a post he retained until his death. On 10 November 1903, he was appointed brigadier-general, 6th and 11th Brigades, 2nd Army Corps, Southern Command, at Portsmouth. On 24 June 1904, Brigadier-General Browne was appointed Companion of the Bath. He retired from a distinguished army career on 10 November 1906.

During his short retirement he took up residence at Gun House, Hampshire Terrace, Southsea, Portsmouth. He also lived at a house named La Rouvenaz, Commune de Chatelard in Montreux, Switzerland. He died at Montreux on 16 July 1907 aged fifty-four, and he was buried at Clavens Cemetery, Montreux. In 1909 a memorial was dedicated to Brigadier-General Browne at St John's Priory, Brecon, and there is a memorial at Portsmouth Garrison Church.

The Victoria Cross came into the care of his eldest son, Colonel Maurice Browne MC, who served with the Middlesex Regiment. Before his death in 1961 he gave the medal to his regiment, along with several more mementos. They are now in their rightful place with the South Wales Borderers Museum (The Royal Welsh) at Brecon. Brigadier-General Browne's set of miniature replica medals were owned by his other son, Major Edward Browne OBE, and he presented them to the South Wales Borderers in 1962.

John Power was eighteen-and-a-half years old when he enlisted into the 1st Battalion, 24th Regiment at Waterford in Ireland on 30 November 1874, and soon went with his battalion on active service in South Africa. He was a member of the Mounted Infantry, with which unit he was noted for gallant conduct on a number of occasions; under Lieutenant Browne VC and, later, Major Russell. In October 1878 he distinguished himself in a decisive action at Galetza Heights during the operations in West Griqualand. During the Zulu War he was named as one of the few Mounted Infantry survivors of iSandlwana, and he was noted for gallantry at the battles of Khambula and Ulundi.

Power's award of the Distinguished Conduct Medal was announced in the *London Gazette* in September 1879. He received the medal from Queen Victoria during the same ceremony at Windsor Castle on 9 December 1879, when Major Leet and Corporal Allan received their Victoria Crosses. He was photographed with his medal in 1880 wearing the home service helmet which has the old badge of the 24th that was used on the shakos and on the foreign-service helmet. He also has a marksman's badge on his left sleeve and a good conduct stripe on his right sleeve. Power was serving with his battalion at Kilkenny in Ireland when he died after falling from a horse. A tombstone was erected in the local churchyard by his officers and comrades.

Chapter 8

Operations at Ulundi

Reinforcements arrived from Britain ready for the re-invasion, including a new cavalry division formed from the 1st (King's) Dragoon Guards and the 17th Lancers, the famous 'death or glory boys' of the Charge of the Light Brigade fame, and Lord Chelmsford decided to make two main thrusts back into Zululand. The first would be made up the coast by a newly-formed 1st Division, and the second thrust would come from the north-west, following the line of the original central column, which would move down and eastward to pass the region north of iSandlwana. Lord Chelmsford accompanied this column, and General Wood took charge of a flying column, which was to work in unison with the Second Division.

When Lord Chelmsford's final advance towards Ulundi began, the Frontier Light Horse was brought back to full strength and Lieutenant D'Arcy was placed in command. The mounted troops continued to go out on patrols to maintain pressure on the Zulus, and a funny incident occurred while the troops were camped near Utrecht. Lieutenant D'Arcy's native servant, who was named Ketchwayo, was out foraging when he was approached by a British scouting party. The scouts were astonished when he openly told them his name and they immediately arrested him and took him back to camp in the belief that they had captured the Zulu king. One can imagine their disappointment when they learned who he really was, and the ridicule they must have suffered because of the misunderstanding.

At the end of June, British forces came in sight of the White Mfolozi River, with the Zulu capital at Ulundi beyond it, and they established a camp on the near bank of the river. Cetshwayo tried several times to open negotiations, and Lord Chelmsford ordered that the Zulus were to return all captured weapons, and lay down their arms as an act of submission. The demands were not met, and on 3 July 1879 the British commander broke off any further communication. He knew that his replacement, General Garnet Wolseley, had arrived in South Africa having been appointed to the rank of general and been given supreme power as military commander, with the intention of taking over command in time to bring the war to a close himself, and Chelmsford was determined not to have that glory taken away from him. Chelmsford disregarded Wolseley's messages of 'concentrate your force immediately and keep it concentrated,' and 'undertake no operations with detached bodies of troops. Acknowledge receipt of this message at once!' However, Chelmsford would not even recognise Wolseley's superior authority in the field. When he was negotiating with Cetshwayo he ignored Wolseley and dealt directly with London.

At noon on 3 July, Chelmsford asked Colonel Buller to cross the river with two columns of mounted troops to reconnoitre the area in readiness for the British advance across the Mahlabathini Plain planned for the next day. Among them were Captain William Beresford, of the 9th Queen's Royal Lancers, and Lieutenant Browne, Lieutenant D'Arcy and Sergeant O'Toole. As they crossed the plain they flushed out some Zulu snipers who had been spying on the columns from some bluffs, and gave chase. Colonel Buller became ill at ease when he noticed there was no real sense of urgency among the fleeing Zulus. He suspected a trap, but before he could announce this to his men, Captain Beresford, who had singled out a warrior who was struggling to keep up with the others, spurred his horse forward and gave chase. As the noble Irishman moved in and prepared to strike, the Zulu raised his shield above his head as a sign of surrender, but Captain Beresford did not know the significance of the action. With the momentum of his charge, the weapon smashed through the shield and into the man's body. Captain Beresford dismounted, picked up the warrior's *assegai* as a war trophy and galloped back to his unit calling out 'first spear!'

Suddenly, about three thousand warriors raised themselves up from hiding in the long grass on three sides of them and steadily advanced towards them. The troops retired in the face of this oncoming horde, but several horses became unnerved and threw off their riders. An officer of the 17th Lancers stated:

> They had pushed towards Ulundi, where swarms of Zulus were known to be assembled, mostly hiding in hollows behind rocks, and in the thick, high grass. All at once the Zulus opened fire, and

> there was nothing for the little band to do but to make a bolt to safety. Just as they were dashing off, a sergeant of the 24th [John Fitzmaurice] was thrown from his horse, and it looked as if the Zulus would get him, for they swarmed around only a few yards away. Lord William saw what had happened, and instantly he cut his way through the enemy.

Sergeant Fitzmaurice's horse had rolled on to him, trapping his legs. Under serious threat, Sergeant O'Toole tried to keep the Zulus back with rifle fire as Captain Beresford offered his hand and gestured to Fitzmaurice to mount up behind him. Dazed and hurt, the soldier shook his head and told his would-be rescuers to leave him to his fate.

Captain Beresford became firm: 'Come along, you f— b—. If you don't I'll punch your b— head for you!' Realising that, even though the Zulus were upon them and moving in for the kill, Captain Beresford had no intention of leaving without him, Fitzmaurice struggled even harder and managed to free himself, and holding out his hand he was dragged up into the saddle.

He was nearly pulled out of the saddle, for a wounded man is a heavy weight to handle, but Lord William never let him go, and while he bore him off Sergeant O'Toole shot down the nearest Zulus with his carbine. Stunned and almost senseless, the sergeant reeled and rolled in front of the captain, who was slashing away with his sword, and as he fired his carbine Sergeant O'Toole helped the officer to keep Fitzmaurice in the saddle. At last Sergeant O'Toole had to throw away his weapon to make his hands free and help to hold the sergeant in place on the horse. At the same time Captain D'Arcy was doing much the same thing as Captain Beresford.

With complete disregard for his own safety, D'Arcy rode back to assist Trooper Raubenheim. The enemy were coming on fast, but he kept his cool and dismounted to help his comrade onto his horse. Cecil then remounted himself, but the horse reared and threw them both off and Cecil injured his back as he hit the ground with a thud. In spite of this he managed to keep hold of the reins, calmed the animal down and tried again to get Raubenheim mounted. The effort caused agonising pains to shoot up his back which forced him to let the trooper fall to the ground again, where he lay unconscious. The Zulus were almost upon him when he at last got onto the horse's back and he had no choice but to gallop away and leave the trooper to his fate. His badly mutilated body was recovered the next day. Troop Sergeant-Major Simeon Kambula, of the Natal Native Horse, also behaved with great gallantry during the retreat, for which he was awarded the Distinguished Conduct Medal. The official *Narrative of Field Operations* stated:

> Sending a portion of his force by the ford of the wagon track, Buller with the main body crossed at another ford lower down, and moved against the southern end of the hill overlooking the river between these two fords. This hill, which had been occupied by the enemy's skirmishers, was promptly evacuated, and when Buller's party emerged from the bush bordering the left bank of the river, a number of Zulus were seen hastening over the open country in front. These were pursued to a distance of nearly three miles [five kilometres] from the Umfolozi, when Buller's party suddenly came under heavy fire from a force of about five thousand Zulus who were concealed in the valley of the 'Mbilane stream. Numbers of the enemy also appeared on both flanks of the reconnoitring party, pushing boldly forward with the object of encircling them and cutting off their retreat. In this attempt they were unsuccessful and Buller ultimately withdrew his party, having lost three men killed and four wounded.

At first light on 4 July 1879, the British force crossed the river, moved into the classic square formation of infantry and guns, with the cavalry in reserve within the square, and braced itself for an attack by 20,000 warriors. Because of his injured back, Lieutenant D'Arcy had to remain in the camp. The Zulus came on in a vast crescent and advanced at a jog to their last great battle. It was reported that not a single one of them got to within thirty paces of the British lines. A hail of lead from rifles and Gatling guns scythed down wave after wave of fearful yelling warriors. The British had become more and more ruthless as the campaign dragged on, and a war correspondent present in the square wrote 'their noble ardour could not endure in the face of the appliances of civilised warfare'.

When the fury of the Zulu attack faltered, the right face of the British infantry in the square moved aside and the 17th Lancers light cavalry unit charged out to chase the fleeing warriors and deliver the final blow, impaling warriors on their lances as they galloped along. The Zulus left 1,000 dead on the battlefield.

One Zulu section is said to have got to within about ten paces of one of the corners of the square, but none of the warriors got near enough to the British lines for any hand-to-hand combat, or the need for men to risk their lives to rescue comrades, so no further Victoria Crosses were gained. However, during the battle Gunner William Moorhead, of the

Royal Artillery, who had only arrived in South Africa on the day of the Battle of Khambula, was serving his gun inside the square when he was so severely wounded in the foot that he was rendered incapable of working the gun. However, he refused to go to the field hospital. He was determined not to remain idle and crawled to where the drums of the Gatling battery were being filled with cartridges and insisted on helping the sergeant to charge them. He did this for half-an-hour under fire. For this gallant service he received the Distinguished Conduct Medal. The DCM was also awarded to the previously mentioned Private John Power, of the 1st/24th Regiment, attached to the Mounted Infantry, and Colour-Sergeant James Phillips, of the 58th (Rutlandshire) Regiment, later the Northamptonshire Regiment. Also in the ranks of the 58th were Lieutenant Alan Richard Hill and Private James Osborne, who were later awarded the Victoria Cross for rescuing wounded comrades under fire from Boer commando units during the Transvaal War in 1881.

As the British force was approaching Cetshwayo's *kraal* at Ulundi, Colonel Buller called out: 'who's to be first in Ulundi?' Several officers responded and spurred their horses towards the gate, but Captain Beresford used his steeple-chasing skills to jump over the thorn fence which surrounded the compound to be first among the huts. From that day he was known as 'Ulundi Beresford'.

That night the flames of revenge lit up the sky as the British set fire to the Zulu capital. Rumours that treasure could be found in Cetshwayo's royal 'palace' turned out to be false. It was no more than a single-storey hut just like the others, and it is said that disappointed officers who searched the building found only useless items, among which were gin bottles, old newspapers and a box of boot brushes. The hut was burnt to the ground.

Fifty years earlier, Shaka, the great founder of the Zulu nation, had predicted his country would be 'trodden flat by the feet of a great white people'. His prophecy had come tragically true.

Lord Chelmsford had his victory. He resigned shortly afterwards, and returned home in near disgrace, leaving Wolseley to take charge of the mopping-up operations and try to impose a peace settlement. Chelmsford sent a report dated 6 July 1879 concerning the Battle of Ulundi, which stated:

> Cetywayo, not having complied with my demands by noon yesterday, 3 July, and having fired heavily on the troops at water, I

returned the 114 cattle he had sent in, and ordered a reconnaissance to be made by the mounted force under Colonel Buller. This was effectually made, and caused the Zulu army to advance and show itself. This morning a force under my command, consisting of the 2nd Division, under Major-General Newdigate, numbering 1,870 Europeans, 530 Natives and eight guns, and the flying column under Brigadier-General Wood, numbering 2,192 Europeans and 573 Natives, four guns, and two Gatlings, crossed the Umvolosi River at 6.15 a.m. and, marching in a hollow square, with the ammunition and entrenching tool carts and bearer company in its centre, reached an excellent position between Unodwengo and Ulundi about half-past eight. This had been observed by Colonel Buller the day before. Our fortified camp on the right bank of the Umvolosi was left with a garrison of about nine hundred Europeans, 250 Natives and one Gatling gun, under Colonel Bellairs.

Soon after half-past seven, the Zulu army was seen leaving its bivouacs and advancing on every side. The engagement was shortly after commenced by the mounted men. By nine o'clock the attack was fully developed. At half-past nine the enemy wavered. The 17th Lancers, followed by the remainder of the mounted men, attacked them, and a general rout ensued. The prisoners state that Cetywayo was personally commanding, and had made all the arrangements himself, and that he witnessed the fight from Lickazi Kraal, and that twelve regiments took part in it. If so, 20,000 men attacked us. It is impossible to estimate with any correctness the loss of the enemy, owing to the extent of the country over which they attacked and retreated, but it could not have been less, I consider, than 1,000 killed.

By noon Ulundi was in flames, and during the day all the military *kraals* of the Zulu army and in the valley of the Umvolosi were destroyed. At 2.00 p.m. the return march to the camp of the column commenced. The behaviour of the troops under my command was extremely satisfactory. Their steadiness under a complete belt of fire was remarkable. The dash and enterprise of the mounted branches were all that could be wished, and the fire of the artillery very good. A portion of the Zulu forces approached our fortified camp, and at one time threatened to attack it. The Native Contingent, forming a part of the garrison, were sent out after the action, and assisted in pursuit. As I have fully accomplished the object for which I advanced, I consider I shall now be best carrying out Sir Garnet Wolseley's instructions by moving at once to Eulongamite, and thence towards Kamaguasa. I shall send back a portion of this force with the empty wagons for supplies, which are now ready at Fort Marshall.

An officer of the 58th Regiment left an account in a journal of the Northamptonshire Regiment concerning the action during the Ulundi operations:

> We got our orders on the morning of the 3rd to fall in an hour before daybreak, and after being shown our places we all lay down to sleep. Officers were in front of their respective companies, which were posted all round the laager. Our rest was soon disturbed by the Zulu army singing their war song. The noise appeared to come from about two miles the other side of the Umvolosi River in the direction of the Unodwengo *kraal*. It had a wonderful effect, about 20,000 men all joining in, they kept it up for about an hour and then all was silent. It looked like business for the morrow.
>
> No bugle sounded the rouse, but we were all awake and had breakfast in the early morning. Luckily it was brilliant moonlight, and in about an hour the division was formed up and ready to start. It was broad daylight when the order to advance was made. The formation was a square, the English infantry forming the sides. The irregular cavalry went in front, the artillery, native troops and ammunition carts in the centre of the square, and the 17th Lancers brought up the rear. In this order the Umvolosi was crossed, and then had about a mile of very irregular and bushy ground to get over before getting onto the plain of Ulundi.
>
> Luckily we were not opposed here or our loss might have been very heavy. No sign was seen of the enemy. We went steadily on until we had passed on the left of the Unodwengo *kraal*, a large kaffir town with hundreds of huts: not a Zulu was there. The square was halted and the cavalry sent forward to reconnoitre, some of them being sent to burn Ukandampanivu *kraal* which was in our left rear. This was soon in flames. The Zulu were now seen coming down the sides of the hill to our left about three miles off. Our square was advanced a little, about one thousand yards beyond the Unodwengo *kraal* and a position was taken up on top of some gently rising ground. Now we had time to look about us and we began to think we should not be attacked after all.
>
> Our doubts were soon dispelled. Down the hillside on our left and front they began to move in beautiful formation. It seemed like endless companies in line all marching at regular intervals. Our place was in the rear of the square, so I can only describe what took place on our side which was in the direction of our camp. Soon the very ground we had marched over coming from the river was swarming with Zulu. As yet they were not within rifle range, but the cavalry began to retire on the square. Suddenly a heavy fire

began from where as yet we had seen no enemy, namely from the right of the Unodwengo *kraal*, and the irregular cavalry were seen coming over the brow of the hill and firing as they retired. In another minute the ground they had just left was covered with a swarm of Zulu who opened fire on us. The bullets began to whistle about us and one of our men fell back and was carried away on a stretcher.

The men were ordered not to fire until the cavalry had retired, which they did in good order, openings being made in the square for them to pass through. While this was being done, the Zulu opened terrific fire upon us from all sides. Our artillery now began on them and sent their shells bursting where they were thickest, but they still came on in swarms, shouting and yelling. We now sent volleys into them by sections at 600 yards range and mowed them down. This did not check their advance, however, and they made a rush for a hollow piece of ground about two hundred yards from our side of the square and were lost to sight.

They must have been collecting for their final rush, for in another minute I could see (being mounted) a great mass of them, all bending nearly double to avoid our fire and making a rush for our corner of the square. As soon as they appeared our men opened on them such a murderous fire that nothing could live before it; guns at the corner also blazing canister [shot] into them as fast as they could. In a few minutes we ceased fire and when the smoke cleared the Zulu were seen flying in every direction. We sent up such a cheer, and helmets went flying into the air, such was the delight of our men.

Now was the time for the cavalry, and in a minute they were out of the square and pursuing the Zulu, cutting them down, spearing and shooting them. Numbers of them turned at bay and fired, killing and wounding a good many horses and several officers and men. The Zulu were in full retreat and got onto the hillsides where the cavalry could not follow, so the guns kept on shelling them till they got out of sight. We now got the order to advance to Ulundi. Cetewayo's enormous *kraal* and two other military *kraals* about a mile beyond Ulundi were burnt and soon the sky was black with smoke. The men were now allowed to rest and have dinner, so we lay on the grass and watched the burning *kraals* and began to count the casualties.

The loss of the whole force was about thirteen killed and seventy wounded, wonderfully small considering the converging fire we were exposed to for more than an hour. The bullets hummed and whistled all about us and there were many narrow escapes. Luckily the Zulu as a rule cannot shoot and trust to close quarters and the *assegai*. If we had been in the Zulus' place and they in ours not a man of them would have got away. Our men were very steady and confident of beating off the attack. They knew, as we did that defeat was death. The strength of the Zulu is estimated at about twenty thousand, our strength was 5,000. It looks rather heavy odds to contend with, but nothing could touch us in square with our deadly musketry fire. After halting for about an hour, we began to retire towards our camp about sunset, tired but rejoicing at the result of the day's work.

Captain William Leslie de la Poer Beresford VC

While writing a biography of Lord William Beresford, which was published in 1917, Mrs Stuart Menzies described him as 'one of the most charming characters and greatest personalities of the age, possessing an extraordinarily generous nature'. Lord Cromer wrote to the author stating 'I hope you will allow me to bear testimony to his great charm and character, his characteristically national sense of humour and his staunch loyalty to both his country and his friends'. Mrs Menzies also wrote 'the Beresfords have for generations been keen sportsmen, high-spirited, unspoilt, straight-forward gentlemen'.

William Leslie de la Poer Beresford was a descendant of William the Conqueror and the Marquess of Waterford. He was born on 20 July 1847 in the village of Mullaghbrack, Markethill, County Armagh, Ireland, the third of five sons to John Henry de la Poer Beresford (1814-66), who was rector of Mullabrack for ten years until 1859, when he became the 4th Marquess of Waterford. His mother was Christiana (1820-1905), daughter of Colonel Charles Powell Leslie, of Glaslough, who was member of parliament for County Monaghan, Ireland. William later declared that he would 'rather meet an army of Zulus than his reverend father in a bad temper'.

George Beresford, 2nd Earl of Tyrone, was created 1st Marquess of Waterford in 1789. Lord William's uncle, Henry, was the notorious 3rd Marquess of Waterford, who was one of the main suspects behind the brutal attacks on people perpetrated by the mysterious character of bizarre appearance known as 'Spring-Heeled Jack,' who was said to leap to extraordinary heights to escape the scene of his crimes. The true identity of this sinister individual has never been established. The 3rd Marquess was well-known in horse racing circles. He entered two horses for the second running of the Grand National at Liverpool in 1840, riding The Sea to fourth place, and finished third on Columbine in

1842, after leading for much of the race. He was killed in 1859 when he was thrown from a horse and broke his neck, and Lord William's father took over as 4th Marquess. This incident was the first in a number of misadventures which prompted the family to believe they were the victims of a malevolent curse.

Lord William's oldest brother, John Henry, the 5th Marquess, shot himself in 1895, having been worn down by years of suffering after a crippling hunting accident. His son Henry, the 6th Marquess, after having narrowly escaped being mauled to death by a lion while big game hunting in Africa, drowned in a river on his estate in 1911, aged only thirty-six. The 7th Marquess was killed in a shooting accident in the gun room at Curraghmore, aged only thirty-three. Lord William's youngest brother, Delaval, became a rancher in North America and was killed in a railway accident in Texas in 1906, and a Mr C. de la Poer Beresford lost his life while attempting to stop a runaway horse in 1910.

Lord William was educated with his older brother, Charles William (1846-1919), at the Reverend George Renaud's Preparatory School at Bayford in Hertfordshire from 1856 to 1858, before going to Eton College. He was a boisterous lad, being described by a school friend, Edmond Warre, who later became the provost of Eton, as: 'I always liked him. His Eton record is chiefly connected with schoolboy sports, and skirmishes with masters at Windsor Fairs, and other places. He kept many bulldogs, and was of a turbulent disposition'. His Eton reputation was that of being good at outdoor sports, playing practical jokes—and fighting!

Behind the gasworks was the usual place where scores were settled, and boys fought blow-by-blow until one of them was on the ground unable to get up. Mercifully, it was bad sport to strike a boy when he was down. Nevertheless, these fights were brutal, and in 1925 Lord Shaftesbury's brother was carried home to die after fighting for two hours. His friend, Lord Langford, stated: 'I think Lord Bill often paid a visit there!'

It seems he was not particularly bright academically, preferring to be on the river or on the back of a horse. His writing was always kept brief, and it is remembered that he constantly wrote to a friend as Jhon, not John. When it was suggested he write variations of the words down on paper and the look of the word would tell him which was right, he replied: 'I always do write it down on a piece of paper and never doubt its being right'. This was usually accepted by all, who feared an invitation to settle things behind the gasworks! He made several unofficial trips to the Ascot races, and although he was severely punished on his return he developed a love of racing which was to stay with him for the rest of his life.

He left Eton in 1863 and went to Bonn to study languages, and during the Easter of 1866 he was one of a party of boys who embarked on a trip into the mountains of the Austrian Tyrol, under the guidance of their tutor, Doctor Perry, when they became lost and were dangerously exposed to the elements. They came upon an isolated hut which gave them some shelter as night came on, but their situation remained perilous. Dr Perry decided to brave the weather and went out into the darkness to try to get help from the nearest village. When he did not return after some time, young Beresford, realising that he had got into difficulty, went out several times to look for him, eventually rescuing him, while keeping everyone's spirits up until they were found. His dogged determination undoubtedly saved the lives of Doctor Perry and the whole of the party.

Charles Beresford entered the Royal Navy as a cadet on HMS *Britannia* in 1859. Having become an excellent horseman suited for cavalry, Lord William also chose a military career, and he was commissioned as a cornet in the 9th Lancers on 8 June 1867. He joined them at Island Bridge Barracks in Dublin, being promoted to lieutenant at Aldershot on 6 July 1870. He served at various home stations from 1867 until 1874, becoming a member of the 9th Lancers polo team, which won the inter-regimental polo tournament in India five out of the seven times it was played between 1877 and 1885.

The 9th Queen's Royal Lancers had been raised as Wynne's Dragoons for service to help put down the Jacobite Rebellion of 1715. They became 9th Dragoons in 1751. The queen from whom they take their title was Adelaide, consort of William IV. During the Indian Rebellion of 1857-58 the 9th Lancers won twelve Victoria Crosses, mainly for operations around Delhi, and it became known as 'The Delhi Spearmen'.

In 1869, Lord William became a patron of the turf and established a racehorse stud on Epsom Downs in Surrey, his mounts winning many valuable races in the Beresford colours of light-blue with black cap. In 1874 the famous 'Brothers Race' was run at the Curraghmore between himself and Lords Marcus and Charles. Lord William won the event, which caused a great deal of controversial interest at the time.

In 1874, Lieutenant Beresford embarked for India on his first tour of overseas duty, mainly in an administrative capacity. He was appointed aide-de-camp (extra) to Viceroy Northbrook on 7 December 1875, and remained as ADC to Lord Lytton when he became viceroy on 13 April 1876. He was promoted to captain on 27 December 1876. His duties in India were, according to a newspaper report '…organiser of the vice-regal tours; the promoter of race meetings, and a most reckless rider at them; a hunter of tigers; a driver of four-in-hands; an amateur theatrical manager; a player of polo; and the entrepreneur of innumerable picnics'. On 1 January 1877, Queen Victoria was proclaimed empress of India, and both to celebrate the occasion and to impress local Indian princes, Lord William helped Viceroy Lytton to stage a durbar 'of almost absurd magnificence'.

However, he had a desire for active service and in October 1877 he gained leave of absence to join General Keyes and his force of 2,000 British and Indian troops on an expedition to put down an uprising by the Jowaki Afridis, who controlled the strategically important Khyber Pass and were one of the more war-like of the various tribes on the wild, mountainous North-West Frontier along the border with Afghanistan and India.

The British Government was suspicious of Russia's expansionist visions and the Tsar's growing influence in Afghanistan, which they believed posed a threat to India—the jewel in the crown. In 1877, Lord Lytton made many proposals to Amir Sher Ali for closer relations with Afghanistan, but the amir refused to accept a British resident. In the following year a treaty was signed between the amir and the Russians which enraged Lord Lytton, and when a British mission was met with anti-British resistance at the Khyber Pass, the Second Afghan War was declared on 21 November 1878.

Captain Beresford heard about the exploits of the 9th Lancers against Afghan tribesmen, so with superb horsemanship he made a daring ride across dangerous hostile territory to join them with the Peshawar Field Force, under the command of General Sir Sam Browne VC, which was preparing to attack the Ali Musjid Citadel, a massive, heavily-defended fortification high up on the gorge overlooking the Khyber Pass. A second main column which crossed the frontier was the Kurram Field Force, under artillery bombardment followed by determined skirmishing assaults, but they had not succeeded in their objectives when darkness fell. The Afghan army abandoned the fort during the night and British forces occupied the citadel without opposition next day. The retreating Afghans were later rounded up and their leaders were taken prisoner. For his part in the action Captain Beresford was mentioned in despatches and received the Afghanistan Medal with Ali Musjid clasp.

Having been requested to return to his ADC duties in India, Lord William was engaged in equestrian activities at Calcutta when devastating news was received concerning the British army's serious losses at the Battle of iSandlwana in South Africa. The war against the Zulus was going badly for the British. Cavalry reinforcements were requested for active service at the Cape, and seeing another chance for military adventure, Captain Beresford applied for six months leave to go to South Africa independently of his regiment to take up an appointment as ADC to Colonel Redvers Buller, whose previous ADC, Captain Ronald Campbell (of the Coldstream Guards), had been killed in action during the disastrous engagement with the Zulus on Hlobane Mountain.

Captain Beresford arrived in Durban in April 1879, and after a punch-up with some army officers in a hotel he travelled to the British camp at Khambula, where the Flying Column was being assembled, and he spent most of his time at the side of Colonel Buller patrolling hostile territory to gather intelligence as the troops advanced on the Zulu capital at Ulundi.

Colonel Buller had a deep distrust of the press, and on one occasion he asked Captain Beresford to deliver a message to Charles Fripp, special artist with the *Daily Graphic*. Fripp made a disparaging remark about Buller for causing him inconvenience, to which Captain Beresford took offence and threatened to thrash Fripp for his insolence. The artist suggested they settle the matter that night and boldly arrived at Captain Beresford's tent to ask if he wished to carry out his threat. During the fierce fight which followed, Captain Beresford injured his arm, and though he wanted to carry on, Fripp suggested it would be more fair to finish the fight another day. They treated each other with mutual respect from then onwards. Colonel Buller said:

> My task has been materially lightened by Captain Lord William Beresford, 9th Lancers, my staff officer, who came from India for the Zulu War, and has been of immense assistance to me. Energetic and untiring, he is always at hand when wanted, while his marked gallantry in the field and his pleasant address secured the respect and ready obedience of men.

Captain Lord William Beresford was mentioned in despatches and received the South Africa medal with 1879 clasp. The process for the award of the Victoria Cross to him was completed in just two days. The secretary of state approved it on 22 August 1879, Queen Victoria received the recommendation and approved it on 23 August, it was announced in the *London Gazette* on the same day, and having returned to England, he was summoned to Osborne House on the Isle of Wight on 24 August for the investiture. While he was there he graciously expressed to Queen Victoria that he could not accept the award unless the two men who had shared the danger with him were similarly rewarded. The sovereign was much impressed by Lord Beresford's chivalry and awards to Captain D'Arcy and Sergeant O'Toole followed. The official citation for the award to Captain Beresford states:

> For his conspicuous courage and bravery on several occasions during the campaign, and especially for his conduct on 3 July 1879, at the close of the reconnaissance before Ulundi, in assisting to rescue Sergeant Fitzmaurice, 1st/24th Mounted Infantry, whose horse fell and rolled on him, as the troops retired before great numbers of the enemy. When lifted up behind him by Lord William Beresford, the man, half-stunned by the fall, could not hold on, and he would have been left had not Sergeant O'Toole, who was keeping back the advancing Zulus, given up his carbine and assisted to hold Sergeant Fitzmaurice on the horse. At the time the Zulus were rapidly closing on them, and there was no armed man between them and Sergeant O'Toole.

Lord William returned to India in 1880. On 28 October 1881, he replaced Major George White VC as ADC to the viceroy, Lord Ripon. On 13 December 1884, Lord Dufferin took over as viceroy and Lord William remained as ADC and military secretary, being promoted to major two days later.

Thibaw, the king of Upper Burma, had been showing anti-British feeling for many years, and in November 1885 a British force occupied Mandalay. A swift, almost bloodless, campaign followed which became known as the Third Burmese War. On New Year's Day 1886, Lord Dufferin proclaimed annexation of Upper Burma to the British Crown, to be administered as a province of India as 'a New Year's present to the queen'.

Lord William was appointed Knight Commander of the Indian Empire on the same day as the annexation, and for his services in Burma he was mentioned in despatches and received the Burma Medal with 1886-87 clasp. In February 1886 he accompanied Lord Dufferin on an expedition to Burma. He returned to India, where he helped to found the Gaiety Theatre in Simla, which opened on 30 May 1887 to celebrate Queen Victoria's golden jubilee. The Simla Amateur Dramatics Company was established there, and Lord William is known to have saved the company from financial ruin.

He was promoted to brevet lieutenant-colonel on 1 July 1887, and he became ADC to Viceroy Lansdowne on 10 December 1888. He was appointed lieutenant-colonel of the 9th (Queen's Royal) Lancers 1890-94, being promoted to colonel on 1 January 1891. He retired in 1893, and on 30 December a farewell banquet attended by many prominent people was held at the Calcutta Town Hall in recognition of his distinguished service.

Lord William became the third husband of Lillian Warren (born 8 June 1854 at Troy, Rensselaer County, New York), the daughter of Cicero Price, a commodore in the United States Navy, when they married at St George's Church, Hanover Square, London, on 30 April 1895. She had become the widow of George Charles Spencer-Churchill, 8th Duke of Marlborough, in 1892. She had lived at 3 Carlton Terrace, London, and rented Deepdene, a superb mansion at Dorking in Surrey, where they made their home together, and received many distinguished visitors, including Edward, Prince of Wales, and Winston Churchill. They worshipped at the local St Martin's Church. As a member of the Dorking Lodge of Freemasons, Lord William generously provided funds for local institutions, including the Dorking High School. A son named William Warren was born at Deepdene on 4 February 1897, and Lord William was devoted to him, but he was not destined to see him grow up.

In 1897 he entered into a horse-racing partnership with Pierre Lorillard, and an American called Mr Whitney, who introduced Todd Sloan to the circuit. The horses were trained by John Huggins at Heath House in Newmarket, the old home of champion jockey Fred Archer. The last three years of the nineteenth century were very successful for the Beresford stable, and their mounts won twenty-seven races. At Newmarket on 30 September 1898, Todd Sloan almost did a 'Frankie Dettori' when he won five races and came second in another out of seven mounts in the Beresford colours. In 1899, Sloan rode Sibola to win the One Thousand Guineas at Newmarket, and the same partnership came second in the Oaks. In the same year, Sloan rode Caimen into second place in the Two Thousand Guineas and the St Leger. Democrat was acquired in 1899, which won seven of his eleven races as a two-year-old, and was given to Lord Kitchener, who rode him in King Edward VII's coronation procession in 1910. Man and horse is the subject of an equestrian statue which was erected in Calcutta in 1913.

Lord William was second in the list of winning owners to the Duke of Westminster in 1899, and Edward, Prince of Wales, in 1900. In 1901, he leased Vladyovski, a horse which he believed would fulfil his ambition to win the Epsom Derby. The horse achieved its potential, but Lord William did not live to witness it, and because of his death his name does not appear in the record books.

While out with the Wareham stag hounds, Lord William had suffered the most serious of his many riding accidents when he fell off a horse while trying to jump a fence, apparently in an effort to outdo a lady rider. He broke his pelvis and never fully recovered. In December 1900, already weak from one of his bouts of dysentery, he became ill with peritonitis.

Lord William Beresford died of heart failure at Deepdene on 28 December 1900, aged fifty-three. His body was transported for burial in the family vault at Clonagham Churchyard. The 9th Lancers sent a floral tribute of chrysanthemums to Deepdene, which was 'a facsimile of the camp bed used by Lord William when in the Zulu War'. A memorial service was held in Dorking the next day and his passing was universally mourned. A tribute in verse by 'Ballyhooley' appeared in the *Sporting Times* for 5 January 1901. There is a marble memorial plaque in Mullaghbragh Church, and a memorial plaque in Armagh Church of Ireland Cathedral. The headstone at the family vault shows his year of death as 1906. Lillian died at Dorking on 11 January 1909, and was buried with her husband, and William Warren, having been left an orphan at the age of eleven, died at Sunninghill Park, not far from Royal Ascot Racecourse in Berkshire, on 28 January 1919, at the age of twenty-one. The house later became the home of Prince Andrew, Duke of York.

Captain Henry Cecil Dudgeon D'Arcy VC

Henry Cecil Dudgeon D'Arcy (usually known as Cecil) was born at Wanganui on the north island of New Zealand, on 11 August 1850, of Irish descent. He was the seventh of nine children to Major Oliver Barker D'Arcy and his wife Angela Martha. Major D'Arcy had served in two famous Irish regiments, the 18th (Royal Irish) and the 27th

(Inniskilling), and he was with the 65th Regiment (York and Lancaster) on garrison duties in the aftermath of the 1845-47 Maori Uprising when Cecil was born. Major D'Arcy also took part in the Maori Wars of the 1860s. He went to South Africa and settled at King William's Town, becoming an officer in the Cape Mounted Rifles. Cecil's uncle, Robert, was a magistrate in Kimberley, who raised D'Arcy's Horse for service during the Siege of Pretoria in 1881. He was wounded in the knee during the fighting at Bronkhorstspruit and the injury later caused his death. D'Arcy Road in Kimberley was named after him.

Cecil gained employment as a clerk in the civil service at Grahamstown, Cape Colony, and on the outbreak of the Cape Frontier War in 1877 he resigned and enlisted for active service with the Albany Mounted Volunteers, rising to the rank of sergeant-major. After the unit was disbanded he went to King William's Town and joined Colonel Carrington's Frontier Light Horse. Edmund O'Toole enlisted at the same time. Showing good potential, he was promoted to lieutenant on 20 December 1877. He saw action quickly, and his bravery became apparent during a confrontation with Gaika warriors. A sniper had pinned down the troop, and Lieutenant D'Arcy gesticulated to deliberately attract the warrior's attention while one of his men took the opportunity to kill the sniper. When Chief Sindili, of the Gaikas, was killed in June 1878 the uprising stopped and Lieutenant D'Arcy and Sergeant O'Toole were among the troops who formed an official representative at his funeral.

After gaining his commission, Cecil was informed that his resignation from the civil service had not been fully accepted, and during his absence he had been appointed a justice of the peace and inspector of licences for the King William's Town and Pedi Districts. However, the authorities accepted that he could not fulfil both military and civilian duties to the best of his abilities and his resignation was formally accepted in 1878. The Frontier Light Horse came under the command of Colonel Redvers Buller, and received orders for active service in the Sekhukhune campaign, joining at Pretoria. When the operation was aborted his unit joined the 4th Column for the advance into Zululand on 6 January 1879.

For his gallant conduct at the Mfolosi River, he became the first man from a non-imperial regiment to be awarded the Victoria Cross when it was announced in the *London Gazette* for 9 October 1879 that Lieutenant Cecil D'Arcy had been awarded the Victoria Cross. He received the medal from Lord Wolseley at Pretoria on 10 December 1879. He also received the South Africa Medal with 1877-8-9 clasp.

Speaking in April 1879 of his part in the Hlobane Mountain fighting, Lieutenant D'Arcy stated:

> All the mounted men had to take a very strong position on a mountain called the Hlobane. We got up there, driving the natives before us at every point, although they fought very well. Williams was killed as we charged up the hill, the baron on the top while he was in command of his troop, a Zulu spotted him from above and shot him right through the head. Barton was sent down a hill with 'C' Troop, and just as we got down we saw about three thousand Zulus below us, trying to get between us and our camp; we at once crossed the hill to come down a most awful steep place; the Dutchmen got to the place, rushed to their horses, and bolted as hard as they could go. My troop was left behind, and Blaine, myself and Hutton got them to go quietly down the hill, which was really a fearful place. I had of course to leave the top of the hill; the Zulus all this time were giving us awful pepper from Martini rifles. I saw, I thought, all of our men down, and then considered I had to think of myself, and got halfway down when a stone the size of a piano came bounding down; I heard a shout above, 'Look out below,' and down the beastly thing came right on my horse's leg, cutting it right off. I at the same time got knocked down the hill by another horse, and was nearly squeezed to death. I had taken the bridle off, and was about to take the saddle when I heard a scream. I looked up, and saw the Zulus right in among the white men, stabbing horses and men. I made a jump and got down somehow or other and ran as hard as I could with seventy rounds of ball cartridge, a carbine, a revolver, field-glass, and heavy boots.
>
> I went some 300 yards when a fellow called Francis got a horse for me, but no saddle or bridle, a riem did for both, when one of the Frontier Light Horse got wounded through the leg, and I had to jump off, put him on my horse, and run again. Colonel Buller saved my life by taking me up behind him on his horse, then Blaine, who had been keeping the natives off in the rear, saw me (as after I got my breath I got off the colonel's horse) and he nearly cried when he met me, all the fellows thinking I had been killed on top of the hill. He behaved as he always does, and stuck to me, and pulled me through the second time. The third time, a major of the artillery, Tremlett by name, took me up behind.
>
> Our men and officers all behaved well, but the other volunteers were what Major Robinson would call a 'big rabble'. We lost many white men and a number of natives. The Frontier Light Horse lost three officers and twenty-four non-commissioned officers and men,

> and sixty-six horses. Each of our men arrived in camp with another man behind him.

It seems the last duty of the Frontier Light Horse was when a hundred hand-picked men were formed into two troops, under Lieutenant D'Arcy, to deal with Boer disturbances at Middleburg. Cecil was rewarded for his services by being appointed captain in a squadron of his father's old regiment. On 31 October 1880, he led his squadron in an engagement with native warriors at Lerothodi's Kraal during the Basuto Rebellion. He served the unit with distinction, but he resigned amid controversy and disagreement on 15 April 1881.

Cecil had been confined to his bed with stomach pains and fever at Pietermaritzburg. He was aged only thirty-one, but he also suffered with asthma, and depressed by constant illness he took to drinking too much. On 4 August 1881 he arrived at the St Matthew's Mission Station at Keiskammahok, near King William's Town, suffering with malaria and bilharzia (schistosomiasis), which is a form of tropical disease caused by drinking contaminated water. He went to bed early that night and in the morning his host, the Reverend Taberer, discovered his room was empty. Local people were alerted and a search for him was organised, but it was called off after only a few days because of a misunderstanding. On 28 December 1881, the body of a man was discovered in a cave in the Amatola Forest in the Perie Bush, and was identified as being that of Cecil D'Arcy. It is believed he left his room in a state of delirium and he had died of exposure. It has been suggested that the act was a deliberate attempt at suicide. He was buried with his parents at the King William's Town Eastern Cape Cemetery, where there is a headstone.

His Victoria Cross came up for sale at auction in September 1992, and on reporting on the event the *Daily Mail* stated:

> But was it really his body? A box of papers recently discovered at the Killie Campbell Africana Library in Durban seems to contradict the fact.
>
> It belonged to a Mr V. G. Sparks and contained a note which reads: 'Captain D'Arcy was supposed to have perished in a snow storm in the Perie Desert. While walking through the snow, Captain D'Arcy saw a dead man lying in the snow. He changed clothes with him and made a getaway.

> The note adds that Sparks had been playing cricket at Newcastle, Natal, in 1925, when he recognised D'Arcy from a photograph. When approached, D'Arcy had pleaded with him to tell no one, as he wished to remain dead to the world.

A cairn of stones was placed by natives at the place where his body was found. This was later replaced by an iron cross surrounded by an iron railing. Apparently, all that remains now are the bolts cemented to the rock which were used to secure the memorial. A headstone was erected in September 1964 by his great-nephew, R. E. D. D'Arcy. D'Arcy Place at Taradale, Napier, on the North Island of New Zealand is named after him. His medals remain with his family. There is a walking stick on which is carved a list of encounters at the Kaffrarian Museum in King William's Town.

Sergeant Edmund Joseph O'Toole VC

Edmund Joseph O'Toole was born in Dublin in 1848, as he was baptised as Edmond Joseph Toole at St Andrew's Church in Westland Row, Dublin, on 23 July 1848. He was the fifth child of seven to Charles Lawrence Toole, of Wilford in Bray, and his wife, Mary Helena Burke. The family had a nursery and seed merchants business in Kevin Street, Dublin, known as 'Toole and Company'. His older brother, William Vincent, attended Ushaw College in Durham from 1854 to 1859, and the 1861 census records that Edmund was attending the college that year with his brother, Luke.

Described as a 'rip-roaring Irishman,' Edmond enlisted into Baker's Horse, presumably as Edmond O'Toole, which was a colonial mounted unit raised in the Port Elizabeth region of Natal, and was garrisoned at Kokstadt. He went to King William's Town in December 1877 and entered Colonel Carrington's newly-established Frontier Light Horse. Cecil D'Arcy enlisted at the same time. He served in the Cape Frontier War of 1877-78, being present in several skirmishes with Xhosa warriors, and when Chief Sindili, of the Gaikas, was killed in June 1878 the uprising stopped and he and Lieutenant D'Arcy were among the troops who formed an official representative at his funeral.

The Frontier Light Horse came under orders to muster at Pretoria for active service with Colonel Rowlands' column for the advance to capture Sekhukhune's stronghold, and under the command of Captain Robert Barton, of the Coldstream Guards, they travelled over 1,000 miles from Pietermaritzburg to get there within a month. When the column fell back, Colonel Buller took them to join the 4th Column for the invasion of Zululand on 6 January 1879. Having been promoted to sergeant, he served with conspicuous courage throughout the difficult war with the Zulus, showing outstanding bravery on several occasions.

Edmund had been overlooked by the authorities for all his previous brave deeds, and it seemed that he might not have been considered for a gallantry award had it not been for Lord William. While he was at Windsor receiving his Victoria Cross he graciously expressed to Queen Victoria that he could not accept the award unless the two men who had shared the danger with him were similarly rewarded. The sovereign was much impressed by Lord William and awards to Captain D'Arcy and Sergeant O'Toole followed. Because of this, the *London Gazette* of 9 October 1879 announced that he had been awarded the Victoria Cross. He received the medal from General Clifford during a special parade of the troops at Fort Napier in Pietermaritzburg on 16 January 1880, which was the same investiture as James Langley Dalton, of Rorke's Drift fame.

Lord Wolseley disbanded the Frontier Light Horse as soon as hostilities ceased in August 1879, and on 15 October 1880 Edmund joined the Herschel Native Contingent as a captain. In 1890 he was serving with the Mashonaland Pioneer Corps as part of the Rhodesian Field Force to deal with a serious rebellion there. He also saw service in the Protectorate Police.

It has been suggested that he emigrated to America in 1898, but his Victoria Cross pension was paid until 1899, and at the time of the Boer War of 1899-1902 a journal called the *Black and White Budget*, dated 4 August 1900, includes Edmund O'Toole in a list of VC holders who were believed to be in South Africa at that time, referring to him as 'a resident of the Cape'.

In a book written by G. H. Tanser, which tells the history of Salisbury from 1890 to 1900, it states that Edmund was given a plot of land at Hatfield Hill in Salisbury, as part of the dividing up of the Cape Column. He is said to have called the land Toole Farm. W. C. Scully published a book in 1913 in which he states that he met Edmund O'Toole, who was working as a horse-drawn cab driver in Cape Town, and suggests that Edmund died a few years before his book was published.

It has also been suggested that he may have been a victim of an epidemic which the Cape suffered in 1901. There is an entry for Edmund on the 'Find a Grave' website which suggests he is buried at

Harare in Zimbabwe, which was formerly Salisbury in Rhodesia. No facts about the circumstances of his death have ever been confirmed, and the location of his Victoria Cross is not known.

Simeon Kambula grew up in Edendale, the Methodist mission station near Pietermaritzburg. His father was Elijah Kambula, the respected interpreter to Major Anthony Durnford RE. He took part in the Langalibalele Rebellion of 1873, and while riding next to Durnford on the Bushman's River Pass in the Drakensberg Mountains on 4 November 1873, the party of eighty mounted troops was ambushed by bushmen, and Elijah was killed, despite Durnford's efforts to rescue him.

When the government asked the elders of Edendale to raise a mounted troop, there was no hesitation. 'We all know the cruelty and the power of the Zulu king,' they told their people, 'and if he should subdue the queen's soldiers and overrun this land he will wipe out all the native people who have dwelt so long in safety under the shadow of the Great White Queen. Shall we not gladly obey her, when she calls for the services of her dark children?'

Volunteers were quickly forthcoming. Within a few days a fine body of some one hundred young men, mounted, accoutred and uniformed at their elders' expense, complete with boots and spurs, gathered to receive their missionary's blessing at a solemn service in the Edendale Church. Then off they marched to war, with their leader, John Zulu, at their head, Troop Sergeant-Majors Simeon Kambula and Learda as the senior NCOs in their ranks. Kambula and Learda became the first native black members of a non-imperial unit to be awarded the Distinguished Conduct Medal.

TSM Kambula's award of the Distinguished Conduct Medal, which would have been similar to that of TSM Learda, was announced thus:

> This non-commissioned officer has also set an excellent example to the men of the troop, of courage and ready obedience under fire. At the White Umvolozi River on the occasion of Colonel Buller's reconnaissance towards Ulundi, the day before the Battle of Nodwengo, Simeon Kambula saved the life of an officer of the Frontier Light Horse, by bringing him out of a very heavy fire behind him on his horse. He was present at iSandlwana, Hlobane, Khambula and Nodwengo; besides many smaller actions, and has taken part in every patrol of the mounted troops of the Flying Column, since 14 March 1879.

Appendix

Gallantry Medals Awarded for the Anglo-Zulu War

iSandlwana, 22 January 1879

Victoria Cross:

- Lieutenant Nevill Josiah Aylmer Coghill, 1st Battalion, 24th (2nd Warwickshire) Regiment
- Lieutenant Teignmouth Melvill, 1st Battalion, 24th (2nd Warwickshire) Regiment
- Private Samuel Wassall, 80th Regiment (Staffordshire Volunteers)

Rorke's Drift, 22/23 January 1879

Victoria Cross:

- Lieutenant John Rouse Merriott Chard, 5th Company, Corps of Royal Engineers
- Lieutenant Gonville Bromhead, 2nd Battalion, 24th (2nd Warwickshire) Regiment
- Corporal William Wilson Allan, 2nd Battalion, 24th (2nd Warwickshire) Regiment
- Private Frederick Hitch, 2nd Battalion, 24th (2nd Warwickshire) Regiment
- Private Alfred Henry Hook, 2nd Battalion, 24th (2nd Warwickshire) Regiment
- Private Robert Jones, 2nd Battalion, 24th (2nd Warwickshire) Regiment

Private William Jones, 2nd Battalion, 24th (2nd Warwickshire) Regiment
Private John Williams (Fielding), 2nd Battalion, 24th (2nd Warwickshire) Regiment
Surgeon James Henry Reynolds, Army Medical Department
Assistant-Commissary James Langley Dalton, Commissariat and Transport Department
Corporal Ferdinand Christian Schiess, 3rd Battalion, Natal Native Contingent

Distinguished Conduct Medal:

Gunner John Cantwell, 5th Brigade, Royal Regiment of Artillery
Private William Roy, 2nd Battalion, 24th (2nd Warwickshire) Regiment
Colour-Sergeant Frank Bourne, 2nd Battalion, 24th (2nd Warwickshire) Regiment
Corporal Francis Attwood, Army Service Corps
Corporal Michael McMahon, Army Hospital Corps (later cancelled)

iNtombi River, 12 March 1879

Victoria Cross:

Colour-Sergeant Anthony Clarke Booth, 80th Regiment (Staffordshire Volunteers)

Hlobane Mountain, 28 March 1879

Victoria Cross:

Colonel Redvers Henry Buller, 60th Rifles (King's Royal Rifle Corps)
Major William Knox Leet, 1st Battalion, 13th (Somerset) Light Infantry
Lieutenant Henry Lysons, 90th (Perthshire) Light Infantry
Private Edmund John Fowler, 90th (Perthshire) Light Infantry

Distinguished Conduct Medal:

Bugler Alexander Walkinshaw, 90th (Perthshire) Light Infantry
Corporal William Dommett Vinnicombe, Frontier Light Horse
Trooper Richard Brown, Frontier Light Horse

Khambula Hill, 29 March 1879

Victoria Cross:
- Lieutenant Edward Stevenson Browne, 1st Battalion, 24th (2nd Warwickshire) Regiment

Distinguished Conduct Medal:
- Corporal Edward Quigley, 7th Brigade, Royal Regiment of Artillery
- Private Albert Page, 1st Battalion, 13th (Somerset) Light Infantry
- Private John Power, 1st Battalion, 24th (2nd Warwickshire) Regiment (also for Griqualand West and Ulundi)
- Troop Sergeant-Major Learda, Edendale Troop, Natal Native Horse

White Mfolosi River, 3 July 1879

Victoria Cross:
- Captain William Leslie de la Poer Beresford, 9th (Queen's Royal) Lancers
- Captain Henry Cecil Dudgeon D'Arcy, Frontier Light Horse
- Sergeant Edmund Joseph O'Toole, Frontier Light Horse

Distinguished Conduct Medal:
- Troop Sergeant-Major Simeon Kambula, Edendale Troop, Natal Native Horse

Ulundi, 4 July 1879

Distinguished Conduct Medal:
- Gunner William Moorhead, 7th Brigade, Royal Regiment of Artillery
- Private John Power, 1st Battalion, 24th (2nd Warwickshire) Regiment (also for Griqualand West and Khambula)
- Colour-Sergeant James Phillips, 58th (Rutlandshire) Regiment

Research Sources and Further Reading

Abbott, P. E., *Recipients of the Distinguished Conduct Medal, 1855-1909*, 1975

'An Interview with Sergeant-Instructor Booth VC—How he won the Victoria Cross', in the *County Express*, 9 April 1898

Ancestry.com

Bancroft, James W., *Cotswold Soldier Henry Lysons* published in *Cotswold Life*, July 2008

_____________, *Devotion to Duty*, 1990

_____________, *Rorke's Drift: The Zulu War, 1879*, 1988

_____________, *The Fight for Rorke's Drift*, 2016

_____________, *The Zulu War VCs*, 1992

Barfield, Doreen, 'For Valour' At Fugitive's Drift', *Military History Journal*, Vol. One, No. 6, June 1970

Baynham-Jones, Alun, *Biographical records of the men who served with the 24th Foot (Later the South Wales Borderers, the Royal Regiment of Wales 4th/41st Foot, and now The Royal Welsh) in South Africa, 1 February 1875 to 12 January 1880*, 2011

Bennett, Colonel Ian H. W., *Rorke's Drift: The Story of the Commissaries, Parts 1 and 2*, 1978

Black and White Budget, 4 August 1900

Booth VC, Sergeant Anthony, Letter from Luneburg dated 14 March 1879

Butler, Lieutenant-Colonel Lewis, *Sir Redvers Buller*, 1909

Calverley, Reverend Henry Calverley, Letter published in the *Daily Telegraph* on 7 March 1879

Cameronians (Scottish Rifles) Museum in Hamilton

Cartlidge, Mrs Jill, Letters to the author concerning Major Chard, 2 October 1999 and 26 January 2000

Census Returns from 1841 to 1911

Chard, John R. M., *Letter written to Lord Chelmsford concerning the application of Victoria Cross to Corporal Schiess*, 22 October 1979

Clarke, N. M. P., Lt-Col. W. J., *My Career in South Africa*. The Killie Campbell Africana Library

Coghill, Patrick, *Whom the God's Love—A Memoir of Lt N. J. A. Coghill VC* (Including a first-hand account by Lt Higginson), 1966

Currey, R. N., *Vinnicombe's Trek: A Family Chronicle of the Time of the Zulu and Boer Wars*, 1990

Dalton VC, James Langley, *Statement to General Wolfenden with reference to the part taken by Surgeon Reynolds AMD*, 28 March 1879 (WO138/3)

D'Arcy, Patricia, *What Happened to a VC*, 1973

Delavoye, Alexander Marin, *Records of the 90th Regiment (Perthshire Volunteers)*, 1880

Dunne, Commissary Walter Alphonsus, 'Reminiscences of Campaigning in South Africa, 1877-81', *Journal of the Army Service Corps*, February 1892

Edinburgh Evening News, 27 September 1888

Edmund O'Toole VC Research Group

Emery, Frank, *The Red Soldier: Letters From the Zulu War*, 1977

Essex County Standard, 3 April 1926

Everett, Major-General Sir Henry, *A History of the Somerset Light Infantry (Prince Albert's) 1685-1914*, 1934

Exeter Flying Post, 9 September 1905, 6 June and 4 July 1908, 9 June 1911

Findmypast.co.uk

Fortescue, Sir John William and Beadon, Colonel R. H., *The Royal Army Service Corps: A History of Transport and Supply in the British Army (2 volumes)*, 1930-31

Fripp, Charles E., 'Reminiscences of the Zulu War', in the *Pall Mall Magazine*, 1884

Frost, Maureen and Kidd, Leonard, 'A Study of Samuel Wassall VC', in The *Midland Ancestor*, December 1988

Fynn, H. F., 'My Recollections of a Famous Campaign', in the *Natal Witness*, 22 January 1913

Greaves, Adrian and Knight, Ian, *Who's Who in the Zulu War, 1879*, Vol. 1, 2006

Hallam-Parr, Captain Henry, *A Sketch of the Kafir and Zulu Wars. The Experiences of an Officer of the Somerset Light Infantry in South Africa, 1877-79*, 2010

Hamilton-Brown, Colonel George, *A Lost Legionary in South Africa*, 2009
Harford, Colonel Henry, *The Zulu War Journal of Col. Henry Harford, CB.*, 1978
Haythornthwaite, Philip J., *The Colonial Wars Source Book*, 1995
Hobson, Mark, *The Bloody Affair at Myer's Drift*
Holme, Norman, *The Noble 24th*, 1999
Hope, Robert, *The Zulu War and the 80th Regiment of Foot*, 1997
Ian Knight's Anglo-Zulu History Group
Illustrated London News, 1879-80 (various)
Jerrold, Walter, *Sir Redvers H. Buller VC*, 1900
Jones, James P., *A History of the South Staffordshire Regiment*, 1923
Kent Express, 28 December 1962
Killie Campbell Africana Library in Natal, South Africa
Knight, Ian John, *Anatomy of the Zulu Army*, 1995
_____________, *Brave Men's Blood: The Epic of the Zulu War, 1879*, 1990
_____________, *British Forces in Zululand, 1879*, 1991
_____________, *The Zulu War: Then and Now*, 1993
_____________, *There Will Be An Awful Row At Home About This*, Victorian Military Society: Zulu War Study Group, 1987
Knox-Leet VC, William, *His Last Will and Testament*, Twickenham, 1898
Laband, John, *Fight Us in the Open: The Anglo-Zulu War Through Zulu Eyes*, 1985
Lock, Ron, *Blood on the Painted Mountain*, 1995
London Gazette, Victoria Cross citations dated 2 May, 17 June, 23 August, 9 October, 17 November and 29 November 1879; 23 February 1880; 5 April 1882; 7 January 1907
Lovegrove, Peter, *Not Least in the Crusade: A Short History of the Royal Army Medical Corps*, 1951
Lummis Files held at the National Army Museum on behalf of the Military Historical Society
Lysons, General, Sir Daniel, *The Crimea from First to Last*, 1895
Lytton David, 'The Struggle for the Cape', in the *British Empire Magazine*, BBC Time-Life Books, 1971
Mackinnon, J. P., and Shadbolt, S. H., *The South African Campaign of 1879*, 1880
Manning, Stephen: *Evelyn Wood VC: Pillar of Empire*, 2007
Melville, Lieutenant-Colonel C. H., *Life of General Redvers Henry Buller VC*, 1923
Menzies, Mrs Stuart, *Lord William Beresford VC*, 1917
Mitford, Bertram, *Through the Zulu Country*, 1983

Morris, Donald, *The Washing of the Spears*, 1965
____________, 'War on the Veld', in the *British Empire Magazine*, BBC Time-Life Books, 1971
Natal Witness, 5 February 1880, 17 December 1881, 6 February 1885, 2, 4 and 6 November 1899; and 21 January 1961
National Archives, The Lysons Family of Gloucester, 1607-1963
National Army Museum in London
Newark Advertiser, 12 March 1879
Newark Magnus
Newnham-Davis, Lt-Colonel N., *The Transvaal under the Queen*, 1900
Norris-Newman, Charles, *In Zululand with the British throughout the Zulu War of 1879*, 1880
North Devon Herald, Letter from Private John Snook, 29 May 1879
North West Evening Mail, 28 May 1917, 5 February 1927 and 22 February 1985
Oldham Chronicle, Letter from William Sweeney, 24th Regiment, 26 April 1879
Penn-Symons W., Glennie F., Paton G., *Historical Records of the 24th Regiment*, 1892
Penn-Symons, Captain William, His Report Written in 1879 which is held at the South Wales Borderers Museum
Reynard, Frank H., *Ninth (Queen's Royal) Lancers, 1715-1903*, 1904
Reynolds, Surgeon James Henry, Account in the Appendix to the Report of the Army Medical Department, 1878, Royal Army Medical Corps Museum at Aldershot
Richardson, Colin, *In the Face of the Enemy: The Complete History of the Victoria Cross and New Zealand*, 2006
Ritter, E. A., *Shaka Zulu: The Rise of the Zulu Empire*, 1955
Scully, William Charles, *Reminiscences of a South African Pioneer*, 1913
Smith, Reverend George, Account dated 3 February 1879, published in the *Royal Army Chaplains Department* Journal, July 1936, Royal Army Chaplains' Department Museum at Aldershot
Smith, Reverend George, 'The Defence of Rorke's Drift by an Eyewitness', in the *Natal Mercury*, 7 April 1879
Smith-Dorrien, General Horace, *Memories of Forty-Eight Years' Service*, 1925
Somerset Light Infantry Museum in Taunton Castle
South African Military History Society
South Wales Borderers Museum in Brecon

Stafford County Express, 9 April 1898, 16 December 1899, 8 June 1964, 10 April 1965

Sunday Express, 16 October 1994

Surrey Advertiser, 5 January 1901

Sussens, Josiah, Letter to the *Transvaal Argus* concerning the massacre at iNtombe River

Symons, J., *Buller's Campaign*, 1963

Symons, J. P., *Reminiscences of the Zulu War by a Natal Carbineer*

Tanser, G. H., *A Scantling of Time: The Story of Salisbury, Rhodesia, 1890-1900*, 1965

The Times, 18 October 1879

Thompson, Paul, *The Natal Native Contingent in the Anglo-Zulu War, 1879*: Historical Studies Department, University of Natal at Pietermaritzburg.

Thornton, Neil, *Rorke's Drift: A New Perspective*, 2016

Tucker, Major Charles, Letter from Luneburg dated 19 March 1879, published in the *Journal for Army Historical Research*, 1943

Vale, Colonel W. L., *A History of the South Staffordshire Regiment*, 1969

Walker, Anthony Julian Bromhead, Letter written to the author concerning Major Bromhead and his ancestors, 5 June 2001

Wallace, Lieutenant-General, Sir Christopher, T*he King's Royal Rifle Corps—60th Rifles—A Brief History: 1755 to 1965*, 2005

War Office Army Lists 1878-1888

War Office Papers, including *The Narrative of the Field Operations Connected with the Zulu War of 1879*, 1881

Wassall VC, Samuel, 'The Last Stand at iSandlwana', in The *London Magazine*, Vol. 31, No. 38

Watkins, Reverend Owen, Article in the *Methodist Reader*

Western Mail News, 7 December 1939

Wood VC, Colonel Evelyn, *From Midshipman to Field Marshal*, 1906

____________, Letter from Khambula dated 6 April 1879

____________, 'One of the Bravest Deeds I Ever Saw: Captain Ronald Campbell's Heroism in the Transvaal', in *Pearson's Magazine*, February 1896

Wood, Walter, 'The Story of Samuel Wassall VC', in *London Magazine*, No. 38

Index

Recipients of Gallantry Awards

Allan *VC*, William Wilson 30 34 43 44-45 75-76 149 173
Attwood *DCM*, Francis 55 174
Beresford *VC*, William Leslie de la Poer 151-152 154 158-164 170 175
Booth *VC*, Anthony Clarke 102-110 174
Bourne *DCM*, Frank 29 55 61 66 79 174
Bromhead *VC*, Gonville 24-25 27 32 34 35 36 39 46 47 49 53 55 58 61 62 63 68-74 89 91 93 96 173
Brown *DCM*, Richard 113 174
Browne *VC*, Edward Stevenson 112 115 140-141 143 145-149 151 175
Buller *VC*, Redvers Henry 61 62 111 112 115 117-121 126 132 135 144 151 154 155 162 171 174
Cantwell *DCM*, John 44 174
Chard *VC*, John Rouse Merriott 26 27 29 30 31 33-34 39 45 46 49 53 54 55-67 73 89 91 92 95 96 119 173
Coghill *VC*, Neville Josiah Aylmer 10 11 12 14-16 18 71 105 173
Dalton *VC*, James Langley 24 29 31 36 38 45 62 74 89 90-93 96 170 174
D'Arcy *VC*, Henry Cecil Dudgeon 112 113-114 115 119 143 150 151-152 153 163 165-168 169 175
Fowler *VC*, Edmund John 116-117 128 130-138 142 174
Hitch *VC*, Frederick 27 32 34 36 37 43 47 49 77-78 81 92 173
Hook *VC*, Alfred Henry 27 41-43 44 52 59-60 61 79-80 91 173
Jones *VC*, Robert 43-44 59-60 81-82 173
Jones *VC*, William 43-44 59-60 61 83-84 174
Kambula *DCM*, Simeon 152-153 171 175
Learda *DCM* 141 171 175
Leet *VC*, William Knox 114-115 122-127 149 174
Lysons *VC*, Henry 116-117 128-129 131 133-135 142 174
McMahon *(DCM)*, Michael 38 44 55 61 174
Melvill *VC*, Teignmouth 11 12 16 17-19 105 173
Moorhead *DCM*, William 153-154 175

O'Toole *VC*, Edmund Joseph 112 113 115 141 143 151-152 163 166 169-172 175
Page *DCM*, Albert 142 175
Phillips *DCM*, James 154 175
Power *DCM*, John 141 149 175
Quigley *DCM*, Edward 141 175
Reynolds *VC*, James Henry 25 28 38 43 45 52 60 74 86-89 91 119 174
Roy *DCM*, William 55 61 174
Schiess *VC*, Ferdinand Christian 25 36 37 39-40 47 59 61 94-98 174
Vinnicombe *DCM*, William Dommett 113 174
Walkinshaw *DCM*, Alexander 134 135-136 138 174
Wassall *VC*, Samuel 13-14 20-23 173
Williams (Fielding) *VC*, John 40-41 42-43 44 79 84-85 88 96 174

Regiments and other units
(In Order of Precedence)

Royal Navy 2 97 160
Artillery, Royal Regiment of 55 112 139 141 153-154 174 175
Engineers, Corps of Royal 10 26 55 56 62 67-68 95 173
9th (Queen's Royal) Lancers 151 160 165
12th (Prince of Wales's Royal) Lancers 54 111 146
17th/21st Lancers 19 150 151 153 155
Coldstream Guards 117 131 169
3rd (East Kent) Regiment (The Buffs) 58
4th (King's Own) Regiment 69
13th (Somerset) Light Infantry 21 104 112 123-127 139 142 143 144 174
24th (2nd Warwickshire) Regiment 11 12 14-17 18 19 25-26 55 58-61 69 72-74 75-77 77-78 81-82 83-84 85 87 112 141 144 146-147 152 173-174 175
32nd (Cornwall) Light Infantry 73
36th (Herefordshire) Regiment 87
54th (Dorset) Regiment
58th (Rutlandshire) Regiment 154 156 175
60th Rifles (King's Royal Rifle Corps) 111 118 120 121 174
80th Regiment (Staffordshire Volunteers) 13 21-22 23 99-102 173 174
90th (Perthshire) Light Infantry 116-117 128-136 139 144
Army Medical Department 25 87 88 174
Army Hospital Corps 24-25 38 55 61 91 174
Army Service Corps 24 55 90 94 174
Commissariat and Transport 24 174
Frontier Light Horse 111 113 116 119 141 146 150 166-168 169-170 171 174
Natal Native Horse 141 152 175
Natal Native Contingent 13 25 30 32 58 59 95

South Africa

Boers/Boer Republics 4 19 21 82 93 104 120 121-122 154

Buffalo River 10 12 19 27 146
Cape Frontier Wars 9 18 20 24 75 77 80 83 85 87 91 95 119 128 130 141 166
Cape of Good Hope 4 9 17 18 20 21 56 72 93
Durban 56 78 97 168
Gingindlovu 145
Helpmekaar 13 27 28 33 53 54 58
Hlobane Mountain 22 99 111-117 132 139 143 145 147 162 167 174
iNtombe River 100-102 111 174
iSandlwana 9-13 18 26 28 35 105 131 141 144 145 146-147 150 173
Khambula Hill 61 99 112 114 115 116 129 132 133 139-145 147 148 149 154 162 175
Pietermaritzburg 75 84 92 93 97 168 170
Rorke's Drift 3 10 13 17 21 24-54 57-61 71 73 80 85 87 89 92 96 111 141 146 174-175
Ulundi 62 88 97 128 147 149 150-158 162 171 175
White Umfolozi River 147 152-153 156 166 171 175
Zulu Warriors 4-8 10 11 13 22 26 28 33-53 59-60 97 112-117 126 139-145 147

United Kingdom

Aldershot 75 88 90 94 120 129 160
Barrow-in-Furness 23
Birmingham 14 20-21 83 84
Brecon 14 16 18 19 74 75 79 80 98 148
Bristol 83
Cambridge 17 68 145
Chatham 56 63 66 77 103 136
Colchester 76 137 138
Cornwall 17 18 19 55 122 129
Cumbria 23
Devon 26 55 63 65 103 117-118 119 122 127 146
Exeter 63 117-118 119 122
Gloucestershire 17 79 81 83 127 128 130
Hampshire 83 122 147
Herefordshire 82
Hythe School of Musketry 74 90 124
Ireland 14 15 16 19 22 68 86 88 90 103 109 120 122 124 129 130 136 137 148 149 158-159 165 169
Kent 19 56 63 66 88 127
Lincolnshire 26 68 70 73
London 2 14 17 27 77-79 80-81 88 90 91 93 127 129 138 148 151 164
Manchester 84
Monmouthshire 75 76-77 80 81 82 83 84-85 86 147
Northumberland 75
Nottingham (Shire) 66 71 102-103
Plymouth 55 63 65 87 137
Portsmouth 72 74 90 148
Scotland 65 68 120 130 137 147
Somerset 55 66 127 130
Staffordshire 109 128
Surrey 164
Windsor Castle 73 75 84 122 131 149
Worcestershire 83
Yorkshire 11 75 148

World

Afghanistan 69 118 161-162
Ashanti (Expedition) 20 34 69 70 119
Burma (Myanmar) 69 127 129 163
China 1 34 118
Crimean War 1 2 3 27 34 67 69 87 128 150
Egypt 14 20 120 129 130 136
France 27 68 138
Gibraltar 73 80 82 146
India 2 14 17 19 74 82 87 98 110 118 129 130 160-161 162 163 164
Indian Mutiny 2 3 14 34 67 99 103 160
Mauritius 21 75 90 104
New Zealand 19 165-166 169
North America 19 20 68 69 90 118 128 145 159 164 170
Perak 104
Sudan 69 120 129 136
Switzerland 94

Personalities

Byrne, Louis Alexander 24 39 61 91
Campbell, Captain Ronald 117 131 134-135
Cetshwayo 7-8 10 35 37 48 140 141 150 151 154-155
Chelmsford, 2nd Baron 9-10 14 15 21 26 54 57 62 111 119 147 150 154-155
Clifford VC, Hugh Henry 93
Dunne, Walter Alphonsus 24 27 29 39 47 60 74 91 93
Durnford, Colonel Anthony 95 171
Glyn, Colonel Richard 11 12
Harford, Henry 54-55 87 92
Pulleine, Colonel Henry 11 12
Rowlands VC, Colonel Hugh 104
Shaka 4-7 8 154
Sihayo ka Xongo 10 11 41 96 146
Smith, Chaplain George 28 32 38 49 74 92 95
Smith-Dorrien, Lieutenant Horace 11 26
Victoria, Queen 1 2 18 63 64 65 73 78 84 119 122 131 136 146 149 161 163 164
Williams, Private Joseph 40-41 61
Witt, Chaplain Otto 24 25 28 32 37
Wolseley, Sir Garnet 9 17 22 62 69 73 80 82 90 97 105 106 118 119 120 122 129 147 151 154 155 166
Wood *VC*, Colonel Evelyn 21 22 61 99 104 105 111 116-117 119 120 124-125 128 129 131 140 142 143 145 147 150 155

Miscellaneous

Distinguished Conduct Medal 1 113 138 141 142 149 152 154 171 174 175
Eton College 117-118 159-160
Great War 19 110 122 148
Haileybury College 14
Harrow School 17 19 117
London Gazette 2 3 18 56 72 75 78 82 83 85 87 93 97 119 125 128 130 147 149 163 166 170
Royal Military Academy, Sandhurst/Woolwich 14 19 56 129 146
Sports 19 160 164-165